D1197359

LUCKY LIFE
A Personal History

W. Scott McLucas

with Susan D. Brandenburg

Charlotte Moore at Sardi's, wearing One World Foundation Medal

Foreword
by Charlotte Moore

Twenty three years ago when Scott McLucas first encountered our burgeoning little theater in a shabby, 84-seat space on West 18th street in Chelsea, he had neither the look nor the air of, "A Knight in Shining Armour." His generosity and vision have since proven us to be short-sighted. Through his painful early experiences, he has emerged a strong, brave and fierce supporter of good causes. He observes and acts with no self aggrandizing bluster. Early on in our quests, we knew we had a champion; someone we could count on who would wander with us through our self discovery and hard transitions with quiet support. In those tough years, the Celtic Tiger was barely growling; Frank McCourt had yet to set pen to paper and win the Pulitzer Prize, and Yeats' "rough beast's hour" was only beginning to come round at last. An avid student of social background and class politics, Scott saw what was coming, and encouraged us to dare to grow, to show our emotions, and speak our minds. We took his advice and flourished. In 1995 we named our studio theatre *The W. Scott McLucas Studio Theatre* in honor of his vision and unwavering support. Ciaran O'Reilly and I spoke at the naming ceremony of our fondness for Scott and Nancy, and of our strong, sweet memories of our times together. We said then, and we say now: Scott McLucas is THE REAL THING.

Charlotte Moore
Artistic Director and co-founder with Ciaran O'Reilly
of the Irish Repertory Theatre, NYC

The Tree and The Book

Hamilton Simpson McLucas

The Tree

Without a story from beginning
A family tree's a barren thing.
Broken limbs are dreams abandoned.
Around the base, lost hopes still cling.
Roots are earthbound lines enclosed by
Dates, carved on the trunk's gray mast.
Like fallen branches, long forgotten,
Lifeless names no shadows cast.

The Book

The yearning to hear distant voices,
Stirs the sap — by pride caressed.
The search along the path behind us
Starts new growth, at spring's request.
Leaves twice green, by memory quickened,
Nourished by awakened past.
Blossoms, born of love remembered,
Give promise to the tree at last.

My mother, Hamilton Simpson McLucas, was a talented writer and poet.
- W. Scott McLucas

Introduction
by W. Scott McLucas

As a beginning author, I have learned that writing a memoir is a search for interesting ways to please readers while telling historical truth. Thus, I am grateful to the New York Times Book Review of July 24, 2011 for introducing me to the books of American historian and Pulitzer Prize winner, Gordon S. Wood. In his 1992 book, *The Radicalism of the American Revolution*, Wood wrote of a sweeping revolution from 1760 to 1825 that "was as radical and social as any revolution in history, but... in a very special 18th century sense." Wood noted that "one class did not overthrow another; the poor did not supplant the rich. But social relationships — the way people were connected one to another — were changed, and decisively so."

Decisive and radical change management in the area of social relationships, as referenced by Wood, has run rampant throughout my family history. My two great-grandfathers, for example, were powerful change-agents during the antebellum period of America. Although each man held different philosophies on the issue of slavery, one was an abolitionist and the other an attorney who, though a slave owner, defended the rights of free men, including former slaves; they ultimately contributed to the future of their nation. Walter S. McLucas, the grandfather whose name I have borne proudly these eight decades on earth, was a most decisive and radical banker at a time in our history when his visionary actions were integral to the future of the automobile industry. As to the changing, lost and found aspect of personal social relationships, Grandfather McLucas lost and then found respect for my father due to the influence of my mother, a woman of high social standing and extraordinary beauty. At her insistence, and due to her powerful place in the family and community, Grandfather McLucas changed his attitude toward his son and awarded him a good position at the bank. The masterful way my mother managed change in connecting my father and grandfather was just one more example of American radicalism at its finest. Many years later, in the early days of the internet, my lifelong fascination with distance learning took a radical turn toward the future when my foundation partnered with the Gertrude Stein Repertory Theatre to present one of the world's first simultaneous global productions. From tiny vignettes in private moments to dramatic scenes on the world stage, my life has been rife with radical social change.

This memoir tells the story of my life and that of earlier generations of my ancestors in the United States of America. I feel that the majority of them showed courage, passion and gentility as they worked to build their lives and our country. Unfortunately, I stupidly lost much of my self-respect at age 21 and spent many years privately ashamed and hiding from reality while publicly building a career in professional theater, television production and advertising. By the time I came into my main inheritance, I was also free of an ugly, lost period in my life; free to join with honorable co-producers of plays and eventually to establish a new professional orchestra which became a brilliant organization in southern France. I hope you enjoy reading this story of challenge, change and growth in my life and in the lives of my ancestors. Included are some mavericks, I myself being one of those who has, in recent years, sought to balance my flaws with creativity in the arts and education. This is a personal history of my lucky life… what has been lost and what has been found.

CONTENTS

CHAPTER 1

Pioneering Family

PART 1
"Don't fire until you see the whites of their eyes!"
Private John Simpson's role in the battle of Breed's and Bunker Hill
June 17, 1775

John Simpson was a militiaman from Deerfield, New Hampshire, who volunteered to fight against the British because of his rage at their slaughter of fellow American militiamen at Concord and Lexington, Massachusetts. John Simpson was my great-great-great-grandfather on my mother's side of the family.

Because John and other American militiamen had spent most of the previous night digging earthworks on the summit of Breed's Hill, overlooking Boston Harbor, and had been rewarded with little food, water, or sleep for their labor, their ire was up. As they watched British troops debarking 200 yards below them, they were more than ready to open fire.

It must have been quite a sight: seemingly vast numbers of red-coated British soldiers with knapsacks, muskets and bayonets being rowed ashore in small boats, protected by massive 50 and 60 cannon British ships. American militia officers encouraged their men, most of whom had never fired their muskets in anger, to be patient and aim true at the right time. After spending the entire morning debarking and assembling, the British began their impressive advance up the face of Breed's Hill, with over 3,000 redcoats, arranged in three ranks, marching, pausing to load and fire, and continuing forward.

The familiar admonition, "Don't fire until you see the whites of their eyes," has become a part of American lore and is attributed to commanders in several revolutionary war battles. However, on Breed's Hill, historians record that American Colonel Stark instructed the men in his part of the line not to fire until the British had arrived at a certain point designated by him, which was within 40 paces of the American works. Nevertheless, when the redcoats had advanced to within the distance that young John Simpson called a good shot for a deer, he could not withstand such an opportunity. He fired and dropped his man. That shot prompted the commencement of firing along the whole militia line.

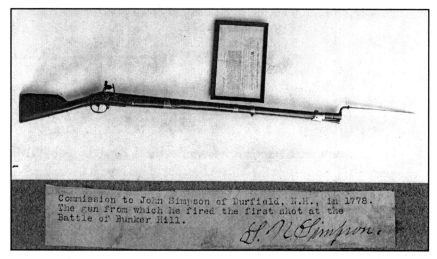

Commission to John Simpson of Durfield, N.H., in 1778. The gun from which he fired the first shot at the Battle of Bunker Hill.

When Simpson was reproved for disobeying orders, he replied that he could not help firing when the game which he was after came within gunshot. Rather than being charged for disobeying an order, young John Simpson was recommended for a lieutenant's commission. He served throughout the remaining years of the American revolutionary war and was discharged as a major at its end.

John Simpson is first on my honors list in this memoir and I am very proud that he was my early relative.

Deerfield, New Hampshire, still honors its native son, John Simpson, as the man who fired the first shot at the Battle of Breed's and Bunker Hill. The musket belonging to that brave young man remains in the possession of my family to this day and continues to inspire the pioneering spirit in all of us. As a boy, I had the privilege of holding that heavy iron musket in my hands and trying to imagine the calm courage my ancestor displayed in that furious battle so long ago.

Historic Footnotes:
*The Battle of Breed's and Bunker Hill [the first battle of the Continental Army] was fought valiantly by a young, courageous and disciplined American militia, but it was not a victory for them, although the British casualties were staggering, with their officer corps losing one-eighth of their total number for the entire American Revolution.
*Over 100 African American and native American soldiers participated in the battle of Breed's & Bunker Hill.

PART 2
Courageous Ancestors Take Stands in a Divided Nation

The enslavement of human beings has been a powerful economic force and a source of moral outrage for thousands of years. Responsible nations around the world began restrictions on the international slave trade about three centuries ago. Officially, it took the first 40 years of the 19th century for law courts and legislatures of three continents to put a legal end to this ghastly commerce.

While slave trading in the United States declined through the 1830s, '40s and '50s, the new accords preventing international slave trade were often challenged, disrespected and ignored locally. Two of my ancestors, Samuel Newell Simpson and Hamilton Rowan Gamble, were among the abolitionists and others arrayed against slavery.

On November 29, 1798, my great-great-grandfather, Hamilton Rowan Gamble, was born in Winchester, Virginia, the youngest of seven children of Joseph and Anne Hamilton Gamble. Scots-Irish, the Gambles had emigrated in 1784 from Northern Ireland. Gamble studied law and, at age 19, was accepted to the bar in Virginia. In 1818, he moved to St. Louis, Missouri, to join his elder brother, Archibald, a clerk in the St. Louis Circuit Court. Great-great-grandfather Hamilton Gamble became a Missouri barrister at a crucial time in history, as 1818 was the year when Missouri lawmakers petitioned Congress for admission of their state to the union. Passage of that petition was delayed by New York representative James Tallmadge in February 1819, when he proposed an amendment barring slavery in Missouri. Its defeat and the ensuing storm of controversy eventually resulted in the passage of the Missouri Compromise on March 3, 1820.

On May 10, 1821, Missouri was admitted to the Union under the terms of the Missouri Compromise, allowing Missourians to hold slaves. An aspiring young attorney at the time, Hamilton Rowan Gamble was a Missouri slave-holder, as before.

The Missouri Compromise prohibited slaves elsewhere in the Louisiana Purchase (including the territory that became Kansas).

One of the largest land sales in history with the United States paying France approximately $15 million for over 800,000 square miles of land, the Louisiana Purchase was touted as one of the greatest achievements of Thomas Jefferson's presidency, but the Missouri Compromise posed a problem in political philosophy for the former president.

"In the gloomiest days of the Revolutionary War, I never had any apprehensions equal to what I feel for this source…" said Jefferson. "The Missouri question is the most portentous that ever threatened the Union."

The reasons for Jefferson's gloom were probably due to changes in motives for secession. During the creation of the U.S. Constitution, Jefferson had written about secession as an option for a dissident state, but in conference with other framers of the documents, he had voted not to include secession because it had no place in a document devoted to the creation of a unified republic. For an effective secession, causes of dissension had to be manifested and these were directly opposite to causes and principles of an agreed union of states.

However, Jefferson was sadly aware that the cause of secession was honored in both the constitutions of New York and Virginia. In 1820, Jefferson called an act of secession a "fire-bell in the night," meaning that the crisis over slavery could easily cause war between states.

In 1824, Hamilton Rowan Gamble was appointed secretary of state, moving to St. Charles, Missouri, which was then the capitol. When the capitol was moved to Jefferson City in 1826, Gamble returned to private legal practice in St. Louis. Although a slave holder, Gamble defended slaves in court. That same year, he became a member of the American Colonization Society, which supported the resettlement of free blacks to Liberia.

In 1827, Gamble married Elizabeth J. Coalter of Columbia, South Carolina. Elizabeth's sister was the wife of attorney Edward Bates of St. Louis, who was later appointed President Abraham Lincoln's attorney general during the Civil War.

After an illustrious legal career, and being elected to the Missouri Supreme Court, the first justice from the Whig party, my great-great-grandfather Gamble quickly rose to chief justice. Though still a slaveholder, he dissented in the 1852 Missouri Supreme Court decision of the Dred Scott v. Emerson case, winning national recognition. Gamble maintained that Scott was free because he had been held illegally as a slave while residing in a free state, basing his dissent on the 28 year old precedent set in the 1824 ruling of "once free, always free," in Winney v. Whitesides. The court ruled against Dred Scott, but he and his lawyers vowed to continue fighting for his freedom.

Hamilton Rowan Gamble

While Gamble, my mother's maternal ancestor, was dissenting on behalf of a slave in Missouri, my mother's paternal grandfather, Samuel Newell Simpson, was heading west toward Lawrence, Kansas. The grandson of John Simpson (our family's revolutionary war hero), Samuel Newell Simpson was a member of an anti-slavery group whose objective was "saving Kansas" so it could be voted as a free state in accordance with the Kansas-Nebraska Act of May 1854.

The Kansas-Nebraska Act became law on May 30, 1854, when the U.S. Congress established the territories of Kansas and Nebraska, adhering to a provision submitted by Stephen Douglas, chairman of the Senate Committee on Territories, that the question of slavery should be left to the decision of the territorial settlers themselves. This was the famous principle that Douglas called popular sovereignty, flatly contradicting the provisions of the Missouri Compromise (under which slavery was barred from both territories). In fact, an amendment was actually added to the act specifically repealing the Missouri compromise. Enraged by the bill's adoption, anti-slavery forces immediately began marshalling citizen groups to keep Kansas a free state.

Great-grandfather Samuel N. Simpson was a member of such a citizen group, called the Emigrant Aid Company, and was one of the aggregate of 1,240 settlers that came to Kansas.

Samuel N. Simpson, born into a family of pioneers, was one of six founders of Lawrence, Kansas. A man who revered oral and written history, my great-grandfather was the one who suggested that the new Kansas town be named Lawrence, in honor of abolitionist and philanthropist Amos A. Lawrence of Boston, Massachusetts. Upon being informed of this honor, Mr.

Samuel Newell Simpson

Lawrence sent a draft for $10,000 to the town, directing that the money be used for educational purposes. Later, the fund was increased to $14,000 and the City of Lawrence offered it for the establishment of Kansas State University, provided that it was located in Lawrence, which it was.

Samuel N. Simpson was proud to be one of the founders and was recognized by his peers as a man of action and vision. He worked on the town plat, creating streets, parks, and zones, for a proud city of the future. To reinforce the stability of their new town, Samuel and his brothers, Henry M. and William A. Simpson, joined together to build and run the Simpson Bank.

As a member of the Emigrant Aid Company that sponsored his family's emigration to Kansas, Samuel did not ignore anti-slavery politics. He worked diligently to bring Kansas into the Union as a free state. Threatening, however, were violent confrontations on the Kansas/Missouri border involving "Jayhawkers" (radical anti-slavery Kansans) raiding into Missouri and pro-slavery Missouri "Bushwackers and Border Ruffians." In addition to their aggression at the border, the pro-slavery forces installed Missourians in Kansas as "short-term residents," thus infiltrating Kansas for voting purposes only.

Scarcely a month after his arrival in Lawrence, Kansas in 1854, Samuel N. Simpson and his fellow Kansans faced a massive wave of armed pro-slavery

Border Ruffians (mostly Missourians) pouring into Kansas in an attempt to steal the election to Congress of a single territorial anti-slavery delegate. As a result, less than half the votes were by registered voters and the pro-slavery forces won the election. It appeared that the 1854 Kansas/Nebraska Act was all but dead, with illegal forces of such magnitude stacked against it.

This vicious "foreign" attack galvanized the leaders and townspeople of Lawrence and many other Kansas communities to prepare to defend themselves.

On March 30, 1855, the Border Ruffians, in ever greater numbers, rushed over the Missouri border armed with printed sheets containing the names of Kansas candidates likely to vote pro-slave in the coming election of Territorial Legislators. Once again, fewer than half the ballots were cast by registered voters and, at one location, it was recorded that only 20 of the 600 votes were cast by legal residents. Thus, the pro-slavery legislature was elected, making a complete mockery of a representative election.

An enraged Samuel Newell Simpson was soon heading up the Free State Vigilance Committee of Lawrence, acquiring arms and ammunition from the East to aid in defense of the town. Individuals were asked to give weekly hours to training and drilling. It was hoped that groups of 30 to 40 volunteer home guards might be quickly assembled in the face of attack and provide sufficient protection for the town. Ostensibly sent by his church to solicit aid and sympathy from the young nation's leaders and thinkers, Simpson traveled throughout the east and midwest contacting known abolitionists who would subsequently support the defense of Lawrence, Kansas from pro-slavery forces. Placing them in a magazine (crate), Simpson received a shipment of Sharp's Rifles ordered by a good friend in Boston, Rev. H.W. Beecher. The crates were cleverly labeled "Beecher's Bibles."

Abolitionist John Brown moved to Lawrence in October 1855, joining heartily with Simpson and his friends in the preparation of Lawrence for defense against all attackers. Unfortunately, those preparations were insufficient for the kind of armed attack Lawrence was destined to face next.

On the 21st of May 1856, 800 Southerners, led by Sheriff Samuel Jones, gathered close to Lawrence. A large force was stationed on Mount Oread, where Charles L. Robinson (first governor of Kansas) resided. Planting a cannon at Mt. Oread to cover and command the town and blocking all pathways of escape, the attackers flew two flags that day: a blood-red flag, on which was inscribed "Southern Rights," floating side by side with the Stars and Stripes.

Sacking a town with a citizenry that was outnumbered and virtually unprepared for battle of this magnitude, the pro-slavery forces attacked two printing offices, destroyed the presses and threw the racks of type into the river. Before they rode out of town, they had blown up the Free State Hotel

Samuel Newell Simpson, in later years

and burned down the private dwelling of Charles L. Robinson on Mt. Oread. Amazingly, there was only one fatality as a result of the first sacking of Lawrence — a slavery proponent killed by falling masonry.

On first reading about the sack of Lawrence, one cannot help but be dismayed by the total lack of defensive preparation. Nevertheless, readers will recall that an unrealistic 30 to 40 volunteer home guards were on call as a defensive measure at that time. So, when confronted with 800 armed and mounted fighters, it would be inconceivable for intelligent leaders to throw their pathetic forces piecemeal at this sizeable enemy without risking total disaster.

At the request of his family in his later years, great-grandfather Samuel Newell Simpson recorded his memories in writing and it was noted that, due to modesty, he avoided the pronoun "I," preferring to refer to himself in the third person. With personal detachment and candor, his well-written narrative provided a first-hand look at the experiences of those early abolitionist settlers of Lawrence. Excerpts of the narrative by Samuel Newell Simpson, taken from Volume 4, pages 1999-2002 of *A Standard History of Kansas and Kansans*, can be found in Addendum A at the back of this book.

Violence became so commonplace in Kansas that renowned newspaper publisher Horace Greeley labeled the torn and turbulent territory "Bleeding Kansas."

During John Brown's activity in Kansas, Great-grandfather Samuel N.

Simpson was supportive, helping to supply guns and ammunition to Brown. The relationship between Brown and my great-grandfather was probably strengthened by Brown's angry reaction to the attacks on Lawrence, and his resulting retaliation in several confrontations prior to his legendary raid on Harper's Ferry, Virginia.

Following his raid on Harper's Ferry, Brown was arrested and found guilty of treason against the Commonwealth of Virginia. Family legend has it that while awaiting trial, John Brown received a visit from his friend, Samuel Newell Simpson, and was urged by Simpson to plead insanity and escape the hangman's noose. Brown countered that he was fully aware of his guilt in breaking the sedition laws, in addition to the earlier charge of treason. He knew that he would face the gallows in any case. On December 2, 1859, the day he was hung, Brown penned his last prophecy for posterity:

> *"I John Brown am now quite certain that the crimes*
> *of this guilty land: will never be purged away; but with*
> *Blood. I had as I now think: vainly flattered myself that*
> *without very much bloodshed; it might be done."*

Residing in bordering states at about the same period in history, my two ancestors, Gamble and Simpson, held many of the same social and moral values. They were destined to be forever connected not only by their courage and action, but by family ties through the marriage of their descendants, Mary Minor Gamble and Charles Lyon Simpson.

In 1857, Gamble's earlier dissent in Missouri still resonated in the hearts and minds of abolitionists when Dred Scott again lost the decision, this time with seven out of nine Justices of the United States Supreme Court declaring that no slave or descendant of a slave could be a U.S. citizen, and that he must, as a non-citizen with no rights, remain a slave.

The Court's decision enraged presidential candidate Abraham Lincoln, who publicly spoke out against it, noting that there were nearly four million slaves in America and that the ruling affected the status of every enslaved and free African-American in the nation and pointing out that black men in five of the original states had been full voting citizens dating back to the 1776 Declaration of Independence.

After Lincoln was elected President in 1860, the Southern slave states, led by South Carolina, seceded from the Union in protest of his opposition to slavery. By the time Lincoln was inaugurated President on March 4, 1861, despite his protestations that he had no plans to end slavery in those states where it already existed, war was imminent. Determined to resolve the national crisis without bloodshed and put an end to the Southern secession, Lincoln continued to seek a balance even after the war began. As an example, he welcomed Kansas into the Union as a free state in 1861. That same year, Gamble attended the State Convention at the insistence of his brother-in-law, Edward Bates, who by then had been appointed attorney general in President Lincoln's administration. The state convention was being held to determine whether or not Missouri should secede, and, as his brother-in-law had hoped, Gamble became the main proponent for Missouri to remain in the Union. Delegates elected him chairman of the Committee on Federal Relations.

In June of 1861, Gamble was appointed provisional governor of Missouri after Governor Claiborne Fox Jackson, a Southern sympathizer, fled the capital with fellow supporters.

It is said that when confirming the appointment of the provisional governor of Missouri, President Lincoln wrote a letter to Gamble, attempting to verify that he was no longer a slave owner. In response, Governor Gamble is said to have written: "Dear President Lincoln, I am no longer a slave owner as of three months ago."

As provisional governor, Gamble remained committed to keeping Missouri from seceding from the Union as well as to maintaining law and order. He sought to restore peace and issued special orders to kill guerrillas in Missouri. Guerrillas were civilian combatants who worked to sabotage Union military efforts. During the Civil War, Gamble supported a gradual system of emancipation rather than an immediate end to slavery.

One of Governor Gamble's first challenges was dealing with "The Great Pathfinder," Union General John C. Fremont, who declared martial law in Missouri on August 30, 1861, initiating an Emancipation Proclamation that unilaterally freed all slaves there. So smug was Fremont in his role of leadership, and so certain was he that his orders would be instantly obeyed, the general even went so far as to have his emancipation proclamation published in the August 31 edition of The Democrat, a Missouri newspaper. Governor Gamble was fully aware that President Lincoln and Congress were desperately attempting to keep the border slave states from seceding by insisting that the war was not about slavery, but about restoring the Union.

Knowing that Fremont's proclamation would fuel the fires of dissension and alienate conservative support, Gamble reported Fremont's actions to the President.

A tug-of-war ensued between Lincoln and Fremont, with the President at first requesting some modifications to the proclamation. Fremont stubbornly refused to change the proclamation without a direct order from the President, even sending his wife, Jessie, to the White House to plead his case to the President. Lincoln biographer Benjamin P. Thomas wrote: "Jessie did not help her husband's case. President Lincoln recalled that 'She sought an audience with me at midnight and taxed me so violently with many things that I had to exercise all the awkward tact I have to avoid quarreling with her… She more than once intimated that if General Fremont should conclude to try conclusions with me he could set up for himself…'"

Historian James M. McPherson wrote: "A wiser man would have treated Lincoln's request as an order. But with a kind of pro-consular arrogance that did not sit well with Lincoln, Fremont refused to modify his proclamation without a public order to do so."

On September 11th, the morning after Jessie Fremont's midnight visit, President Lincoln ordered Fremont to rescind his emancipation proclamation and then give up his official command in Missouri and depart for assignments elsewhere. However, it was to Governor Gamble's credit that he stood up for the President's principles of preventing further secession that kept Missouri in the union and out of range of a "loose cannon" Brigadier General.

Proper timing for taking initiative was a common thread that bound my predecessors, Gamble and Simpson.

It was on a hot August morning in 1863 that Great-grandfather Samuel Newell Simpson made a decision to protect members of his family from Quantrill's Raiders by hiding them in a Kansas cornfield. Crouching among the cornstalks was not Simpson's style, but it was a necessary act considering the alternatives for the Simpson family. They watched in terror as Bushwacker William Clarke Quantrill, a Confederate guerilla leader and former school teacher, led a ragtag army of more than 400 on horseback out of the burning city of Lawrence and down the road toward their property. Quantrill and his raiders were bent on preserving the rights of slave-owners in Missouri and their intent was to burn every house and kill every man in Lawrence. Their vicious early morning attack resulted in the murders of 183 men and "boys old enough to hold a rifle." Often, the savage raiders dragged men and boys from their burning houses and executed them before the eyes of their families. Only the quick thinking of Great-grandfather Simpson saved the men of our family that day.

A year later, in 1864, Samuel Newell Simpson married Kate Lyon Burnett, daughter of Judge Calvin Burnett, one of the most influential citizens of Lawrence. She was a lady of superior culture, well-educated and a successful teacher, including drawing and French among her subjects, and became the mother of three children: Charles Lyon (my grandfather), who attended M.I.T. in Boston, and became a successful realtor; Bernett Newell, a lawyer who graduated from Harvard University; and Nellie Josephine, who became the wife of William A. Ackenhousen, a merchant of Kansas City, Missouri.

That same year, Governor Hamilton Rowan Gamble died while in office due to complications from a broken arm that became infected. When he died, Great-great-grandfather Gamble left behind him his wife, Elizabeth, and their three children, Hamilton (the father of Mary Minor Gamble, my maternal grandmother), David and Mary Coalter Gamble.

An old flint-lock musket once fired by American militiaman John Simpson has been handed down through the generations of our family. It is one of the few tangible evidences of the courage and tenacity displayed by both the paternal and maternal sides of my mother's family. The musket is a fitting symbol of the American spirit that flows in our blood.

Author's Note: In addition to their great integrity and determination, both Samuel Newell Simpson and Hamilton Rowan Gamble possessed talents that distinguished them from other men of their time. Their special ability was to work closely with others and, without wasting time, define an issue and provide a workable solution for it.

Hamilton Gamble and President Lincoln formed a unique partnership that saved the State of Missouri for the Union, and, until his death in 1864, Governor Gamble managed as well as anyone could, the most fractious and violent state in the Union. Missouri suffered from the ravages of Quantrill and his gang, the James brothers, the Daltons, two Confederate armies, and hundreds of other desperadoes.

Samuel Newell Simpson served causes he believed in with a wide range of significant people such as John Brown, anti-slavery firebrand, Carrie Nation, prohibitionist and liquor-bar smasher, and U.S. Army generals (whether they were leading their troops with or against Kansas as a free state). Later in life, he worked closely with mayors and governors in both Kansas and Missouri on real estate issues and the founding of new towns. He also dealt with authoritative Indian braves and tribal chiefs over land ownership claims.

Samuel Newell Simpson and Hamilton Rowan Gamble were vital to their nation and I am extremely proud to be their descendant.

CHAPTER 2

Power in the Ground

The first McLucas to come to America was John, born in 1764 in Londonderry Down, Northern Ireland. He was my great-great-great-great-grandfather who, with his bride, Martha Thompson, lived as a farmer in Westmoreland, Pennsylvania.

In 1795, just a year prior to the birth of John and Martha's son, John McLucas, Jr., the U.S. victory won at the Battle of Fallen Timbers* brought about a new spirit of peace. Marked by the signing of a treaty at Greenville, Ohio, between American Indians and the U.S. Government, the treaty favored the growth and reputation of families like mine. For several years, native American Indian tribes had wreaked havoc on settlers and their communities in the Northwest Territory until troops led by General "Mad Anthony" Wayne had been summoned by President George Washington to bring peace and order to the frontier. "Mad Anthony" Wayne had command of a large body of quickly but properly trained troops calculated to completely defeat the native Ohio/Indiana Indian tribesmen.

General Wayne's new force had superior numbers but one can imagine the diehard character and barbaric look of the enemy warriors as they

* *The Battle of Fallen Timbers was fought on August 20, 1794, and is famous for the decisive victory of the United States over a confederacy of Indian tribes. The fight took place between the two at Fallen Timbers, which was an area full of trees toppled by a tornado, and was just to the north of the Maumee River.*

gathered before the Battle of Fallen Timbers: the Shawnee, Mingo, Delaware, Wyandot, Miami, Ottawa, Chippewa and Potawatomi. This native Algonquin force was soundly defeated with modest losses to General Wayne's troops and signaled the beginnings of an uneasy truce.

On opposite sides of the Battle of Fallen Timbers were two emerging historical icons, Shawnee Chief Tecumseh and William Henry Harrison, future governor of the newly formed Indiana Territory. Tecumseh was not among the signers of the Treaty of Greenville or the later Treaty of Fort Wayne, vigorously opposing the treaties and massive land acquisitions that allowed settlers into Ohio and Indiana and appeased Indians with large subsidies of money and liberal distribution of liquor prior to negotiations. A talented orator, Tecumseh traveled widely, urging other Indian chiefs to join him in resistance of U.S. land acquisition. He strongly warned Governor Harrison to rescind the Treaty of Fort Wayne, in which a delegation of Indians ceded three million acres of Native American lands to the United States.

In August 1810, Tecumseh led 400 armed warriors to confront Harrison, who rejected Tecumseh's demand and argued that Tecumseh's interference was unwelcome by the other tribes of the area. Until Tecumseh's death in the Battle of the Thames during the War of 1812, pockets of violence continued to erupt on this new frontier due to his passionate determination to save Indian lands. In the main, however, the attitudes of the Native American Indians had changed. Their tribes began to seek living space elsewhere in America and pioneers seeking farmland began to settle in Indiana. The newly peaceful territory of Indiana became a state in 1816.

For farming families like that of John McLucas, Jr., who brought his bride, Malinda Brooks, to Indiana in 1820, the wild frontier slowly vanished. Freedom abounded, with the ability to plan cultivation of their land, to plant and harvest crops, and to be able to enjoy life with fishing, hunting, and gathering of nature's riches. They stored supplies for the long winters, as the Indians had done before them, and communicated with other people of like mind, participating actively in social, civic and political affairs.

My great-great-grandfather, Wilson T. McLucas, the son of John and Malinda, was born in 1823 in Harrison County, Cadiz, Indiana. Wilson was eventually drafted and fought in the Union Army during the Civil War from 1863 to 1865. He and his wife, Elizabeth, raised six children in

Indiana, including my great-grandfather, John Calvin McLucas.

John married 17-year-old Lewessa Belle Cooper in 1874 and on July 18, 1875, in Newcastle, Indiana, their son, my grandfather, Walter Scott McLucas was born. Shortly after the birth of their son, the McLucas family moved to Fairbury, Nebraska, where John Calvin McLucas became a successful farmer, and where Walter received his early schooling. Due to his acute perception of practicalities, young Walter also learned a great deal about modern farming, especially the importance of tools and efficient systems for their employment. His powers of observation and his utilitarianism would serve him well in later years.

Prior to his graduation from the State University at Lincoln, Nebraska, Walter asked advice from his father and others in agriculture and livestock-raising and thus obtained a lead on a job with Byers Brothers Livestock in Omaha, Nebraska. Diploma in hand, the enterprising young McLucas spent the next 18 months learning about the livestock commission and loan business in Nebraska's largest city.

Meanwhile, another, smaller Nebraska burg called Beatrice held a romantic interest for McLucas — namely, a fair young woman named Grace Nichols, descended from a fine family with a historical legacy that qualified her as a member of the National Society of the Daughters of the American Revolution (DAR Number: 62271.)

Walter and Grace were married in Beatrice in 1898. A daughter, Marjorie, was born of their union in 1899 and a son, John (my father), was born in 1904.

My grandfather's interests in those early years turned from livestock and agriculture to the study of law and humankind under pressure. After intense study of shorthand, he became official court reporter for Judge Charles B. Letton in the First Judicial District of Nebraska, serving for a period of three and one-half years. His stint at court reporting enhanced his ability to remember names, facts and figures as well as his entrepreneurial bent, which he next applied to opening his own office in St. Joseph, Missouri, for Byers Brothers Livestock.

The following year, young Walter Scott McLucas opened a Byers branch office at Kansas City and organized a Missouri corporation to handle the company's affairs in this state, he being part owner, secretary and treasurer.

Walter McLucas began his banking career in 1908, when he gained control of the Merchants Bank of St. Joseph, Missouri, of which he became

Walter S. McLucas

vice president and cashier. In October 1912, this bank and the First National Bank of St. Joseph consolidated, and my grandfather took office as its first vice president.

Walter McLucas was a visionary who learned a great deal about banking and enough about several other industries in the midwest to realize the importance of the automobile in the American economy. So vital was the key relationship of the automotive industry to all transport in America, it permitted an exciting view into the future as any far-sighted man could see. Grandfather McLucas knew many of the risks and major problems of promoting new industry, so he wisely narrowed his sights to those responsible for the production of automobile fuel — petroleum in the ground to be extracted, refined and brought to a market as large as the planet itself.

By 1915, Walter McLucas was privileged to become acquainted with William Thornton Kemper, President of the Commerce Trust Company of Kansas City, Missouri, the midwest's largest bank. When Mr. Kemper and his board invited my grandfather to accept a vice presidency and board membership of the Commerce Trust Company of Kansas City, Missouri, he accepted enthusiastically. As vice president of the First National Merchants Bank of St. Joseph, Missouri, Walter McLucas had visited some of the Oklahoma and Texas oil fields to canvass prospective clients for bank loans. Consequently, my grandfather's ability to provide funds to qualified business borrowers was at its summit and he was ready to embrace the role of best lender in the oil fields of the United States. He mustered all his business ability learned and developed over 40 years to back up this decision, and went to work immediately contacting prospective clients for new loans to finance oil field drilling.

The results were unprecedented. He became a banking legend in the oil fields for his luck and his masterful ability to make loans to reliable clients over the next 38 years.

In business terms, Walter Scott McLucas's successful one-on-one deals with petroleum producers were the quintessence of that special American model of communication described so eloquently by Historian Gordon S. Wood in his Pulitzer Prize-winning book, *The Radicalism of the American Revolution*.

My grandfather admired these adventurous oil men and enjoyed being with them — eating, drinking and card-playing. Being a conservative in all three activities, Walter managed his life on the petroleum road with aplomb.

When first proposing these expansive new oil field loans to the board of the Commerce Trust Company, he encountered some opposition. "Walter, we are and have been primarily in the feed and grain business," they protested. "We know nothing about oil."

"Wait a minute," said he. "My confidence that these loans will be repaid on time is very strong, gentlemen. If you will approve these loans, I will put up my stock in the bank as security for them." That was how my grandfather earned the nickname, "Wait-a-Minute McLucas."

One of my grandfather's favorite people in the oil fields was Wade Phillips, president of the Phillips Petroleum Company in Bartlesville, Oklahoma. Wade Phillips was a great teacher and my grandfather thus learned much from him about the oil business.

At about age four, I was with my mother on an automobile trip in Oklahoma when she became lost and needed to seek directions. She knew of only one source of helpful information in the town of Bartlesville, Oklahoma, and that was the legendary Mr. Wade Phillips, whom she had never met. When she knocked on the door of his home, she was surprised to be greeted by Mr. Phillips himself.

My resourceful mother smiled charmingly at him and introduced herself as the mother of Walter McLucas's grandson and namesake, which child was at the time peeping shyly from behind her skirt.

One glance at me, and Mr. Phillips burst out laughing. "I'd recognize that face anywhere!" he declared. "He is the spitting image of his grandfather! Mrs. McLucas, what can I do for you today?" She asked for and received information on how to reach our next destination, for which she thanked him and went on her way. A portrait of my grandfather, father and me attests to the fact that we were, indeed, family.

Three Generations of McLucas Men

Another of my grandfather's rich

friendships, garnered from his connections with the oil fields, was with a man named Harry Sinclair. Harry was the founder of the Sinclair Oil Company. From 1915 to 1921, they developed a great friendship, with implicit trust between them. They shared information concerning individuals and business activity in the oil fields. Nevertheless, in 1921, their relationship had to change drastically. Harry was under indictment by the court system for a variety of infractions related to the Teapot Dome Oil Scandal.* So, to protect my grandfather's position with the Commerce Trust Company of Kansas City, their business relationship had to cease and communication between them lapsed until much later.

*Note: The Teapot Dome Oil Scandal concerned a cartel of important U.S. oil companies and their associates who attempted to commercialize privately most of the country's state and national oil reserves. The cartel's associates in the scandal included President Harding and his entire cabinet and the Secretary of the Navy, Secretary of the Interior and Secretary of the Treasury. The ten-year campaign in U.S. law courts against the unprincipled villains responsible for the scandal was led by the heroic Senator Thomas J. Walsh, Dem., Montana. Most of the criminals were punished and Senator Walsh won back most of our nation's integrity.

Having become president of the Commerce Trust Company of Kansas City in 1917, my grandfather took temporary leave in 1921 to accept the vice presidency of the First National City Bank of New York, where he served as head of the country bank division. After more than a year of working with some of the most important bankers in America, he returned to resume his presidency of the Commerce Trust Company. That year and a half spent at First National City Bank served as a catalyst for success throughout the remainder of his career and his life. He gained mastery of his gift for banking while in New York, using it as a classic model from that time forward, having learned how important it was to always maintain contact with national bank operations and principles as a source of information.

When he renewed his responsibilities as president of the Commerce Trust Company, his primary goal was to help make it the most important bank in Missouri and potentially the best in the midwest! Together with a great team of seasoned executives such as James T. Kemper. Sr., Jo Zach Miller, and others (brilliant young visionaries from all parts of the country) he went to work creating new business in the growing metropolis of Kansas City.

During the early 1920s, one of the most important chapters in American economic history began to emerge. Despite prohibition, the Teapot Dome Scandal and the rising criminalization of many cities and towns, one of the most impressive economic expansions of all time came from the United States. In that decade, there was great economic growth and prosperity throughout the nation, engendering new interests in technology, modern science, fashions, the arts, theatre and music. Kansas City, for instance, developed a reputation for great jazz, which attracted visitors as well as local townspeople to enjoy a new and exciting style of music.

Innovation was the name of the game and it occurred in banking, too. W. T. Kemper's initiatives concerning the need for a friendly atmosphere in which new businesses could flourish resulted in new employment practices that changed the face of banking forever. One of the Commerce Trust Company's most popular new features became its Women's Department, located in the main office on Walnut Street. In earlier days, women had not been given credit for any ability to handle financial matters (after all, they had only won the right to vote in 1920!), but now Mrs. Ralph Beebe was put in charge of the Women's Department and she did more than help women with banking matters. She answered daily requests that ranged from how to give a speech on "Women in The Business World," to figuring an estimate on costs of wallpapering an entire house.

In a bank article listing these daily requests, Mrs. Beebe commented, "People go to their doctor to talk of their aches and pains, to their minister to talk about their souls and to their bank to discuss all the subjects just mentioned, as well as for business and financial reasons." Especially true for women, in those early years, their business was more personal than commercial.

Obviously, caring about the customer included providing more than actual banking services, and that philosophy brought tremendous growth to the Commerce Trust Company. Through providing good customer service, as well as undergoing several mergers and acquisitions, by the early 1920s, the Commerce Trust Company bank capital stood at $6,000,000 and surplus at $2,000,000.

We have seen that my grandfather's high number of loans to oil drillers in Oklahoma and Texas brought a new resource of revenue to his bank. Earlier, when the Kansas City, Mexico and Orient Railway was declared bankrupt, W. T. Kemper (then president of the Commerce Trust Company) was declared its receiver. Mr. Kemper, now totally cognizant of the benefits to be derived from power in the ground, immediately ordered that test oil wells be dug along the railroad's right of way, thus saving the bankrupt line. Without fanfare, successful oil wells were opened at several places along the railroad's tracks, and by 1925, the railroad was recapitalized and divided into the Kansas City, Mexico and Orient Railroad of Texas and the Kansas City, Mexico and Orient Railroad of Kansas. Another piece became the Quincy, Oklahoma and Kansas City Railroad, and in 1928, the railroad was acquired by the Atchison, Topeka and Santa Fe Railroad.

Many other Commerce Bank-financed industries grew steadily during the 1920s, including those of automotive and aircraft manufacturers. My grandfather excelled in nurturing these new and exciting industries. Unfortunately, the end of prosperity came abruptly on October 29, 1929, with the great stock market crash. This was followed by the Great Depression.

As an interesting aside, popular legend has it that a strange culture had grown prevalent in the oil fields during that time of power in the ground. It was a culture that was as old as mankind himself, but as new as the black gold flowing from the fields of this young nation. A simplified explanation of the way the new oil field culture worked follows: Oil Man A (very successful) and Oil Man B (moderately successful) are in love with the same Lovely Lady. To the regret of Oil Man B, the Lovely Lady accepts the marriage proposal of Oil Man A and marries him. Eventually, Oil Man A falls on hard times while Oil Man B begins to prosper. Assets eroded, Oil Man A is afraid of having to go out of business, but Oil Man B sees his plight and offers a solution. "Pal," he says, "I see you're having a hard time. If you'll divorce Lovely Lady, I'll pay you $5,000 for her." Oil Man A agrees to that proposal and Lovely Lady, quite content with the new arrangement, happily marries the now wealthy Oil Man B. The culture of "wretched excess" reigned in the oil fields, and it eventually spread throughout the nation. It was most certainly one of the causes leading inevitably to the deprivation of the Great Depression.

One day and one month before the crash of 1929, I was born to Hamilton Simpson and John Nichols McLucas at a hospital in Kansas City, Missouri. My parents honored me by naming me after my grandfather, Walter Scott McLucas.

Today, we know much more about the Great Depression — how enormous it was all around the globe and the effects of rising political extremism in Germany, Italy, USSR, Bulgaria, Romania and other nations, which led to World War II. The crash of 1929, which spread so quickly to stock markets worldwide, deeply affected both my father and my grandfather, whose lives had been entwined with the banking business in America for many years. Especially shocking to them were the bank failures everywhere, regardless of state or national boundaries.

However, the bank failures contained a totally unexpected advantage for my grandfather. It had nothing to do with *Schadenfreude* (a German expression for gaining advantage intentionally from the misfortunes of others). Rather, my grandfather's good fortune came about because he was believed to be the ideal person in the U.S. to create and head up a new source of funding for a depression-battered builder of automobiles and trucks — General Motors! Who decided that Walter McLucas was the best banker in America to revive its most important automotive company? The answer was that several executives of General Motors, together with Mr. Jess H. Jones, head of the Reconstruction Finance Corporation (RFC), newly created by the Hoover Administration to rebuild crippled industry, chose my grandfather over several other candidates. Other politicians representing banking and the oil industry also contributed to the final decision.

What happened was that all the banks in Michigan collapsed in 1932, leaving the automotive industry in dire straits, unable to meet their payrolls and costs of manufacturing new cars without borrowing. Ford and other manufacturers apparently had enough reserves to eke out their cost of sales for a while, but General Motors found that they no longer had sufficient cash to continue business as before. They did, however, have sufficient cash to help finance a new bank in which the major investment was to be made by the RFC.

My grandfather felt terribly conflicted about certain aspects of his decision to accept this new role. He hated giving up the chairmanship of the Commerce Trust Company in Kansas City, particularly at a time when his bank was suffering badly in the Depression and his departure might be looked upon as an act of cowardice. However, his new position would require building a sizeable new bank from the bottom up, and he could not resist the challenge. He felt that if he surrounded himself with a great team of talented and innovative executives, the challenge would be met.

So, he went traveling to meet powerful people in Washington, New York and Michigan to gain their support, and during the first months of 1933, he concentrated on careful hiring and planning work for his staff at the new bank.

On March 5, 1933, President Roosevelt gave his inaugural address to the nation and announced a four-day national bank holiday to end on March 10. He also announced that on the 11th, some banks would reopen for business, but others might still be delayed in reopening. On the 10th of March, he announced that, indeed, some banks had reopened, some were still delayed in so doing, and unfortunately, others would not reopen. However, the president stated that great hopes remained for more re-openings and that there would soon be new national banks which would open for the first time.

On March 24, 1933, the brand new National Bank of Detroit, Inc. opened for the benefit of the citizens of Detroit, the citizens of the State of Michigan, and new corporate clients such as the General Motors Corporation, which would be served from that day onward.

My grandfather was elected chairman and president of the National Bank of Detroit (NBD) and numerous innovations in banking were introduced under his guidance. The General Motors Acceptance Corporation (GMAC) was financed by the bank to enable customers to buy vehicles on time. Also, at the end of the first six years of operation, the NBD Bank had paid off its initial loan from General Motors and by the end of the seventh year, NBD had paid off its RFC Loan as well.

The impressive history of General Motors production of vehicles — flying, crawling and rolling — is forever tied to the history of the National Bank of Detroit, and the friendship that developed between my grandfather and the then head of General Motors, Alfred P. Sloan, is legendary. They were like two sides of a coin, each of them American pioneers in their own right.

Grandfather Walter S. McLucas was at the helm of the National Bank of Detroit from the day it opened in 1933 until his death in 1953. It was, at that time, the 13th largest bank in the United States.

Author's Note: Excerpt from General Motors website regarding World War II: "From 1940 to 45, the Company produced defense material at a value of 12.3 billion dollars. Decentralized and highly flexible local managerial responsibility made possible the almost overnight conversion from civilian to wartime production. GM's contribution included the manufacture of every conceivable product from the smallest ball bearings to large tanks, naval ships, fighting planes, bombers, guns, cannons and projectiles. The Company manufactured 1,300 airplanes and one quarter of all U.S. aircraft engines." (This illustrates the "industrial version" of Pulitzer prize winning Historian Gordon S. Wood's concept in his book, The Radicalism of the American Revolution, wherein he describes the social relationships and how "the way people were connected one to another — were changed, and decisively so." My grandfather, throughout his illustrious career in banking, had a way of "connecting" with people who were world-changers.)

CHAPTER 3

Silver and Gold

My maternal grandfather, Charles Simpson, was fortunate in following his father's footsteps with great success in real estate. You may recall his father, Samuel Newell Simpson, was one of the founders of Lawrence, Kansas, and fought hard against land and vote-stealing border ruffians to preserve and protect his property there. Eventually, that property extended up to the outskirts of Kansas City, Missouri, and beyond, and the pioneering Simpson family was credited with much of that growth.

Proud of their patriotic lineage and their success as developers and landowners, both father and son enjoyed emulating historic land barons of days gone by. They particularly admired heroic military men on horseback, men such as Napoleon Bonaparte! A treasured family heirloom still in my possession is an old reproduction of a famous David portrait of Bonaparte crossing the Alps on horseback during his second Italian campaign. Also remaining from the collection of Samuel and Charles Simpson are commemorative urns of two Napoleonic victories, one at Wagram, Austria and the other depicting the victory at Friedland, East Prussia.

Charles was unquestionably a stylish horseman who prided himself on managing teams of two, four or six horses while on the seat of an appropriate carriage, invariably impressing his passengers with the level of his skill. Hamilton, the daughter of Charles, admired her father and enjoyed horseback riding and other sports (including tree-climbing — definitely not encouraged for most girls). In fact, Hamilton's father had hoped for a boy and, thusly, had irretrievably given her a boy's name in spite of her true gender. So it was not surprising that Hamilton became somewhat of a tomboy. Charles took his little "Hammie" out to New Mexico and taught her how to ride a horse properly. Horseback riding and all things equestrian were to forever remain a passion for my mother.

While Hamilton eventually picked up the endearing nickname of "Hammie," her older sister, Dorothea, was called "Sister" by those close to her, including her younger sister. Both nicknames followed the girls into adulthood.

My grandparents, Charles and Mary Simpson, traveled often to Europe and even to the Middle East. Their travels in the early 1900s were arranged by Thomas Cook & Son, Ltd., virtually the only travel organization allowed to rent to affluent tourists such unusual amenities as a team of six horses and a carriage, as well as the right to drive those horses wherever they pleased throughout the Holy Land. Following his last dashing tour of the Middle East, Grandfather Charles was, forever after, one extremely proud modern Crusader who spoke often and at length of driving behind a splendid team of horses through the Holy Land.

Hammie as a young girl

Thomas Cook & Son, Ltd. also arranged acts of diplomacy where necessary since Jerusalem and other places dear to Christian believers were all under Turkish administration, with commercial concessions to the British and the French. While touring the Holy Land, the Simpsons even heard rumors of petroleum being extracted between the Tigris and Euphrates Rivers and being refined to make fuel which could someday replace coal. Imagine that!

The way home, prior to World War I, varied from trip to trip, but was long. From the shores of Acre on the Bay of Haifa to Marseilles and then across France to the Atlantic and finally home in Kansas City, it took over one tiring month.

Welcomed home by their two daughters, the Simpsons were soon to hear about a new teacher at Ms. Barstow's school, where Hammie was a student. Miss Babbit, recently arrived from Boston, had captured the heart of Uncle Bert, brother of Charles and a recent widower. Soon, Uncle Bert and Miss Babbit were wed. Thus, Miss Babbit became Aunt Miriam Simpson who took up residence with Uncle Bert on the edge of The Plaza in Kansas City, one of the biggest early shopping centers in America (started in 1906). The two of them traveled the world throughout the 1920s. They became the most traveled relatives in my family. They brought back china, glass and jewelry from the Mediterranean and the Orient and a great deal of the same from Europe, as did many affluent tourists of the time.

Aunt Miriam Babbit Simpson was very interesting for Kansas City society. She was slightly corpulent and had Latin features that included a rather large mole in an unfortunate part of her cheek. The startling thing about Aunt Miriam (in addition to the mole) was her accent. She had the thickest Boston Brahmin accent and expounded academically in it at all times. The leading families of Boston would have envied anyone who could lay it out the way she did in her beautiful Bostonian English. She played the grande dame to the hilt, albeit that she was a school teacher when she arrived in Kansas City. It took her about five minutes to charm the dames of high society in Kansas City. She was just large enough to be imposing and she lorded her superior accent over those who spoke in the Missouri whine. Aunt Miriam's face was a mystery — a pie-shaped mystery with a mole in it. I was convinced, as were my cousins, Deedee and Mary, that there were ghosts everywhere in Uncle Bert and Aunt Miriam's huge house, inhabiting every dark cubby hole, and this wonder woman — the strange queenly woman from Boston — was also haunting to us. We terrified one another with delight, hiding from both the ghosts and Aunt Miriam whenever we visited their house.

Many years later, a revelation about Aunt Miriam came to me most unexpectedly. I was traveling in the Azores (islands off of Portugal) and got stuck there by TWA for several days. While there, I studied the geographical mockups they had at the lodge and discovered that there were three or four islands filled with fishing villages. When I finally boarded the TWA plane going to Boston, the stewardess very snobbishly and inappropriately welcomed me to the "cattle car." There were many people aboard under the command of a labor organizer, she explained, flying to Boston to work in the vegetable and fruit fields at harvest time. I looked around the plane and, lo and behold, there were several Aunt Miriams! It tied in with what I had seen of the fishing people in the lodge who, for generations, had been taken by ship from the Azores to New England to plant and harvest vegetables. Mother told me that most of what Aunt Miriam inherited was destined for

Hammie - Belle of the Ball

relatives back east. Now I understood. In the American tradition, she had risen socially and was operating magnificently. She and Uncle Bert traveled the world and not a soul in Kansas City ever knew what I knew... until now.

As a member of one of Kansas City's most prominent and respected families, Hamilton Gamble Simpson was a sought-after belle of the ball.

The triumphant debut into Kansas City society of the intelligent, vivacious beauty was soon followed by her marriage to John Nichols "Jack" McLucas, the privileged son of another prominent Kansas City family. Each of my parents brought to their marriage the thin veneer of wealth and the powerful force of their unique individual personalities.

My father was the pampered son of a doting mother and an extremely busy father who was more devoted to his business interests than to his family. A highly respected banker, Grandfather Walter S. McLucas rarely noticed his son, John, and when he did, he must have been somewhat disappointed at his son's apparent laziness and lack of ambition. With everything handed to him on a silver platter by his mother, Grace, and the servants of the household, there were few challenges that my father faced, except for pleasing his father, which was nearly impossible.

John Nichols McLucas grew up in the shadow of a domineering and rather distant father who had little patience with incompetence. When he failed the entrance exam to Princeton University, he was sent to a cramming school for tutoring until he was able to pass the test and be admitted. Even with that helpful leg-up, Princeton requested that he not return following his sophomore year, thereby attracting his father's wrath and possible "punishment" when he was sent to work on a sand barge in the Missouri River. Unfortunately, young Jack lost the sand barge job, possibly as a result of sleeping off hangovers in the shade of the sand barge instead of working on it.

It was following his brief sand barge career that my father met and married my mother, Hamilton "Hammie" Gamble Simpson. A stunningly beautiful young woman whose family frowned upon this match, considering their breeding and position in society to be superior to that of his family, my mother later admitted that her attraction to Jack McLucas could be traced to one quality: He made her laugh.

Walter McLucas, then president of the Commerce Trust Company in Kansas City, was doubly outraged at his son's inability to hold a simple job and now the news that he was about to be married!

"To whom, for God sake?" demanded Walter of his son, Jack. "Have you made her pregnant?"

When Jack replied, "To Hammie Simpson — oldest and best family here — and no, I haven't made her pregnant," Walter McLucas was still not satisfied.

"I want you out of this city!" he growled. "So, after you marry, I will get you a job working for a telephone company somewhere, to which you will go and never return! You will not remain an embarrassment to me, your mother, or any family member. You will hear more about the telephone company job later, but get married while I can still stand to see you breathing!"

Jack married Hammie in the spring of 1926 and took off with her for Temple, Texas, in a new Ford sedan. After acquiring a cheap rental apartment, the young couple settled in and he proceeded to learn the rudiments of telephone line repair and maintenance for the Temple Texas Telephone Company. This long linesman job included climbing poles 18 to 25 feet off the ground. It got cold in Temple, Texas, and my mother had trouble with the wood stove in their apartment. She spent hours every evening bathing my father's battered, bloody hands in warm medicine baths before bed. It was killing work.

By the next spring, the newlyweds were thoroughly fed up with Temple, and everything it connoted. They drove back to Kansas City to try to convince my grandfather that his son's family debts had been paid. Part of Jack's plea to his father was that Hammie would surely leave him if he was forced to continue splicing wire.

Upon arrival in Kansas City, my grandfather coldly refused to bargain with them as a couple, so each spoke separately to him. Hammie was most effective because she was not about to sacrifice her life or married happiness to a cruel and vengeful father-in-law. Walter McLucas admired her courage and finally gave a reprieve to the young couple. John Nichols McLucas then started at the bank as an assistant teller and began his respectable life as a banker.

Prior to their courtship in Kansas City society and marriage, Hammie had attended Miss Bennett's School, a fashionable two-year Junior College in Millbrook, New York. She graduated from Miss Bennett's, but she was much shaken by the school's very modern teachings, such as that God was dead and that there were many new troubling thoughts circulating in the world, even though women could at last vote. A woman well ahead of her time, Hammie had already formed many of her thoughts and habits through working for her family's business, Simpson Realty Company.

Having been raised in a prominent real estate family, and having worked in their parents' business most of their lives, the sisters took over the real estate business in 1933 after their parents died, with the intention of closing it out. Instead, they remained property managers for many years, motivated by their concern for their downtrodden tenants. The real estate was in the Missouri River bottoms, serving a needy population. Hamilton and Dorothea were philanthropists at heart.

The girls manipulated a chap who was in charge of the "abstracts" of property in the Kansas City area, which were not to be shared without proper documentation and preparation. The abstracts (histories of property bought and sold, for how much and by whom), have since been incorporated into the title, so we rarely lay eyes on an abstract anymore. In those days, however, this was a big deal, because Kansas City had only been founded in the 1870s. This poor man who was the city clerk behind the desk got very used to the Simpson sisters and their act. He would greet them when they came in and they would state what they wanted. He had about

18 rules that didn't allow immediate inspection of an abstract by anyone, even landowners, and he would state those rules. At some point during his discourse, Dorothea would start to whimper and cry a bit. This clerk could never resist "Sister's" tearful entreaty. He would blush, lower his head, reach both arms out, turn this enormous record book around on the desk top and walk out of the room with words similar to, "I'll be back in a few minutes and I hope you will have recovered from your distress by then." Everyone benefitted from these minor acts of corruption since the Simpson sisters' records were always known as the most accurate.

Both girls, while attending high school in New York City, had stayed with their "Auntie Hamma" (Hamilton Williamson) who was a woman of some wealth. She had a good number of friends in the literary world who would visit her salon monthly to chitchat about current events and matters of interest to writers and journalists.

Her son, Latrobe, attended Harvard University and, in 1912, got a transfer to a German university in Hamburg. When asked, in 1914, whether he would like to return to the U.S. in view of our possible war with Germany, Latrobe refused, saying that he was enjoying his studies and preferred to stay. In 1917, after the U.S. declared war on Germany, Latrobe again refused to return. He remained in Germany for the duration, a ship's berth for the U.S. not being available until December of 1918.

Here we were at war with Germany and they were supplying my cousin, Latrobe, with food, lodging and education. He was entrenched in studies at a German university. Our family, well known for "sparing no horses" when it came to talking or traveling, was strangely silent about Latrobe's sojourn overseas in war time.

Years later, I asked him point-blank about that time in his life and he responded, "Well, you know, Scott, I was a student and a very serious one. We had an international group varying in members and we all got along quite well together. The only thing that was bad was the food, which was terrible, and a lot of it was supplied by the Red Cross."

The sad thing about Latrobe was that although he became a prolific writer of children's books with his wife, Ruth, he was completely inarticulate about the most important event of his life. His time spent in Germany during the war would have been an interesting read, but it has never been mentioned until now. I have three theories that may explain his silence: one, he may truly have been the classic Victorian scholar — so imbued with loyalty to the rules of scholarship that he thought of nothing else; two, he could have performed spy services for the allies, as well as doing his academic work; or three, he may possibly have been a German sympathizer, about which he would have had to keep secrets for the remainder of his days.

Latrobe Carrol was the be-all and end-all of anomalies. His life in Germany, and then his life in New York City (where he and his wife Ruth were close friends with such literary luminaries as Pulitzer Prize-winning author Willa Cather) were a complete mystery to us midwesterners.

Through my New York cousin, Ellen Adamson, who had befriended Latrobe and Ruth after they moved to the city from North Carolina late in their lives, Nancy and I got to know them well. Ruth was delightful in that she revealed to us a small but complete collection of humorous children's songs gathered from God knows where. At home or in public, Ruth would happily give a mini-concert of these little ditties, complete with special effects such as drumbeats, barks, hisses and cries of joy. Latrobe and Ruth Carrol were charming, intelligent and pleasant people to the very end of their long lives. They both lived to be over 100 years old. Latrobe's story died with him. It will forever remain in a locked closet of our family history.

Hamilton Williamson had a son, Latrobe Carrol, from her previous marriage into the famous architectural family of Latrobe, the architects who worked with L'Enfant in designing Washington D.C. There is a classic family photo of the somewhat stern Auntie Hamma posing with her son, Latrobe, a tall, gangly young man who is looking down toward his mother.

Back in the days when Latrobe was studying in war-torn Germany, my mother and her older sister, Dorothea, returned from their stay in New York City with Auntie Hamma and resumed their lives in Kansas City society. Dorothea married Gilmer Meriweather in 1920, after he graduated from Princeton in 1919. My mother admired and looked up to Gilmer so much that she allowed him to influence her life permanently. Before my father came along, Hammie had a serious two-year relationship with a young man named Robby — a boy that Gilmer and his family disliked intensely. Hammie and Robby would meet regularly for romantic picnic lunches on a bluff overlooking the Missouri River, but because Gilmer declared Robby a fool and advised Hammie that he was unfit to be her husband, she gave him up and married the man who made her laugh — my father, Jack McLucas. "Jack made us all laugh!" declared my cousin, Dee Morris, Dorothea's daughter. It's true. My father was the life of the party whenever possible.

Unfortunately, his penchant for partying was not conducive to a happy marriage. Hammie suffered two disastrous miscarriages before I came along, both of them made more miserable for her by her husband's lack of concern. In 1927, Dad dropped her off at the hospital after her labor pains began and when she lost the baby, he was nowhere to be found. She ended up having to ask for help getting home from the hospital. When she was in the throes of her second miscarriage, she managed to find him in a bar by telephoning all over town and he arrived late, but in time to bring her home from the hospital.

Finally, on September 28, 1929, I was born in Kansas City, Missouri, and named Walter Scott McLucas, II, after my paternal grandfather.

For the first five years of my life, I was loved and influenced by two women — one white and one black — my mother and my nurse, Beatrice Moore. Beatrice had served the same purpose with my father when he was a child.

"Bea" was a motherly woman — soft and gentle. I ate with her in the kitchen until I was about nine years old and then, at age ten, I was "promoted" to the dining table with my parents. Thereafter, I was witness to a perpetual verbal tennis match whenever my parents dined at the table together. I was merely the audience as they fought, tussled and argued about anything and everything. Alcohol was the fuel, and all of the verbal sparring was done in a civilized manner — both of my parents had great command of the English language and came from civilized homes, after all. They were unhappy and mismatched, but civilized.

We lived in my grandfather's house until I was about 10 years old and then he sold the house and we moved to a brand new home outside of Kansas City, just across the state line in Kansas. The last time I saw Beatrice Moore, she was cooking in the kitchen of our new house, soon before World

War II began. It hurt me when she was no longer in my life. I loved her as much as you can love someone who is publicly invisible. There are no photographs of Beatrice Moore, although she was so much a part of our family for so long. The servant class was rarely acknowledged in those days. As an adult, I've thought of her often, and with grateful affection.

I was baptized in the Episcopal Church and raised on traditional American values. I vividly remember, as a boy of about six, sitting in church

Hammie holding her infant son

between my parents as the organ music played softly and people seated themselves in pews on either side of the central aisle. Today, I realize that it was one of my mother's carefully planned scenarios that were meant to make a lasting impression. It certainly did that.

When the gentle organ music ceased, silence reigned for a moment and, suddenly, in thundering chords from the organ, the hymn "A Mighty Fortress Is Our God" blasted the silence. My head spun to the right and I watched, mesmerized by the church parade down the central aisle, two standard bearers leading the way — one supporting the church flag and the other supporting the Stars and Stripes. I was absolutely overwhelmed with admiration and pride in God, church and country. My respect for symbols originated there, and I was destined to spend my life avidly seeking their meaning.

In more recent times, after eight-plus decades of research, through many levels of life and in myriad global locations, I consider myself to be a secular humanist with a rather Gandhian view of the world — very much aware of a spiritual connection to the universe and all beings in it; respectful to all religions and spiritual beliefs, but a slave to none.

That defining moment in church was but one of several carefully planned and staged learning moments that my mother presented to me throughout my childhood.

Typically, she would pick a time that she thought appropriate to expand my experience, and then she would introduce me to something that would remain with me always. Examples of her discerning taste and determination to provide me with the same follow: She introduced me to both the splendor of Verdi's opera, Aida, and the fabulous rhythms of jazz trumpeter Bunny Berigan. She had a couple of Berigan's records which she played for me. She told me he was worth listening to, and I agreed.

She took me out to New Mexico and shared with me her love of horseback riding. In conjunction with her love of horses, another of my mother's carefully orchestrated events to which I was exposed as a boy was The American Royal — the greatest midwest stock and horse show and rodeo in existence at that time. It also involved gaited horse judging with some of the finest equestrian competitors alive — a two-hour show complete with live orchestra and intermissions. One of the main reasons I was taken early on was to see the last act, which was the dressage of a team of four or six magnificent black horses. They were drawing a carriage driven by the Queen of The American Royal, Loula

Scott at five

Long Combs. As she entered the arena driving her matched team of six, the orchestra struck up the tune, "My Old Kentucky Home", and Loula Long Combs led the team in an unforgettable performance. They showed off their gaits — including walk, trot, rack and pace (gallop was ignored for aesthetic reasons).

Loula Long Combs was a horsewoman extraordinaire and much admired by my mother. As mistress of Longview Farm in Lee's Summit, Missouri, Loula was the daughter of lumber baron and philanthropist, L. A. Long, and an early animal rights activist. Her act at The American Royal was one I will never forget.

Mother's inspirational influences extended to a great interest in my reading, which she guided carefully. For example, she introduced me to the writings of the American adventurer Richard Halliburton, who traveled the world and wrote exciting books about his travels, which included a description of the Taj Mahal. My mother and I were enthralled by the story of the love of Shah Jahan who created the Taj Mahal in memory of his late wife, the beautiful Mumtaz Mahal, meaning the "Jewel of the Palace." The Shah used as many as 28 varieties of semi-precious and precious stones to adorn the exquisite inlay work of the Taj Mahal. As a student at Pembroke Country Day School, I once was asked by my teacher, Mr. Wedeen, to read two selections from Richard Halliburton's book — one about the Taj Mahal and how it was built, and one about how Richard Halliburton swam the Grand Canal in Venice. I remember the Taj Mahal speech well because my classmates applauded it loudly.

I attended Pembroke Country Day School in Kansas City from kindergarten through sixth grade, formative years in more ways than one. Although the memory of it is somewhat misty, and I've often wondered whether I dreamt it or it actually happened, it appears that I was sexually "interfered with" at the school. It was either in first or second grade when a female teacher got me alone behind a platform in the middle of the classroom; this had been constructed with a railing around it so that we could sit and read to one another. She proceeded to unbutton my pants and hold my tiny penis in her hand. Of course, I peed instantly. I remember that I found it invasive and I probably cried, but I didn't tell my parents. My teacher may have told me not to tell. I think she probably did. It has never seemed like an important memory, but it may have had some influence on me, although I've had no ill-effects from it that I know of. In fact, I've found such intimacy quite pleasant when attractive women later felt so inclined.

Sometimes, I feel that more importance than necessary is given childhood incidents such as that one. I knew I had been taken advantage of and, somehow, I avoided being sent screaming out of the room by it. I didn't squeal on the teacher. The incident, in my mind, simply made me very aware of the importance of secrets, which may have paid off later on during the period between 1951 and 1986, which I have labeled the period of "Keep Your Secrets, Keep Your Dignity."

At Pembroke Country Day School, I became friends with my classmate, George Ketcham, who was the son of an art teacher there. I believe his father actually painted my portrait at one point. I was next to George one day when he got accused of something by one of the playground bullies.

We generally avoided the bullies because we felt so superior to them, but on this day, this particular bully could no longer ignore our disdain. He made the mistake of roughing up George, who was somewhat pudgy, but carried a secret weapon — a pair of rock-hard hands. George had the strongest hands of anybody I've ever known. George took hold of the bully's free hand and almost broke it. The boy, begging to be released, was brought down to his knees by George. I was so proud of George for that. The bully didn't have a chance. George finally let go of his hand and it was certainly badly sprained. It was a defining moment on the Pembroke Country Day School playground, as neither George nor I were ever bullied again.

Scott at about 8, reading

George and I were members of the school band, but poor George had absolutely no sense of rhythm. He was given the bass drum and, unfortunately, could not manage it. He couldn't seem to pay attention long enough to keep up tempo, and soon dropped out of the band. I played the baritone, a first cousin of the sousaphone, and I found it very interesting to play a brass instrument. The band played marches... not very well, but with great enthusiasm. We played at the so-called commencement services in the spring and our sound was almost sickening, but we invariably got a bit better in the fall. One of our favorite pieces was the 1902 British patriotic song, "Land of Hope and Glory", with music by Edward Elgar and lyrics by A. C. Benson.

I was on the football team briefly at Pembroke Country Day School but somehow convinced a doctor that I had developed a trick knee and no longer had to play.

In 1941, although I was off the team, I became football manager, carrying the water bucket with a sponge and cups. Coach Wedeen, who was the athletic director of the school as well as a teacher, was a wonderful man who was rather long-suffering. He had, after all, to deal with a bunch of spoiled rich kids like me… falling down all over the field and inventing injuries and excuses right and left.

During my fourth or fifth grade, we were being taught about commerce, and I was given the idea of trying to make some money at the school. They had a tiny "storelet" that sold candy bars and gum and so forth, and the idea was that I would be a bank for people who didn't have enough nickels, dimes or pennies to purchase those items. I would charge interest and, thus, make money on the loans. My banker father and grandfather put me up to it, of course, but it soon became much too complicated and I gave it up quickly. It was the accountancy that ruined me. I couldn't remember who owed me the pennies.

I did have decent grades throughout school and I also became very impressed with the lady who taught penmanship. She was a large lady who had very little patience. She was secretary to the headmaster of the school and she really felt demeaned by having to give a course in penmanship. I've never been looked down upon with such disdain as she mustered up for these kids who could barely scrawl out things on the paper. By necessity, we made progress under her direction.

In 1939 or 1940, my parents very kindly offered George Ketcham a trip to a dude ranch in Colorado where we vacationed on two different occasions. We went to the dude ranch right up until World War II broke out, and I enjoyed riding with my mother, the excellent horse woman.

At the dude ranch, George and I rode horse back and threw horse shoes. We dressed up like cowboys and tried to rope calves. I was pretty good with the rope myself, but it was difficult for George. Even with his strong hands, his coordination was nil.

From the time I was nine years old, my dog Scrappy accompanied us when we went to the dude ranch in the summer. There, Scrappy did everything he could to keep up with me, as he was a "one boy dog," and I was the most important being in his life. He quickly discovered that he could not outrun the horses and, inevitably, when I saw him panting alongside of my horse, I would reach down and scoop him up and allow him to ride in the saddle with me. We were quite a pair, Scrappy and I. He was my little hero, because he would keep running behind the horses no matter how fast we rode.

I remember seeing my dad in the conga line at the dude ranch. He was always enthusiastic about leading a dance, and he could get 60 or 70 people together and get them smiling back, too. It was a sort of manufactured

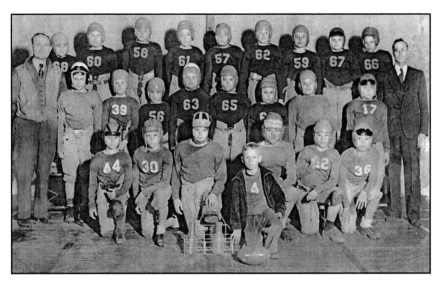

My Pembroke Country Day Football Team (Scott #67)

excitement at the dude ranch. We were all there to have a good time and hilarity was high. Jack led, and everybody followed the dance with shouts of joy and glee. I remember being surprised and fascinated to see that side of him.

Occasionally, Dad took me to the Boy Scout Parade in downtown Kansas City. It was a very big deal, because Eagle Scouts who studied anthropology would learn Indian dances and some of them were excellent dancers. They were truly as good as anything I later saw in any part of the world. The seating was sort of catch-as-catch-can and I remember standing a long while to watch the Indian dancing.

One of my mother's special teaching moments occurred on an early trip to New Mexico during which we visited a small adobe pueblo, San Il Defonso, where Indians lived and farmed near the Rio Grande river. On a certain day in May the Indians there performed a traditional rain dance they hoped would benefit their corn crop. Drumming, chanting and dancing began near a buried ceremonial room, the Kiva, where village elders and medicine men had meetings and also guarded sacred jewelry, clothing, drums and other instruments used in events like the village rain dance. After an enormous amount of drumming, chanting and praying for rain on that dry and dusty community, at days end the pueblo's population changed quickly into everyday clothing and paraded into the local church. Following a few minutes praying and a blessing by their priest, they burst outside, shouted triumphantly, and fired a number of gunshots into the evening sky. Thus, a few bullets became the final symbols sent to induce rain to fall on the Indian corn stalks. Mother and I watched the ceremony all day, including the moment of the bullets in the sky. It was all mesmerizing and nearly intoxicating. As in the past, my mother brought a picnic lunch for us to share, but we remarked how sad it was that my father had no interest in witnessing this day of folkloric celebration and hope.

Dad was principally a duck hunter and duck hunting season in Missouri was extended to other states. It was weekend hunting usually, and they went down into Arkansas and up north into Idaho. My father and his buddies — all hunter types — would go regularly, but he rarely invited me. They would hunt the pools and ponds where the ducks gathered, sitting in huts (or duck blinds) that they brought with them in the trunks of their cars. The one I hated the most was the one I didn't get to know until after WWII, when my father got invited deer hunting in the northern part of Michigan. There, the townspeople would be hired to beat the bushes and scare the deer in front of them to where the hunters were stationed and ready for the kill. I was appalled by this mechanical slaughter. I think my father anticipated my non-wish to participate, because earlier I'd been up to this same hunting ground, which covered acres of Northern Michigan. There were other kinds of game available up there, and I learned to shoot a gun. In fact, I was a sharpshooter. I had a BB gun as a boy and I was a pretty good shot with it. I had no qualms about the gun, but I knew that I could use it only against certain targets.

One of the reasons that I still wear my father's ring, which he abandoned when my mother divorced him, is that I'm grateful to him for saving my life. It happened on a trail: Dad and I were walking one day on the farm owned by my grandparents outside of Kansas City. It was a place for hunters, and he was carrying a loaded shotgun with him. I remember that it was a nice spring day. All of a sudden, my father spun around, making a perfect arc over my head, aimed the gun down behind me and blasted away, killing a poisonous snake that was just about to bite me in the ankle. I've been forever grateful to him for that and for his knowledge of guns and how to use them. He was a good marksman, a sharpshooter, and a fine sportsman (except for the programmed deer kill).

It was simply that there were certain kinds of hunting he did that were repugnant to me. He would, for example, hunt doves in New Mexico, scaring them up out of the brush in the late afternoon at dusk, just as the light is about to disappear. I was invited, but chose not to watch it or participate.

Dad was a vice president at the Commerce Trust Company and Mother was an icon in the business community. She had a good head for business, plus she was quite attractive and often pursued by the business community as well as individual suitors. She was used to that and she knew how to fend off both types of "hunters." It was made difficult by the fact that she was married to Jack McLucas, who was working his way up at the bank. Mother had to be a diplomat in any kind of social gathering she attended with him. The midwest is the midwest, after all. It is not as subtle a place as the American east. Bankers pursued her with offers to head women's

departments at various banks, and she didn't mind that kind of attention, but she politely fended it off because of my father's bank career.

My father's relationship with me was always a problem, because I just never felt that he wanted to fulfill his role of fatherhood. He was definitely jealous of my relationship with my mother, which was a companionable type of friendship that was more conducive to quiet conversation, reading and learning than action-oriented pursuits like hunting, dancing and boxing.

One of the abilities my father took particular pride in was his boxing acumen. It was the only thing he did of note at Princeton. There was

Mother, Dad and me with dogs:
Scrappy on left and Bissie on right

a day in the late 1930s, when I was probably about eight or nine years old, that my father corralled my mother and me at the top of the stairs in our house. He had boxing gloves for me and for him. Mother told him that we could box, but she insisted on being present. As I donned the boxing gloves, I sensed that I was preparing for the worst. I didn't trust him or the place he had chosen for our bout. We were standing on the landing, and a fall could have been mortal. The entire scene defied reason. We sparred for a while and then he hit me rather hard between the nose and cheek. I burst into tears and fell into my mother's arms. That was the end of boxing at our house. He was disgusted and left angry, muttering that I was not much of a son. "If he would just go away without getting mad," was a revealing statement I made to my mother about my father then and again later in my youth.

Earlier, when we lived in a house owned by my grandfather on West 57th Street in Kansas City, my friends Berkie Welch, Joe Hall and George Ketcham were most respectful of me due to an event that occurred there. The house got termites and the building had to be completely fumigated. The house had to be remounted on enormous wooden beams — freed from its underpinnings and its stone foundation — completely lifted up, so to speak, in order to be rid of the termite infestation and perform the fumigation of the era. The process created the damndest World War I scene you can imagine. My friends and I were in rapt admiration of the rubble. We could play there forever, it seemed, as it took months for the fumigation to be completed, with a section of the house being done at a time while we lived in the part of the house that wasn't on wooden beams. Because it was my house, I was the instant hero — the general in charge of every battle. It was paradise for a bunch of boys. The World War I battles of the Somme, the swamps of Ypres, and the fortresses of Verdun were re-enacted with ferocity and imagination. Of course, we knew nothing of the ghastly horrors of 1914-18.

Joe Hall lived in a great big house down another street not too far away. His yard was enormous, but it couldn't compare to the battlefield that was my yard. Berkie Welch was another neighbor boy. He and I loved wheeled vehicles. We were the motorized corps when we played war.

Our family would usually go to Detroit to have Christmas with my grandfather and those holidays were pretty joyful. I don't remember much about my grandmother, Grace. She was sort of a silent partner of my grandfather. I remember her more from their days on the farm near Kansas

City. She really adored that farm, and she was reluctant to give it up when her husband got called to Detroit. She knew it would be a long time before she could talk him into acquiring a farm in Michigan like the one they'd had in Missouri. I associate her with that farm. I don't associate her with the Detroit apartment — but I do see her face there. It was usually quite a large group at Christmas —with some people from the Nebraska side of the family who I didn't know at all. They probably came to Detroit because of my grandfather's great fame. It seemed like there was always a houseful.

While Christmas at Grandfather Walter and Grandmother Grace's apartment in Detroit could usually be counted upon to be an enjoyable family holiday, there was one horrible Christmas that continues to live in infamy in my memory. It had to do with my cousin, Charles Nichols deKuyper, III, the son of my Aunt Marjorie (Dad's sister) and her second husband, a well-known Dutchman, Charles Nichols deKuyper, II. I was put in charge of his son, Charles III, "Nicky," at the annual Christmas party because I was quite a bit older than he was. I was not happy about this chore, and what followed seemed to be an act of vengeance perpetrated by Nicky. He was about four years old and wearing a bluish-greenish knit suit. He decided to do three things: 1) defecate in a manner that was extremely messy and odoriferous, 2) burst into tears, and 3) throw a tantrum… all at the same time. I was responsible for this creature. I was nearly a teenager, and definitely young enough to be embarrassed — cringingly so. He made an impression upon me that has lasted a lifetime.

Aunt Marjorie, Nicky's mother, was beautiful and independent, far more ambitious than her brother, John Nichols McLucas. She had an opportunity back in the 1920s to be in the movies. She had been in a play and may have even been a member of Actor's Equity at one time. She was offered a job working as an actress for a big Hollywood studio, but unfortunately that was when the Fatty Arbuckle scandal had just burst into newsprint (Arbuckle was arrested in 1921 and tried for the murder of a young starlet, but the jury could not find enough evidence to convict him). Grandfather told his daughter that if she wanted to become an actress in Hollywood, she need never cross his doorstep again, and she would be disinherited. So she didn't pursue the offer, but I think she held a grudge against Grandfather forever.

Aunt Marjorie's first husband was a playboy named William "Billy" Huttig. His father had been a champion beet root raiser in Colorado who made a fortune out of sugar beets. Billy Huttig liked to buy very inexpensive old cars and take them up to a certain bluff overlooking the Missouri River, get in them and drive them as fast as they would go to the edge of the bluff. He would leap out just as the car hit the crest of the bluff and tumbled into the river below. They had a child whose name was Barbara Huttig. She had a lovely smile, but was eaten up with a number of complexes. When I was about nine or 10 years old, Barbara came to stay in our house for a few months because she was having a hard time getting along with anyone and she adored my mother. My mother liked to help people and she took Barbara

Barbara Huttig with Scott on Swing
Still friends at the time
(before shoe incident)

on, realizing that she needed someone other than her own sharp-tongued, somewhat bitter mother, Marjorie.

Barbara took so much of my mother's attention that I resented her mightily. The resentment and jealousy grew to the point that I could stand it no longer, and one day, I picked up a high-heeled shoe and whacked Barbara on the back of the head with it. I apologized, knowing that I shouldn't have done it, but it stayed an unforgettable moment in our relationship. Barbara and I made up eventually, although the difference in our inheritances was another factor that separated us in later years.

And then it was December 1941 and our country was at war. My father joined the Army Air Corps and went first to Miami Beach for training, was commissioned an officer and was then assigned to Mather Field in Sacramento, California.

The Kansas City, Missouri, train station was shrouded in darkness as we silently boarded the troop train at 2 a.m. that spring morning of 1942. War-time regulations dictated silent arrivals and departures, and no unauthorized stopping or starting. At age 12, I was excited to be traveling to Sacramento, California, to join my father, now a captain in the Army Air Corps and Assistant Adjutant at Mather Field. Flanked on either side by my mother and my dog, Scrappy, I was ready for adventure… or, so I thought.

Citizens and troops were squeezed into train cars with convertible upper and lower berths. We all slept fitfully during those early morning hours as the train chugged westward, I cuddling close to Mom and Scrappy curled at my feet. The only four-legged civilian aboard, Scrappy was part Chow and part something else: a reddish colored, long-haired medium-sized dog, bright and well-behaved. He had been my best buddy and constant companion from the time I was nine years old; even accompanying me to school earlier that year, where he'd slept on the floor by my desk throughout the class day. Our cherished family pet, in my child's perspective, Scrappy was the heroic dog version of Sir Galahad.

As I opened my eyes and glanced toward the train window, the early morning dawn unveiled a beautiful vista… the endless wheat fields of Kansas rushed by, golden splendor as far as the eye could see. The panoramic vision took my breath away for a moment. Even though I'd traveled through Kansas by train and car before, its vastness always thrilled me. After breakfast, the train quietly came to a halt and I realized it was taking on water at a water tower. Most of the passengers got out and walked about, enjoying the pleasant spring morning. We took Scrappy for a walk. We felt there was no need for his leash out here, as both training and desire caused him to happily trot by my side wherever I went.

We were some distance away when we noticed a few of the soldiers heading back hurriedly toward the train and realized it was about to move (there were no warning bells in war-time). We started off at a brisk walk back toward the train and I called out to Scrappy, but he was having such fun that he wasn't quite ready to return. He was about 25 feet away from me and I began urging him on by slapping my leg and yelling, "C'mon Scrappy!" The train began to move at that point and I reached it as did my mother, almost simultaneously. As she got on, I turned around and looked for Scrappy. He was trotting along rapidly about fifteen feet away. I knelt down and held out my arms, yelling at him with ever-increasing urgency, "C'mon, Scrappy, c'mon boy!"

Like many dogs, Scrappy had a certain curvature of the cheeks that made him appear to be smiling. He smiled a lot, especially when he was having fun, and that is what he was doing now. Scrappy was smiling and his tongue was beginning to protrude as he ran faster and faster. He thought we were playing a game. At the very last minute, I jumped on the moving train,

Scott and Scrappy

reaching out and yelling with all my might for my dog.

"Scrappy! Scrappy! C'mon, boy! You can make it! Run, Scrappy! Run!"

Yelling, I leaned far out, clinging to the hand hold of the metal platform at the end of our train car. My shouts were completely muffled by the roar of the train as the wheat fields whizzed by. No longer able to bear watching my copper-colored best friend getting smaller and smaller as the train picked up speed, I turned my eyes toward my mother. "Mom…" I mouthed in a silent whisper. My mother's eyes were fixed on the eyes of a young Army lieutenant who was standing directly beneath the emergency brake pull. He had witnessed the drama taking place and, after a moment's embarrassed hesitation, the young lieutenant reached up and yanked the brake pull with all his might. In a few minutes, the train came to a stop. Scrappy, now matted and panting, pounded toward me and I leapt down to the ground, scooping him joyfully up in my arms and running up the metal steps to the train.

Licking my face and smiling his odd doggy smile, my bedraggled, tail-wagging Scrappy was the hero of the hour. However, the young lieutenant was clearly the one covered with grace for having pulled the emergency brake of a troop train headed west in war time. Why, after all, was this war being fought, if not for a boy and his dog?

CHAPTER 4

Passages

Truman Capote once said, "It is a scientific fact that if you stay in California you lose one point of your I.Q. every year." The first time, I was destined to stay in California less than one year, thus keeping my Intelligence Quotient intact. When my mother, Scrappy and I stepped off the troop train in Sacramento, California, I was nearly 13 years old and entering 8th grade.

Mather Field in Sacramento was a navigation training headquarters for the Army Air Corps, and Dad was assistant adjutant of the base. I enrolled in the Social Security system that summer, working as a messenger for the PX (Post Exchange). It was my first official summer job, although George Ketcham and I had made a few unsuccessful summer forays into the world of business by setting up Nehi Grape Soda stands in front of his house, selling a grand total of about three sodas a week!

With this California PX job, I was an official government messenger, filling out forms and picking up and delivering registered and insured mail from one point to the other on base. A black enlisted man named Larry was assigned by the "Mo Pool" (Motor Pool) to drive me to and from my appointed tasks. Larry was loquacious about the one subject on which he was an expert... sex. To the impressionable ears of a boy whose only experience with sex had been countless hours of masturbation, Larry's graphic language was marvelous. Larry described in lurid detail a large variety of sexual positions and techniques — always stressing the importance of sex as the most necessary and enjoyable pastime known to man. I knew quite a bit already from reading about sex, but Larry was a great clarifier. I've never forgotten the raw and often hilarious sexual insights provided by Larry, the man from the "Mo' Pool."

In the fall of 1942, I was placed in a large public school with a student body of nearly 1,200. Up to that point, my education at Pembroke Country Day School in Kansas City had been pleasantly challenging, and I had been surrounded by the familiar faces of my peers and classmates in a small, nurturing private school. This huge assemblage of California strangers in an institutional environment marked by a jumble of unfamiliar sights and sounds was a shock to my senses. I was paralyzed with fear... suddenly awash in another civilization. Looking back, I realize the teachers must have recognized an alien in me, as I was transferred from one level to a higher level classroom. They were probably attempting to help me process this new school situation, but it only served to further alienate me. I went home at the end of that first day of school in a nearly catatonic state and absolutely refused to return.

Earlier that summer, my parents had learned how determined I could be to remove myself from an uncomfortable situation. They had sent me to an exclusive summer camp in the Sierras, very near Lake Tahoe, and received a call from the camp counselor that I was unhappy and that I refused to stay at the camp and insisted upon being taken to the nearest bus stop for the ride home. The bus stop sign remains in my memory today. It read: "CalNevaHo."

I was smart, scared and spoiled. My parents relented immediately when I refused to return to the huge public school. They placed me with a tutor in a small private school near Mather Field that specialized in helping navigators in training to brush up on their math skills — trigonometry, calculus and the like. It was nicknamed the "Cram" school because they crammed there for their training under speeded-up wartime conditions. The lady who owned the school and had been hired as my tutor had little time for a young student, nor was she equipped to educate a student of my age and qualifications. She handed me a book entitled Hypatia and advised me to read it, which I did. She then asked me for a book report on it.

Again, in retrospect, I feel that this woman had no intention of teaching me, but simply wanted to share her fantasies with an eager young student.

Hypatia of Alexandria was regarded as the first woman astronomer. She was a beautiful woman and highly regarded as an accomplished mathematician, inventor and philosopher on the same level as Aristotle and Plato. Hypatia lived during the late 4th or early 5th centuries C.E., a time of great change, just as this woman who taught math to navigators was living at a time of great change. She obviously identified with Hypatia and wanted me to experience that complimentary revelation when I read the book. Unfortunately, all I experienced when reading Hypatia, was boredom and frustration. The "Cram" school tutoring was not for me, either. In fact, this waste of time represented one of my early realizations of the evils of waste. Like my mother, I've never been one to waste time or have patience with those who do.

Our next move was to a California sheep ranch, where I was placed in a small country school that was more to my liking. It was easy. I knew it all. When the instructor pulled down a map of the world and began quizzing students about the various countries, I whipped my hand into the air and kept it there. Unfortunately, rather than being impressed with my vast depth of geographical knowledge, the teacher was understandably aggravated. My classmates had not been privileged to have a knowledge of geography as a main hobby that I so arrogantly flaunted, and he was not going to allow me to put them down by showing them up.

However justified the teacher may have been, he allowed his anger to get in the way of his professionalism and chided me publicly, requesting that I give the other students an opportunity to respond, calling me spoiled and denigrating my private school education. I was humiliated and embarrassed. The following day he invited me to come out and discuss the chemistry set that he was going to acquire for the school. He truly did try to make decent amends and we eventually got along alright, but I was still glad when my mother and I returned to Kansas City that same school year.

I was thrilled to return to the welcoming halls of Pembroke Country Day School. It was just the same, but I soon discovered that my California school experiences had changed me I felt a need for more adult progress. My parents approached me about whether I would like to attend the Lawrenceville School in Lawrenceville, New Jersey. It was one of the more important of the Eastern prep schools and I first said yes to the offer, but then had to pass stringent entry exams. We were all somewhat surprised when I failed the Latin portion. Mother immediately hired Doc Foster, one of my favorite professors from Pembroke Country Day School ("PemDay"), to tutor me in Latin and when I retook the Lawrenceville test, I passed. I entered The Lawrenceville School, Cleve House, in the fall of 1944, going into the Third Form (10th grade).

The Lawrenceville School was, and is, one of the most prestigious private prep schools in the East. From the school's website, here is an excerpt on the history of the school:

School History

Lawrenceville was founded in 1810 as the Maidenhead Academy and run under such names as the Lawrenceville Classical and Commercial High School for more than 70 years. It was not until its 1883 "refounding" that it became The Lawrenceville School and discovered its true and abiding identity. At that time, Head Master James Cameron Mackenzie devised Lawrenceville's hallmark House System. The campus, now a National Historic Landmark, began to take shape when renowned American landscape architect Frederick Law Olmsted, the same man who laid out New York's Central Park, designed the School's famous "Circle" in partnership with Boston architects Peabody & Stearns. Just over 50 years later in 1936, Lawrenceville introduced its second distinctive feature—the Harkness system of teaching. Most classes today at Lawrenceville are still held around small oval tables to facilitate class discussions.

With its House and Harkness systems, Lawrenceville grew to occupy a special place in the American imagination. Owen Johnson, an alumnus of the School, first captured the "new" Lawrenceville in his 1910 novel, The Varmint, which recounts the travails and adventures of one Dink Stover as he made his way through Lawrenceville. Stover became one of the country's most beloved fictional characters, prompting Johnson to write a series of Lawrenceville stories. In 1950, Metro-Goldwyn-Mayer released The Happy Years, a Hollywood version of The Varmint along with another Lawrenceville story, The Prodigious Hickey. The movie was filmed on the Lawrenceville campus to ensure authenticity. While Lawrenceville has stayed true to its history and traditions, it has also evolved to reflect changing times. In 1985 the Trustees voted to admit girls, and the first girls arrived in 1987. Less than two decades later, Elizabeth Duffy, the School's first female Head Master, came on board to lead the School into its third century.

The Lawrenceville School continues to benefit from the unique experiences

and perspectives of its students, faculty, staff, and alumni. We're glad you are
now a part of School history.

My first year at Lawrenceville was stimulating. I felt at home there and
enjoyed the qualities of the students and teachers. Soon after I became a
student at Lawrenceville, I learned that the Periwig Club was auditioning
for the popular comedy, "The Man Who Came to Dinner," by George S.
Kaufman and Moss Hart. The play had debuted on Broadway in 1939 and
been made into a movie in 1942, and now, the drama club at my school was
producing it. I was excited at the prospect of being a part of it. Briefly, the
play was about a famous, egocentric New York radio personality named
Sheridan Whiteside who, while visiting a small Ohio town, accepts a
dinner invitation at the home of Ernest Stanley, a well-to-do factory owner.
Unfortunately, Whiteside slips on some ice in front of Stanley's home,
injures his hip, and, confined to a wheelchair in the residence, becomes
one of the world's most irascible and fiendish ogres. The ensuing torment
of the outlandish Whiteside's interminable convalescence at the home of
the long-suffering Stanley and his family is hilariously divided into a three-
act production.

I won the role of Ernest Stanley and, for the remainder of my school
career at Lawrenceville, was remembered for my "Southern drawl" in
the recitation of my first line, "Mistah Whiteside!" Until that time, I had
been unaware that I had a Southern drawl, but that is how my Kansas City
speech pattern played in Lawrenceville, New Jersey in 1944.

Having acted in one of its plays, I automatically became a member
of the Periwig Club and, although I never appeared in another play at
Lawrenceville, I became the actor representative on the Club's board and
later had the great joy of campaigning for and electing a new Periwig
Club President, Zeke Zeckendorf. Zeke's father was one of New York's
most influential real estate barons during World War II and afterwards.
I gathered up a great number of proxy votes in Zeke's favor and helped
him win with them. I was proud of my foray into politics, but the truth
of the matter is that nobody in the Periwig Club really gave a damn about
who was president, including Zeke. In fact, some 30 years later when I
attempted to renew our acquaintance by contacting his office, there was
no great rush on his part to reconnect with a fellow past member of the
Periwig Club.

While membership in the Periwig Club was optional, there was absolutely no option involved with being a member of the Cleve House Football Team. Everyone had to play in at least one sport. It was a rite of passage and a matter of honor, especially for those new to the school. There is one word that comes to mind when I characterize Cleve House football… exhaustion. Exhaustion ruled the daily practices and weekly games between houses, although there were moments of exhilaration as well, where each of us took pleasure in making a really good block or tackle or run… but exhaustion was my overwhelming physical response to Cleve House football. Our colors were green and white, and after about fifteen minutes of play, the uniforms became dun-colored. The nearer you get to the ground in New Jersey in the fall, the less attractive a place it is.

I was a guard or a tackle — playing both offense and defense — hence the exhaustion. Our games lasted all afternoon long — seemingly endless to me. At Lawrenceville and schools like it, your shoes develop wings as you walk and run on the paths of honor. Football was one of the honorable team sports necessary for my completion (we all knew the principles) it was part of the respected tradition.

Our team did have a hero. His name was Digby and he was our quarterback. He was small — much smaller than I — but smart, courageous and filled with energy. He led every single play and was heroic, game after game.

We played our games house against house and, although we weren't the best or the worst, once in a great while, one of our third form newcomers would go from the house league up to the varsity league. Our Lawrenceville Varsity league played other schools such as Mercersburg, The Hill School, and Peddie. We were all in the innocence and honor racket — our job in football and all other sports was to out-honor the other teams. We were a minor replica of the Ivy League teams like Harvard and Yale.

As to our studies, they were challenging and time-consuming. For some reason, I remember my first story assignment well. It was my original story of a military detachment off in some sandy location like Africa that was filled with flies and other insects. This imaginary detachment ended up running close to total destruction because it came within earshot of another fight between African natives and a colonial army. Just because they were so gung-ho to get into the fray, the detachment nearly perished. I called the story "Sundown" and made a fair grade on it. It all came out of my fantasy world which had to do with me being a military hero in some wild part of the world — one of my many fantasies at that age. However, my strongest goal and/or fantasy that drove me was the determination to get through those three years at Lawrenceville and go on to Yale. I liked the concept of achieving honor and excellence in whatever field I pursued. My only drawback was laziness, so in an effort to cover up that slight flaw, I learned acting early. I had observed many in my social strata who were able, with ease, to go around challenges rather than meet them head-on. This seemed an intelligent and advantageous way of doing things as long as honor was not compromised. Fortunately for me, my mother had taught me to think independently and had rewarded my adventures, but I certainly grew up privileged and less challenged than many others simply because I was lucky.

Early in my first year at Lawrenceville, I experienced a defining moment that would help shape the rest of my life. Two young military veterans in full uniform (former members of Cleve House who had returned from war to finalize their high school credits) participated in a debate that made an amazing impression on me. Their eloquence; their extraordinary knowledge and ability to reason quickly and demonstrably in public; their maturity at such a young age… totally astounded me. I was paralyzed with admiration for them, having heretofore been totally unaware that I had contemporaries of such awesome ability. They were champions. They were confident leaders, and as I listened with rapt attention to their every word, a terrific storm was stirred in me… it was as if I were hearing Lincoln's Gettysburg address being spoken for the first time ever. A blast of awareness shook me. This was the reason I was at Lawrenceville! This was a school for greatness. Heroes were made here. That incredible debate between young military men just back from the front was the catalyst that set me on the path to achievement. Their example was one I have spent the remainder of my life attempting to emulate.

There was one fellow student with the unfortunate name of Billy Funk, who most assuredly did not inspire emulation. Billy played the piano in the common room of Cleve House nearly every day, repeating the one piece of music he knew — the score of *Oklahoma* — to the point of driving many of us nearly mad. He didn't play it loudly, but he did play it constantly, and not that well. With Billy Funk tickling the ivories so incessantly, it is a miracle that I was not completely turned off of piano music, but there was a saving grace just outside my window at Cleve House, where an altogether different type of concert ensued. In a small one-story brick building consisting of two tiny rooms, the Lawrenceville music director worked daily with soloists, duets, quartets and instrumentalists. Tutoring talented young musicians nearly every afternoon directly below my window, the music director provided me welcome diversion from the all-too-familiar Funk-rendered interpretations of *Oklahoma*.

I enjoyed being in Cleve House, and although I don't recall the names of my two room-mates that first year, we must have gotten along well. I was used to being alone, and functioned better that way. At the end of Third Form, I was elected house treasurer, most probably because I had a reputation of being good with numbers, and I came from a banking family. I accepted that role and felt honored to have been elected.

Attending Lawrenceville was akin to attending a private college, and the annual prom was just one example of how highly placed the school was in the social scheme of things. Back in 1944, during my first year of attendance at Lawrenceville, the prom featured entertainment by Les Brown and his Band of Renown with singer, Doris Day. There were girls there from private schools all over the East, all there to share in the glory with Lawrenceville boys. The gym at Lawrenceville was limited in its lighting effects — but it was darkened just enough to make the girls and their gowns seem "nightclub glamorous." Miss Doris Day was a brilliant singer and a charming, conservative, graceful dancer who had learned to deal discretely with the nearly constant and embarrassing tumescence of eager teenage boys. I remember nervously dancing with Doris Day to the very danceable swing music of Les Brown and his Band of Renown and, with some relief, giving over when a tap on my shoulder signaled a fellow student was cutting in. It was heady stuff, indeed, to be dancing with a star! Nervous or not, I loved it!

Speaking of dancing and the heady stuff that accompanied being in close contact with a female form, a few of us were more enterprising than others about taking matters beyond the dance. There were those at Lawrenceville whose experience in New York City was extensive compared with that of the first year students, and as our plans for personal exploration advanced, other psychology began its work. Most of us had never experienced a mid-Atlantic fall season... it was certainly my first such discovery... and we found we were confused by the fall winds and buffeting temperatures, feeling very strong one moment and fearful the next. It was an exciting season. Four of us first year students, accompanied by two upper classmen, made the last fall urban trip allowed by the school authorities. We booked hotel rooms in the city (New York), enjoyed a new Broadway play called *Carousel*, and spent some time at a dancehall near 44th Street where a roll of dance tickets could be purchased for 75 cents. In this particular dance hall, the well-trained band played some of the shortest dance arrangements in history and when the dancing was done, we met the girls at the back stairway and went to their hotel (not ours). One of the girls from the dance hall was named Mindy. Dark-haired and charmingly well-curved, Mindy liked to pose in front of the mirror with her evening's guest. We were both so young and we posed joyfully in the mirror, laughing as we admired our bodies. The session, at a cost of $25 to $30, lasted only about 30 minutes, and then I took a cab to my hotel, seemingly a great deal older and wiser than ever before.

Together with a pair of other new students at Lawrenceville, guided by a couple of upper classmen, we celebrated our weekend with drinks in the Biltmore Cocktail Lounge before boarding the train back to school. The waiters had been instructed to serve adult beverages to young men without questioning age, as they might inadvertently be insulting young soldiers.

Autumn, 1944 and our great October adventure in New York City created in me a strange, adversarial attitude, awakening a new sexual drive and awareness that marked my true coming of age. We all had that memorable weekend to discuss for many months ahead, realizing that it was a once in a lifetime experience. Now, we felt more prepared than ever to accept the challenges that Lawrenceville had in store for us.

Meanwhile, back in Kansas City during my first year at Lawrenceville, my mother was doing her part to support the war effort by entertaining troops when they came into town and playing the role of loyal wife to a man in military service to his country. She played her role to the hilt because she respected the social rule that deemed it unpatriotic and harmful to our soldiers' spirits to divorce a serviceman during wartime. Despite many opportunities to stray from her marital vows, my mother maintained chaste behavior throughout World War II, all the while entertaining such dignitaries as General Pete Casava, whenever he could be excused from his main job of piloting General Eisenhower on military missions. I knew her chastity was real, as I occasionally watched mother and the general kiss each other's cheeks like brother and sister as they said their goodbyes on the front steps of our house.

On holiday breaks from school, I sometimes had occasion to spend some quality time with my grandfather. I recall one major mistake I made with him on one such holiday that momentarily endangered his doting attitude toward his favorite grandson and permanently taught me a lesson… never confuse blood with appreciation. We were playing gin rummy for the first time together, and I beat him three times in a row. That was absolutely one of the most idiotic things I've ever done. He was furious. What I should have done was to purposely lose a game earlier in the session. Unfortunately, at that age, I was not that purposeful.

With the end of the war in Europe in May of 1945, Mother finally filed for divorce, and the war between my parents came to an end as well. Their divorce was quickly followed with marriage by each of them to a new spouse.

Dad married Kitty Smith of North Carolina, whom he had met through a mutual friend, Lyle Brush, in Santa Fe, New Mexico. Kitty was attractive and had a good sense of humor. She was a world traveler who wrote a book called The Reluctant Refugee based on her harrowing war experiences. It appeared that she would make my father happy in their marriage. She was like a breath of fresh air to him, as he had endured a miserably cold, bleak, and dangerous experience in his more than three years in the Air Transport Command.

Unfortunately, when Dad took Kitty to Detroit, she did not find favor with my grandfather. Grandfather McLucas was so angry that my mother was no longer in the family, that there was a possibility no one could have impressed him. Grandfather apparently treated Kitty so rudely that she told my father she would not live in Detroit; that she would leave him if she had to stay in the same city as his father. Dad actually got down on his knees and begged her to stay with him. She relented and stayed, but he spent the rest of his life trying to make it up to her.

Mother married William F. Colwes of Kansas City, Missouri, a new car salesman who was tall, handsome and very amusing. Smooth, manly and socially adept, Bill Colwes appeared to be what my mother had been waiting for. All signs were that he would make a good husband for her.

Dramatic change was in the air. No longer were we a small family unit with a home base in Kansas City, Missouri. Just before the divorce was finalized, my parents sold our house in the city and departed with their new mates, my father north to Detroit and my mother to Santa Fe, New Mexico. My family and my childhood home were no more. World War II was finished. The summer of 1945 was a time of important moves and passages.

As for me, I viewed their divorce as about five or six years overdue, and I was happy that each of my parents had found a new and promising mate. At fifteen, having spent a satisfactory first year at Lawrenceville, I was somewhat aloof from what was happening outside of my new world of study and school. My parents' termination of their long and tortured relationship coincided conveniently with my semi-official coming of age, which was in progress as my time at Lawrenceville continued.

CHAPTER 5

Coming of Age at Lawrenceville

During the spring and summer of 1945, and into the following year, my nose remained almost constantly between the pages of Time and Life magazines and newspapers of the day, as well as my eyes and ears being glued to radio programs and newsreels. I was fascinated by the total devastation that had been wrought upon Nazi Germany and Imperial Japan — two world powers crumbling before our eyes. The very fact that both of these cultures were based on neatness and order made it nearly unbelievable that their destruction had been so messy, but the black and white photos before me didn't lie. I devoured the repugnant news with a strange mixture of horror and delight, safely acting as a voyeur from my secure perch at home in the good old U.S. of A. And, with patriotism emanating from my every pore, I was confident that "we" would somehow repair the damage and make things right in the world once again. Nevertheless, I kept up my schoolwork.

And then, there was the delicious horror of watching the villainous Harry Lime (played by actor Orson Wells) escaping through the underground tunnels of Vienna in the movie, "The Third Man." The movie was the epitome of all the evil that had been perpetrated on the world, even including a group of young children in a hospital ward dying from poisonous inoculations. It was a show of pure cinematic symbolism — rich material indeed for a young, imaginative mind. I had an idea, then, of the meaning of *schadenfreude*, the German term for deriving pleasure from the misfortune of others. I would later learn, while working in Germany and other parts of Europe, that *schadenfreude* is a much more frightening reality when personally experienced close up.

I remember vividly a taxi-cab ride in New York with my mother and one of my heroes of the day, Westbrook Van Voorhis, the voice of the Time-Life radio and newsreel series, *March of Time*, and the man who was famous for saying the phrase "Time… marches on." I do not know how my mother knew Westbrook Van Voorhis or managed to have him in the taxi at the same time I was there, but I do know that it was another one of her spectacular teaching moments, as she was well aware of my fascination with the news of the day and knew I would be thrilled to meet Mr. Van Voorhis.

In my second year at Lawrenceville, I got quite caught up in studying *The Aeneid*, an epic Latin poem by Virgil written between 19 and 29 BC, about the travels of Aeneas and his ancestry to the Romans. It was exciting to experience the ancient language with a professor who was a Latin scholar. I scored so highly on my final exam in fourth form that I received the second highest award for Latin.

As treasurer of Cleve House during my second year at Lawrenceville, I collected funds from my fellow students to pay for special events such as parties and picnics and I began to learn the cost of certain items I had never been responsible for purchasing in the past. I had already learned from my mother to disdain waste and was, therefore, appalled when I saw my classmate, Jack Smart, flipping butter patties up at the beautiful 14-foot-high vaulted ceiling. I instantly used my position of authority to give him demerits for his wasteful display. Smart was furious. His organized retribution began shortly thereafter with the christening of a new nickname for me —S-M-I-L-Y. Wailing cries of "S-M-I-L-Y" rang out from the open windows of Cleve House and from other hidden alcoves, until everyone in Cleve House knew of my new nickname and the reason behind it. Somehow, I managed to retain my friendly demeanor, keep smiling, and resist the urge to counter-attack, despite the continued onslaught of verbal abuse. After about five days of wailing "S-M-I-L-Y", Smart and his cohorts grew weary of it and left me alone. At the end of the year, I received the medal for "House Spirit," possibly as compensation for humiliation, and probably as a nod of respect from the House Master for my having done my part to preserve the dining hall ceiling and then taken the higher path when chastised for exercising the power available to me. Today, reflecting back on those days, I feel that Jack Smart and I are about even.

Dad brought his new wife, Kitty, to Lawrenceville to meet me, and I remember being charmed by her. She was witty and pretty and vivacious, yet there was an underlying strength about her that was intriguing. Kitty had survived two Japanese concentration camps, and had married an Englishman and lived in Shanghai. She had been shipped to the Philippines with her tiny daughter, Jinx. Her husband had died and she had been brought back to the U.S. on the Gripsholm, a famous Swedish hospital ship. Her sister lived in Santa Fe, New Mexico, and that was where she had met my father. Kitty was a lovely, strong woman and I think the only reason my grandfather disliked her was because she was not my mother.

Mother's new husband, Bill Colwes, was a tall, well-spoken, distinguished looking gent who had visions of grandeur that never quite materialized. Bill was destined to have a brief and disastrously unsuccessful run for Congress as the Republican senator from New Mexico, but back in the 1940s and 50s, he and my mother had several friends in high places in Santa Fe. One of their most prominent Santa Fe friends was General Patrick Hurley, who retired in 1945 from his Ambassadorship to China, but remained active in military and political circles. As an avid student of military history, I was proud to shake the hand of the hand of the man [General Hurley] who had shaken the hand of mighty Mao Zedong. I was also pleased to note that General Hurley had a pretty daughter who attended a prep school in the East. I even had the pleasure of once escorting the General's daughter to a Lawrenceville Prom.

1945 was also the year people in New Mexico heard of atomic bomb tests in their own state and became concerned about rumors of great danger to the local population. This knowledge paled when not one but two massive atomic bombs were exploded over urban areas of Japan in August 1945. Thus the atomic age began and eveunatly aligned the two most powerful states in the world against each other, until peace, hope and good will returned again for humankind, 50 or 60 years later.

Some time during the school years of 1946, my mother called from her home in Santa Fe to give me sad news. My dog, Scrappy, had died. In the Santa Fe neighborhood where he lived with Mother and Bill, his penchant for play had unfortunately led him into several dog-fights. Sadly, he had not survived one of those fights. I have since had several beloved pets, but none of them possessed the heroic spirit and personality of that copper-colored friend of my childhood.

In the summer of 1946, I became the assistant treasurer and sometimes stage hand for El Theatro de Santa Fe, one of the few summer equity theaters in the west. That first summer I had the pleasure of seeing one of America's greatest actresses in the summer theater. Her name was Jane Cowl, and in 1917 she had starred in a popular Broadway play, *Lilac Time*, produced by top New York producer Joseph Belasco. Jane Cowl was performing on a tour of the U.S. summer theaters in a production of one of her most famous plays, *The First Mrs. Frazier*.

El Theatro de Santa Fe was located in an old Army base theater and the cast members were housed informally at the old barracks, which served more or less as dormitories — one for the males and one for the females. There were approximately three shows a month, with six performances each week and rehearsals occurring simultaneously for the next show. In addition to helping in the box office, I participated in strike nights (dismantling the old set and building the new set) and, once in a while, played a bit part as an extra — a Mexican bandit or part of a crowd scene. Basically modest, I was never comfortable on stage, but was aimed from the very beginning at producing rather than performing.

One of my favorite plays at El Theatro was *They Knew What They Wanted*, starring Harold Perry, who played Mr. Gildersleeve on The Fred Allen Show. I enjoyed hearing his booming voice as Tony in the play, and that show eventually became a musical, *The Most Happy Fella*, with music written by Frank Lesser.

Another favorite play was George Bernard Shaw's *Saint Joan*. The young lady who played the lead role had never done any serious acting, but she was like the Bride of Christ, becoming totally married to the role of St. Joan. She was so wonderful in the role that I fell head over heels in love with her, but found to my dismay, that she was otherwise inclined. She was in love with one of the other actresses.

Speaking of actresses, there was a night when I was invited back to the barracks after rehearsal by a couple of the actresses — both "older women" in their mid to late twenties. They invited me to have a drink with them and proceeded to inform me they had been discussing me and had decided it would be a delightful idea for us to engage in a ménage à trois, as they knew that 16-year-old boys were often perpetual "fountains of joy." I hesitated to accept this seduction for several strange reasons... my mother would be worried about me... it would be an exhausting night that would go until dawn... I had plans for the next day, etc. Eventually, as the discussion continued and the wine flowed, the whole idea fell apart, but as I was about to leave, one of the actresses decided she wanted to leave with me. We went back to my place and had the first of several enjoyable interludes.

When I say "my place," I literally mean that my mother had built a separate efficiency apartment in front and to the left of their home in Santa Fe and it was mine. At 16 years of age, I had a nice bedroom with twin beds, a bathroom and an attractive corner fireplace with brick interior. Behind my locked door, the wine did flow and the fires of love did burn (whether or not a flame flickered in the romantic corner fireplace).

In stark contrast to my torrid summer days and nights in Santa Fe, I aspired to a higher calling at Lawrenceville, having been appointed to the position of Head Chapel Usher for the services in the school chapel during my Fifth Form (senior year). In this role, it was my duty to count the weekly chapel receipts. The count occurred up in my room, so I felt responsible when, one day, I discovered that some money was missing. I had a pretty good idea who the thief was. A classmate from California had taken to visiting my room during my count, sitting on a padded window seat that looked out on the esplanade. He generally sat there as I counted the collection plate and prepared rolls of change. He was a well-to-do student from Pasadena, California, so I reasoned that he must be a minor kleptomaniac, pocketing the change once in a while for no other reason than the thrill of stealing directly from under the eyes of a trusted fellow student.

Luckily, I had a good friend in the Upper House named Nelson Hobart. Nelson was from Kansas City. He was confined to a wheelchair due to polio, but did not allow that to lessen his great sense of humor or his considerable leadership ability. Nelson was president or vice-president of our class at that time and I told him about the theft and my suspicions. He told me he would bring it up to Mr. Churchill, the House Master, and get a recommendation on what to do. Mr. Churchill, from that time on, met me after chapel on Sunday in my room and I handed him the bags of money to count. The visits from the California classmate dried up after that. Ironically, the summer prior to Fifth Form, I had invited him to spend some time with me in Santa

Fe and during the summer, he had perpetrated another theft… that time of an exquisite young lady named Tijaël Éclair. I was in love with Tijaël (who was as lusciously beautiful as her name implied) and the bastard knew it, yet he moved right in on her and she fell for his blonde charm. I heard later that he died young and I often wonder how and why his luck finally ran out.

Another California connection that I had while at Lawrenceville in Upper House was a boy named Mike Todd, Jr., the son of Hollywood film producer Mike Todd, Sr. This was well before Mike Todd, Sr. married Elizabeth Taylor. It was in the fall of our senior year in 1946 that a strange and memorable incident occurred. Mike, Jr. lived not far from me in Upper House and sometimes talked about some of his dad's unusual activities that were beyond my understanding. One weekend, Mike, Jr. was visiting his family's New York apartment when a crazed, knife-wielding woman sliced Mike, Sr. Saving his father's life, Mike, Jr. got him into the car and father and son drove down to the school and parked right there in front of the Upper House. Mike Todd, Sr. retreated into his son's room and stayed sequestered there for the next five to 10 days. He was already quite famous at the time, and we all realized that we had a delicate social situation here and we had to be hospitable.

Mike Todd, Sr., was a lightning bolt. He moved very fast. He was a small man with a big reputation as a rough-and-tumble producer who was famous for his Mafia connections. One of the biggest things he had that year was a giant swimming show up in a large outside hall on Long Island. The irony of the situation with Mike, Sr. and Mike, Jr. during those days at Upper House, was that their roles were reversed — the son became the father and the father, the son. Mike, Jr. wouldn't let Mike, Sr. out of his sight.

I liked Mike Todd, Jr., although we did not stay in touch after Lawrenceville. He was a loner and so was I. He did come out with one fairly amusing nonsensical statement that I recall —something like "Oh, you roam like the Romans roam."

One of Mike, Jr.'s best friends was a young man from South America who had a pornography collection that, I'm sure, rivaled that of the Vatican. It was something we were all enthralled by. Occasionally, when we were tired of studying (or not) we would wander down the hall and ask if we could take a peek. The South American had a stack of photographs in several folders that were absolutely amazing — the envy of every prep school boy this side of the Vatican.

My most triumphant achievement at Lawrenceville happened when I was appointed Varsity Swim Team Manager. It was the high point and fulfillment of my youth and my years at Lawrenceville to be manager of a championship swimming team. By the end of the season, great mutual respect had been developed between the coach, the team and me — we were all champions. I could add figures faster and announce and tabulate results more accurately than anyone else, and I viewed the team with pride and affection. I was not their buddy — I was their manager, and as such, I received respect for what I did. When the team won, I won.

In a 2011 New York Times article, columnist David Brooks requested that readers over the age of 70 submit a Life Report on "What I Did Well." I submitted the following essay on that Lawrenceville championship season:

You mentioned needing a Life Report on "What I Did Well," so an old athletic project of mine came to mind. It concerns a championship season my prep school's swimming and diving team won at the enclosed pool of the Lawrenceville School in 1947. I was the student manager of the team. The scene was the school campus of Lawrenceville, NJ, five miles south of Princeton. I am amused that my set of tasks at that time would be called 'multi-tasking' in today's vernacular. I announced all events for both home and visiting teams in both swimming and diving events. I announced all winners and their times or their points. I kept scores of both teams. Coach Schoenheiter stood four feet away from my podium with his own score cards and lists and, through the entire season, he never had to correct any of my calls or statements. I was truly happy and even made a few sports-oriented jokes in between contests. It was during those glorious afternoons I felt myself acting as one of two people, both of whom were me... and, much like descriptions of Charles Dickens' dual personality... emerging successfully from the shadows only to slide back into them upon leaving the gym.

One great reward for me was the receipt of a silver box with Major L Club Manager of the Year award inscribed thereon. It was presented to me in a separate end-of-school celebration. There were other powerful coaches and teams at Lawrenceville that year, so I was deeply honored that Chief Coach Schoenheiter wanted me to have that award over all the other competitors.

During the two years that I managed the swim team, our able captain was Tim Cutting, who has remained a friend through the years. In 2012, when he heard I was writing my memoir, he was good enough to send me some

47 *Olla Podrida* 47

WALTER SCOTT McLUCAS, II

"Scotty" "Luke" "Mac"

"Wait until spring when I'm in shape."

1312 Madrid Road, Sovato Heights, Santa Fe, New Mexico.

Born at Kansas City, Missouri, September 28, 1929. Cleve House Championship Soccer Team '44-'45, Cleve House Secretary-Treasurer '45-'46, Cleve Charm '45-'46, Periwig Club '45-'47, Actor-Representative '46-'47, Varsity Track Team '45, Assistant Manager Varsity Swimming Team (Numerals) '45-'46, Manager (Minor L) '46-'47, Chapel Usher '46-'47, Head Chapel Usher '46-'47, Honors Average '45-'46, Cheer Leader '45.

Came to Lawrenceville September, 1944. Former House, Cleve. Preparing for B.A. at Yale.

Lawrenceville Yearbook Photo & Write-up

yearbook photos from that championship year of 1947. His hand-written note about me to my assistant biographer, Susan, was quite complimentary. "Scott doesn't get the praise he deserved. He was the best team manager we ever had and he took us through two winning seasons, for which we threw him in the pool with all of his clothes on!"

Memories of that season of 1947 with the swim team are still crystal clear and important in the scheme of things. That small silver box from the coach remains in a place of honor in my home nearly seven decades later. It is the symbol of a victorious apprenticeship for a potentially challenging life full of adult competition.

CHAPTER 6

Yale

In 1947, one approached the Yale campus in New Haven, Connecticut by crossing Church Street and entering the massive Victorian Vanderbilt Hall, a freshman dormitory, through its arches, which offered both a view of the 18th Century Old Campus and entries to Vanderbilt Hall itself.

For the first four months of my life at Yale, that unique old hulk was home and the center of all activities for me and for my three roommates, Dick Cook, Warren Ladue and Stu McNamara. Dick, Warren and I had Lawrenceville diplomas to hang on our walls, and Stu was a hometown boy who had graduated from a school in New Haven, itself. Typical of Stu McNamara, he used all of his Yale quarters as places to hang his Naval Reserve uniforms and white shirts, and not much else, since his family lived so nearby. Few hometown boys lived in the dorm, although Frank Benedict, also a "homie," later became our roommate at Branford Hall. Frank was very bright. He became a physicist.

One of my first memories of Yale was responding to a written invitation sent by a clergyman of the Episcopal faith. Every detail of this meeting remains crystal clear in my memory.

I was directed to a small Victorian chapel on the old campus, not far from the Statue of Nathan Hale, Connecticut Hall, and my entrance door to Vanderbilt Hall. A shout from above brought me up a straight stairway where I turned left (no other way possible) and was told to take a seat in a chair placed there, about 10 feet from my greeter in the far corner of a room where the clergyman, clothed in black with a white clerical collar, was seated at a high carved desk with its back to a wall. The only light in this room came from a lamp on his desk. We introduced ourselves and told one another how happy we were to meet and how we were both looking forward to participating in religious services in one of the original Episcopal churches on the New Haven Green. This was not far from the famous split-rail fence bounding the western part of the green, and I felt a marvelous aura of history in their atmosphere. As I reflected on the historical significance of my surroundings, however, the clergyman's conversation somehow began to veer in a strange direction, and I began to tense up. The man of the cloth's speech took him all the way to Italy and Spain, leading him to lurid tales of nasty and rambunctious sexual activities in these two countries, involving Spanish and Italian boys and girls. The clergyman was obviously a connoisseur of these activities, his eyes sparkling strangely as he delighted in his personal recollections. I cringed, gulped, mouthed a few stilted words, and hastily made my exit. Since that day in 1947, and when in New Haven, I have never felt the need to visit that small Victorian chapel on Yale's old campus.

However, on every occasion in New Haven since graduation in 1951, I have visited my favorite Yale statue, that of American Revolutionary patriot Nathan Hale, whose famous last words, "I only regret that I have but one life to give for my country," have inspired me often when considering decisions involving greatest good, relative costs, and the balance of other human values.

In 1947 and '48, with our nation still reeling from World War II, and fully adult veterans pouring into institutes of higher learning to mix with younger college freshmen like me, the Yale campus was turbulent, to say the least. Contrasting points of view were rampant in those days, as the cold war between Russia and the United States erupted and the tug-of-war between conservative and liberal forces took on new strength. A loosely organized and unnamed patriotic freshman political group attracted me to its meetings, and I became engaged in helping with free distribution of an issue of Time magazine that explained a host of well-written and edited conservative positions. It counteracted a mass of Communist-inspired speeches, writings and publications on the campus. We trooped through halls and porticos with our messages, drawing some attention to our cause and helping to encourage a patriotic movement on campus. What was thrilling to me, in addition to the solid patriotic ideals espoused, was that this group was almost exclusively composed of veterans with both war experience and peacetime goals.

One of the most famous Yale initiatives was its insistence on good posture. All students were scientifically photographed in the nude — with frontal and side views — in order to determine our true posture. Looking back, the possibilities for law suits were enormous. Yes, we lined up, were instructed to disrobe, entered a room and posed for a photographer, and then, as we donned our clothing, the next student was called in to pose. It was something that nobody paid attention to until, years later, girl students entered Yale and that practice was stopped, but this was just a couple of years past World War II. There was no physical testing involved with the photograph — you were simply instructed to stand as straight as you could. The thing I remember was that I was told I had a slight lordosis (curvature of the spine). It wasn't so terribly handicapping, but I was instructed to be careful about it in the future. Some students were more heavily criticized and had to sign up for intensive remedial exercise. I have my doubts about the therapeutic success of this initiative. It also occurred to me that it would be a good thing if the posture check photos were not made available to the clergy.

Just as I went innocently to meet that troubled Episcopalian man of the cloth, I entered my freshman year at Yale with expectation that I would receive something like the same warmth, acceptance and cooperation I'd received from the teaching staff at Lawrenceville. Of course, my hopes were immature, and I had almost completely misunderstood the gigantic problems of educating jumbled generations of students following the most devastating war in world history.

My troubles started with a pair of badly taught courses, both of which were required for graduation. One was straight-forward economics. I'd expected a survey course that included the history of economic theory and its interpretations, or other subjects for which there are full records, such as how Rome managed hundreds of years of Mediterranean trade. As it turned out, the course was straight modern Keynesian theory taught by an uninspired grad student. Somehow, despite the challenges, I passed that course.

The other was nuclear physics — worldwide. The very young teacher (a graduate student) lecturing us was hard to understand when prioritizing what we needed to study and retain. Also, it was "early days" in the field of atomic energy and very difficult to separate its destructive forces from its constructive ones. The lecture course was held in a great auditorium with more than 300 students in attendance and there was little, if any, opportunity to question or discuss concepts. I failed the course.

I was then called to an audience with three senior professors seated behind a long table in a dimly lit room and grilled hard regarding the reason for my failure of nuclear physics. It was intimidating as they asked details about how many hours I devoted to study each night and reminded me that it was completely my responsibility to pass the course to graduate. I was informed that my attitude toward studying needed considerable improvement. I was required to take both chemistry and biology the next semester in order to make up for my failure in physics. No options were permitted.

Another disappointing first year course was Conversational French, which came to a skidding halt when I entered the "drawing room stage-set" classroom, discovering to my amazement that not a single student was speaking exclusively in French. They were lounging around what passed for a living room in all manner of conversational poses, and their comfortable discourse was a combination of French and English. Although I had achieved some slight proficiency in speaking the French language through classes at Lawrenceville, I was certainly not at the level of casual comfort evident in that unusual Yale classroom. Intimidated, I swiftly exited and did not return until some time later, when I had recovered a bit of my self-confidence. I took Conversational French classes for the remainder of my time at Yale, and, upon moving to France several years later, was grateful I did not let my original hesitancy keep me from learning additional spoken French.

After the initial surprises during my freshman year, the remainder of my time at Yale was fairly uneventful, until my senior year in 1951.

As a member of Yale Dramat from my sophomore year onward, I was destined to know several fellow classmates who were invited to be members of the eight secret societies on campus. Sophistication prompts us to desire acceptance by elite inner circles and, like nearly everyone else at Yale, I quietly yearned to be tapped for one of the secret societies, the most well-known being Skull & Bones. Selection to the "Tombs" at Yale was in the spring when all members of the junior class were assembled in Branford Courtyard. By the time I was a junior, I happened to live in Branford Hall, so it was easy to appear somewhat casual about being there. Although I was 99.44% certain that there would be no taps indicating an invitation, there was still that small inkling of hope. There were friends who specialized in running all over Branford Courtyard and slapping people on the backs, joking about false selection to Skull & Bones, and I did receive a few "joke slaps," but no true invitation to any of the secret societies, for which I'm actually somewhat grateful. I learned, through the grapevine, that one of the more disturbing initiation rituals for most of the secret societies was the requirement of lying flat on your back, naked, as you recited your life story to society members. Just as I chose to exit my French class temporarily, I'm sure fellow Lawrenceville grad Hale Matthews would never have endured reciting his life story as he lay naked on his back, however, he did certainly love to share his story.

Hale Matthews had been a year behind me at both Lawrenceville and Yale. His mother was a member of the very wealthy Mellon family of Pennsylvania. While still at Lawrenceville in 1947, Hale had somehow obtained a copy of the novel, Brideshead Revisited, by Evelyn Waugh, even before it was published in the United States. It had been published in England in 1945 and had quite a following by 1947. In fact, Hale Matthews had chosen to adopt it completely — considering it a sacred tome and memorizing every single word of it. By the time he entered Yale, Matthews had two stories to tell — his own and the one he had adopted as his own. Based on adventures of the English upper class, the novel became a part of Hale's persona. He knew every character by heart. A dandy at Yale, sporting elegant attire and cream-colored suits, Hale Matthews was the arch prototype of the affected son in Brideshead Revisited. His flamboyant literary flair attracted a lot of attention to him, and he relished that attention mightily. He actually became a caricature of Waugh's fictional being and lived the words of the novel daily. Wealthy and imaginative, Hale later began to write his own musical comedies and submit them to the Yale Dramat for acceptance. The Dramat turned Hale down two or three years in a row, but he came right back and paid for and produced his own musicals at a local high school nearby.

Secret societies and drama aside, my academic education at Yale was proceeding quite well. My favorite professor was Ralph E. Turner, one of the most popular and controversial professors teaching at Yale in those years. His history class was so popular that I was unable to get in until I was a junior in 1950. Professor Turner vehemently warned his students against Islam conquering the world. I remember at least three lectures devoted almost exclusively to that subject and I sensed prophecy there, although the concept of those "filthy nomads" wielding any power or control over us was anathema to our tender sensibilities. Professor Turner's popularity certainly stemmed from his startling teachings. People lined up for his classes because he was a shocking teacher. We were a "community of disbelief," rolling our eyes and taking notes for the inevitable testing as he lectured at length about the dangers posed by the people of the Middle East. It was truly as though we were in a movie and the professor was just a dramatic performer. He expounded eloquently about the extreme militancy of the people of Islam, and it was in his class that I heard the word jihad for the first time. We admired his courage and were stunned by his views, but we believed him only on a superficial level.

I've always had a thing for the Middle East — the steely heroism of Lawrence of Arabia; the romance of the Arabic language; the tales of the Crusaders. I once wrote a good paper on Ur of the Chaldees, a place mentioned in Genesis that was discovered in the 1920s by archeologists to have been a city of gold — located near where Baghdad is now. All of that seemed so mystical and far removed from my reality until September 11, 2001, when Professor Turner's prophetic words came to life as the Twin Towers tumbled to earth. His words still ring in my ears, and the world continues to approach the conditions he predicted so many decades ago.

Upon contacting the archivist at the Yale University Library for information on Professor Turner, it was revealed that his opinions were much more well-founded than we students realized. The following, from Head of Public Services, Diane E. Kaplan, Manuscripts and Archives, Yale University Library, are excerpts from a brief description of the professor's stellar credentials:

Ralph E. Turner, in full Ralph Edmund Turner (born Nov. 6, 1893, Anthon, Iowa, U.S. — died Oct. 5, 1964, New Haven, Conn.), American cultural historian, professor at Yale from 1944 to 1961, and, as an American delegate to an educators' conference in London (1944), one of the planners of the United Nations Educational, Scientific and Cultural Organization (UNESCO)... He was chairman of the international editorial board preparing a six-volume Cultural History of Mankind, and he lived to see the publication (1963) of the first volume. From 1936 until 1941 he was economic historian for the Bureau of Research and Statistics, Social Security Board. During World War II he served in various governmental capacities as an economic analyst and as cultural-relations officer for the Department of State. His publications include America in Civilization (1925), James Silk Buckingham: A Social Biography (1933), and The Great Cultural Traditions, 2 vol. (1941).

Aiming to earn a degree in Liberal Arts, I took several other interesting courses that had something to do with forming the person I am today, and then there were a few classes that were memorable simply because of their oddity. There was, for example, a South Sea Islands anthropology course that I found interesting, especially when the sexual customs of the queen of one of the tribes were described in detail. There was a bit too much emphasis placed on her reproductive organ, which her devoted tribesmen called "the frisky one," a fact that the professor seemed to relish revealing to the students. It was a bit of childish fun.

Jazz played a large role in my social life at Yale, as I spent many a Sunday afternoon at various fraternity houses on campus enjoying the glorious sounds of Sidney Bechet's soprano saxophone.

Sidney and a group of players would come up from New York City every weekend and play New Orleans jazz while 50 or 60 of us sat at their feet, sipping beer and absorbing the rich music produced by Sidney and his five-man group. I remember that Jack Teagarden was sometimes on trombone and there was always someone on drums and trumpet, sometimes a clarinet or a sax. One of my favorites was Bechet's version of "Oh, Didn't He Ramble," but I loved anything written by Kid Orey. Back in Kansas City during the 1930s, jazz had been king and it seeped into my heart and soul. I still enjoy good jazz and listened to some excellent performances in the clubs in Paris during the 1970s and 1980s, but nothing ever compared to sitting right at the feet of Sidney Bechet in a frat house as he gave us the romance and beauty of the greatest soprano sax player in the world.

Certain life events and certain people have a way of staying with you, and that is how I view my association with the Yale Daily News and its editors, Arthur Milam and William F. Buckley. Arthur and William worked side by side at the Yale Daily News, both as news managers and editors, and yet there could not have been two more different personalities than these two men. Like many Yale students during the late 40s and early 50s of the 20th century, I knew both Milam and Buckley by reputation and held them in high esteem as leaders of thought on campus. Arthur Milam has always held my utmost respect and admiration. I also had the privilege, in recent years, of serving with him for eight years on the Board of Trustees of the Contemporary Museum of Art (MOCA) in Jacksonville, Florida. Arthur Milam was head of the MOCA Board of Trustees, and I always felt comfortable, reassured about the management and the destiny of that museum, as long as he held that position. Arthur is a master of leadership, as he was during the time he spent at Yale.

Following Buckley's publication of the book, *God and Man at Yale*, his reputation as an author and a master of the English language began its ascendency. While I did have some respect for his use of language and his ability to organize an argument and to debate effectively, I came to feel that his grasp of leadership was weak and not convincing. Buckley's attempts at dissimulation of his natural arrogance were total failures. His innate cruelty was evident in his often unprovoked and unrelenting attacks on respectable guests from around the globe. I watched Buckley often bring to their knees, or otherwise destroy, debaters and debating teams. His rapier wit and superior style is still admired by some, but I personally would have been gratified to see a new and humanistic debating champion emerge on the international scene.

Social psychology and abnormal psychology proved to be two of my favorite courses. I also took the "gut course" of geography, along with history, sociology, economics and accounting (including corporate investment and management). I enjoyed art history and toured several art museums, later learning more about the artists and their works when I lived in Europe. My grades at Yale steadily improved throughout the four years and I graduated with an acceptable grade average.

Yale Dramat was the one extra-curricular activity in which I was involved, much of my interest due to my summers spent at El Theatro de Santa Fe. It wasn't until my junior year that Yale Dramat began to play a big role in my life, after having my horizons broadened considerably by a tour abroad during the summer of 1950. This tour abroad was with my Aunt Dorothea and Uncle Gilmer, cousins Dee and Mary Gamble, and Mary Gamble's husband, Robert Adamson.

Our little family group sailed over to Europe on the Pacific and Orient ship, the Stratheden. It was a seven day passage and once in Europe, we visited London, Paris, Rome and some of Switzerland. In Paris, we split the family up, with Dorothea and Gilmer returning home to Kansas City and Dee, Mary, Robert and I going on to Italy, where we visited Rome, Naples and the Isle of Capri.

On the night before we were to split up in Paris, Dee disappeared. Gilmer, her father, got excited and took a taxi cab to a restaurant in the early morning hours to yank Dee from the arms of a young suitor. Gilmer was quite excitable by nature, his face often turning beet-red, and although this Paris adventure was quite innocent, Dee sometimes gave her father good reason for his blood pressure to rise.

On our voyage back, once again on the Pacific and Orient Lines, we found it fascinating to watch the Indian crew members cooking out on the deck. The smells from the various oriental dishes were tantalizing, although we hidebound midwesterners were unimaginative enough to generally stick with our own dining room fare.

Toward the end of the voyage, my imagination journeyed far afield when I met a pretty young girl who was traveling alone. She was strikingly different. Of Jewish origin, and about 16 years old, she was quite innocent, but of strong mettle. I learned later that it is not unusual for Jewish people, either men or women, to travel alone. They are a courageous people. I had never had a Jewish girlfriend and found her hard to resist, as she thought I was Prince Charming. Totally caught up in being her romantic hero, I restrained myself admirably. We didn't neck. We simply held hands and talked at length, conducting a refined shipboard romance if ever there was one. Once back on solid ground, she invited me to her home in New Jersey. There, I was discovered in her bedroom by her father, an angry Orthodox Jew, and summarily escorted from the house. Had her family been more liberal, we might have had a real romance, but as it was, we did not have time to do more than say goodbye. The relationship was on thin ice from the beginning. Neither of us was prepared to commit to any permanence in our romance.

Meanwhile, back at Yale in the fall of 1950, things began to get exciting. I had recently been elected to the one year office of treasurer of the Yale Dramat, and its recently elected vice president was John Manly Johnson, a returning veteran who was a good friend of our president, Dick Kebbon. John proved to be an excellent writer of scenes, music and lyrics as well as an impressive take-charge person. Through his girlfriend, Patrice (Patty) Munsel, a fine coloratura singer at the Metropolitan Opera in Manhattan, he was highly connected to the theatre and the theatre crowd. John managed to obtain U.S. Theatrical rights from author and playwright Clare Booth Luce to adapt her novel *Kiss the Boys Goodbye* for Yale. I was impressed to see a fellow student creating lyrics and music for an original libretto, and auditioning professional performers to come and sing the score. He had composed a number of cleverly fashioned songs, in the style of Broadway tunes of the early fifties.

John's adaptation of *Kiss the Boys Goodbye* was a huge deal for the Yale Dramat. He had even arranged for a tour to New York City, with the play being performed at the Young Men's Hebrew Association Theater with and sponsorship by the Junior League of New York. The stage manager from a current Broadway show was our director and the music was being transcribed for orchestra by Yale graduate student, John Crosby, who later founded the Santa Fe Opera and became head of the Manhattan School of Music. John Johnson even managed to line up professionals, Elaine Stritch and Janice Rule, both excellent choices for musical comedy.

As treasurer of Yale Dramat, I was in charge of ticket sales and expenses. Our tour manager for the production appeared to be jealous of me. He may have wanted to be the Yale Dramat treasurer himself, or to play a bigger part in this New York production. Whatever the reason, he purposely attempted to catch me at a loss when he came running up to me on the morning of the tour, just as the bus was being loaded, and smugly informed me that he would need a payment of approximately $2,000 immediately in order to carry out the tour. His anticipation of causing public embarrassment for the treasurer of Yale Dramat was obvious, but it was not to be. Because of rehearsals and college academic work, I had ignored making Dramat journal entries, etc. I dashed to the bank, withdrew the necessary funds from my own account, put the money in an envelope, and promptly handed it to the tour manager. Having the funds available at a moment's notice was convenient and satisfying. It was a lucky perk of being the grandson and namesake of a prominent banker who trusted me not to overspend. I did not take that trust for granted.

The most important event that occurred with *Kiss the Boys Goodbye* was when the show was almost stopped from appearing in New York by the Council for the Living Theatre (Equity, Stage Hand and Theatrical Union coalition). I found their title ludicrous in terms of what they were trying to do, which was stop our "live show" from happening. Their complaint was that neither Elaine Stritch nor Janice Rule nor our management (Yale Dramatic Association) had made application to the Council for the Living Theatre for our one single appearance in New York City. They didn't care that it was being performed at the YMHA (a non-union house). Their concern was that it was happening in New York City and equity actors were involved. They were determined to stop the show.

It was all quite dramatic. Suddenly, during rehearsal at the YMHA, the doors flew open and a group of tough-looking men in overcoats exploded into the hall. Stalking down the aisles toward the stage, their faces were grim and menacing. They didn't have clubs in their hands, but they might as well have as they roughly attempted to lay hands on the music, all the time loudly shouting threats. The management of the YMHA was called into the auditorium and eventually everyone calmed down enough to hold a discussion in an office at Park Avenue.

The conflict was settled without further disturbance and the show did go on in New York. We gave the one-night performance in a peaceful and orderly fashion. It was enjoyed to a degree by the Junior League, our sponsoring organization, although our Yale orchestra was, frankly, an embarrassment. Certainly, the Junior League members must have enjoyed listening to Elaine and Janice, and found our Yale leading men to be adequately entertaining. While that was our only New York performance, the show had previously been performed twice in New Haven. One of those performances was particularly memorable. The score was played passionately and extremely well on double grand pianos by John and the arranger, John Crosby. When played by those who wrote and scored it, the music proved to be quite spectacular.

I was amazed at the talent, presence and personality of this man named John M. Johnson who had served his country as an officer in the U.S. Army and was now making such great strides for our Yale Dramat. Even with four summers of theatrical experience behind me, I had never in my time with theatre, drama, amateur or professional performance, experienced the excitement, complexity, beauty and pleasing originality by participating in the creative process in action. At the heart of this process was a man I considered a genius, writing from scratch to produce great new lyrics and music.

John was a one man show. For Yale, he was quite extraordinary — even to the extent of having a spectacular girlfriend who was an opera star at the Met! The grandiose picture of him that I had in my mind led me to feel it was an honor to be the friend of such a great guy. I was to learn, to my deep regret, that John was merely a façade who had flashes of creativity and talent, but nothing of true substance that lasted. John Manly Johnson was a narcissist of the first order, whose opinion of himself was far more grandiose than mine or anyone else's.

In the 35 years that I knew him, John never talked about his family or his childhood, except to say that his mother ran off with a traveling salesman when he was very young. He had some relatives in North Carolina, but I never got to know any of them. Much later, I discovered that he had lied about his age and was five years older than he admitted. John was his own invention. He appeared to be a man who was charming, smooth, cosmopolitan and completely in charge, but in reality, he was a spider in search of his prey… which I turned out to be.

When we met, I was a rich boy with a blueblood background and he was not. I was naïve and impressionable at age 22, and lacking real-world experience. He, at nearly 30 years of age and having served in the military, was far from naïve.

John's narcissism manifested itself in several ways: his vanity knew no bounds and he derived erotic gratification from his own and others' admiration of his physical and mental attributes. I played right into his hands by unwittingly pandering to his narcissism and as a result, the events of one strange night in 1951 changed my life forever. I have little recollection of that night except that we stayed in a friend's apartment, two Yale men out on the town and a bit too inebriated to take the train back to New Haven. I awoke in the same bed with John. The train ride back to campus was silent. Humiliated and ashamed, I simply hoped that by ignoring the appearance of evil, it would go away. My hopes were in vain. Two days later, I received a phone call from John. He was desperate, shouting, threatening to kill himself unless I became his partner for life. It was blackmail of the worst kind — a terrifying conversation that I was totally unprepared for, especially when he threatened to inform my grandfather and all the members of my family of my recent sexual activity. To this day, I don't know which was most terrifying — the possibility that I could be responsible for another human being's death, or the possibility that my grandfather would disdain and punish me even more than he had done to my father. I had spent my entire life dealing with the latent fear that I might have inherited some of my father's tendencies and doing everything I could to earn my grandfather's respect. Now all of that was at risk.

From childhood on, regardless of circumstances, my mother had emphasized that I was obligated to do no harm. One pivotal night of being taken to bed by a narcissistic man who had designs on my lifestyle and wallet doomed me to spend the next 35 years of my life often alone, trapped in a "Do No Harm Destiny" of my own making. It wasn't until John's death due to cancer in 1986 that I was released from his constant verbal and silent threats. Between fear of his suicide, and fear that he might do real harm to any woman with whom I had more than a passing fancy, I allowed him to rule my life. John became my roommate and creative business partner over the years, but I knew from the start that he was never my friend. He had no room in his life for friendship with anyone other than the man he saw in the mirror. I was, indeed, lucky that I survived to live the rest of my life with my wonderful wife, Nancy.

CHAPTER 7

Perception

I was now a Yale Graduate of the Class of 51. Before leaving New Haven for a post-graduate life in New York City, John and I traded some confidences and plans, coming to an uneasy understanding that there would be no further insults or threats. Narcissism* was an unfamiliar word to me at that time, and I simply accepted the situation as it presented itself. My parents had been informed that he and I were to be roommates, sharing a rental apartment in the City for the remainder of the year and possibly into 1952. I would do post-grad study at Columbia and John had been hired by Doremus & Company, financial advertisers on Wall Street. He later transferred to Young & Rubicam, to work in their television division.

During the summer of 1951, as I settled into my new life in New York City and awaited the beginning of classes at Columbia, I spent some time sailing with friends on Long Island Sound and the New Jersey Shore. While sailing that summer, I became attracted to a lovely young woman named Joan, with whom I shared a common interest in theater. Joan was also scheduled to begin post-grad work at Columbia in Theater and Communications and would end up being in my acting class, but our budding romance was "nipped in the bud" early by a fellow sailing enthusiast named Edwin Eugene "Buzz" Aldrin. A young trainee in the brand new profession of astronaut, Buzz Aldrin was the heroic type of man I had always admired. Although

*Narcissism – Definition and symptoms – Addendum B.

Joan and I were physically attracted to one another and had enjoyed our time sailing together, I willingly stepped aside for this American hero in the making when it became obvious that he had eyes only for her. He later married Joan, who was to become an integral partner in his preparation for future fame as one of America's first astronauts.

The class work at Columbia was a good distraction from romance. It was interesting, well-taught, and caused my brain to work in a new way; helping me to understand perceptions that I had never before considered. This unexpected benefit occurred when student writers and directors were required to work on scenes from two perspectives: 1) that of live audience in a theater and 2) that of a much smaller audience reacting to drama on a screen. I've since discovered that perception and perspective are among the most fascinating of life's challenges. One of Webster's simplest and most understandable definitions of perception describes it as "the way you think about or understand someone or something."

The most startling new area of perception I've observed in recent years was exemplified in the Fox Network's television program "Bones." In this series, you have a beautiful female expert on pathological aspects of the interior of the human body, but both the perspective and the perception angles have changed in direction, density, and concept. You are required to listen for some minutes to descriptions of body parts of which you have no prior knowledge and which you know you will probably have even less knowledge in the future. What you are supposed to take away from observation of this scene is totally dependent on the translation by the beautiful expert who has pronounced judgment on the condition of the body parts and how they arrived at that condition. Even at Columbia in 1951 and '52, I could never have imagined the detailed perspectives presented by "Bones," or its consequences. Nevertheless, what I have learned through experience and observation is that human beings have an amazing capacity for varying all aspects of perception and perspective to suit specific circumstances.

Thus, my own perception of my life has been characterized in many ways over the years. In the early 1950s, I was living in a suspension of disbelief… discovering my "second-self" and role-playing for keeps. An observance about the two-sided nature of man — perception versus reality — was made by Charles Dickens in his novel *Great Expectations*, with the following quote from Pip: "Pause you, and think for a moment of the long chain of iron or gold, of thorns or flowers, that would never have bound you, but for the formation of the first link on one memorable day." In my case, one "memorable" night created a long chain of events that became my life.

I was one of thousands of students at Columbia and my living situation was of no interest to anyone else. We resided right on the edge of Spanish Harlem on West 90th Street, a somewhat undesirable location that discouraged anyone who was particularly interested in visiting us. It was a sort of "perception protection."

In early 1952 I suspended my Columbia classes for a year, and with the help of Patrice Munsel's agent, Charlie Baker, I obtained an interview at the William Morris Agency, America's oldest and largest talent brokerage firm. I was hired as a messenger in the mail room at William Morris Agency and I felt I was truly getting my foot in the door into professional show business. Back in the 1950s, the Morris Agency was, essentially, the producer of several of the most popular new television shows including *The Milton Berle Show*, *Texaco Star Theater* and *Your Show of Shows*. Being one of the eager, young employees at Morris, I relished every moment of drama connected with the weekly television appearances of such legends as Milton Berle and Danny Thomas.

There is one particular show that stands out in my memory for the sheer "insider glee" that occurred at the agency as a result. It was the *Texaco Star Theater Show* on June 3, 1952. Milton Berle's scheduled guests for the live, one-hour show included vocalists Billy Eckstein and Dorothy Collins; comedians Morey Amsterdam and Henny Youngman; musical/comedy performer Jack Durant; actors Jack Albertson and Billy Barty; and the acrobat and trampoline act, The Schaller Brothers.

It was on that show that "Uncle Milty" performed a hilarious sketch that mercilessly parodied Phil Spitalny and His All-Girl Orchestra (whose show was produced by the competition, MCA). After viewing the show along with thousands of other people in the television audience, I was privileged to report to work the next morning at the William Morris Agency and enjoy the "sequel," as executives walked around grinning like Cheshire cats with a bowl full of cream. The agency opened at 9 a.m. and by 9:15 that morning, Phil Spitalney's lawsuit for libel against Milton Berle was being served upon the agency. I imagine that the resulting courtroom battle, if there ever was one, must have been just about as hysterically funny as the original Berle satire.

It was my fervent hope to ascend the career ladder at the Morris Agency, climbing the usual route from mailroom on up, and when I was offered a job working as assistant agent to George Morris (no relation to the Morris family that started the agency), I was thrilled. Unfortunately, on the day I was to report to work for George Morris, I walked into an office where files were being packed and there was nobody in authority anywhere around. That stark scenario told its own sad story. Morris was out and I had no new job, but as has so often happened in my life, the timing was lucky. I walked out of the Agency and into the role of student at New York's School of Radio and Television Techniques.

This unique school was created by professionals who were well-versed in the new media and earned their salaries by teaching courses in television management and production. This was done through the GI Bill of Rights for Veterans of the Korean War. The purpose of the three-month course was very simple: train students to own and operate a local television station.

Our training in television production included several mock production days in which a typical week of broadcasting was condensed into fifteen-minute segments. In one hour, a whole day of broadcasting was represented. This might include a quarter of an hour devoted to a variety show, the next quarter to a sports show, the next to a news broadcast and the next to a quiz show. As a directorial candidate, I was exposed to every aspect of broadcasting. We practiced and participated as cameramen and writers as well as directors, learning a great deal about television production in this very concentrated course.

While it was difficult to train for every eventuality in live television broadcasting, I was proud to have been specifically trained for football game coverage. The complexity of coverage has increased since 1952 with many more cameras involved now, including remotely operated equipment, but the basic structure of camera placement on the football field has not changed. Main cameras stay in the same places over the field even today, although some cameras now fly.

Our creativity was challenged constantly during this course as we learned how to televise various types of shows. Our training for sports — football, baseball and basketball — took place using boards with camera indications. We learned the programming during our class periods, with programs being filmed through the use of kinescopes (film strips taken with television cameras), combined with live action. The kinescopes preceded videotape. All of this was used for reference and review. We usually had at least one drama and one news show, both of which required our full imagination. Having to spend time as a cameraman and writer as well as a director was an excellent exercise in understanding all that was involved in television technique.

The Army Pictorial Center was located nearby in Long Island City, and I kept hoping that some of the veterans who were training us would make use of that modern movie studio, but we remained in New York City. I even joined the U.S. Army Reserve Signal Corps in hopes that I would get my foot in the door at the Army Pictorial Center, where the Army did many of its training films. However, it turned out that our regular reserve meetings were held in a lower Manhattan office building.

Meanwhile, I wrote direction modules on some of the teleplays and actually directed an early Horton Foote play (a lucky view of future endeavors). Professional actors played the roles in our mock productions and our news shows were sometimes surprisingly brilliant. There was one breaking news item, for instance, that had the newscaster announcing with barely suppressed excitement, that the Queen Mary had capsized in New York Harbor, nearly colliding with Ellis Island as the Statue of Liberty looked steadfastly on. The news team had to rob some old films of shipwrecks to get the footage for that story!

Later, there was an equivalent of the School of Radio and Television Techniques that opened in Los Angeles, but I was proud to be one of the first to attend the first such school of its kind. Television was still the new thing in 1952. This course offered students an opportunity to learn about the new theater of electronics. Creativity and innovation were the keys to this exciting entertainment venue that was piquing everyone's imagination.

When my grandfather announced in 1952 that he was coming to New York for a quick visit, I was still attending the School of Radio and Television Techniques, located at West 57th Street in Manhattan. Our brief meeting was one of my finest productions. I chose a moment when I knew the main studio could be shown off to its greatest advantage. I wanted my grandfather to see cameras, microphone booms, the control room, the scenery and all of the production equipment involved in this exciting new television industry where my future would be. We drank coffee together at a small prop table beneath 50-foot ceilings, bordered by the most modern of lighting and camera equipment. As I talked of my future plans to work in the new television industry, he beamed his approval at me. All of the symbols of that new industry surrounded us. We had an excellent meeting of the minds that day. The smile on his face as he shook my hand for the last time told me how impressed he was. I was never to see him alive again. My grandfather died in February of 1953. I still remember that last meeting with pleasure and pride. It was clear to us both that I would do my utmost to be successful in television production.

After completing the course at the School of Radio and Television Techniques, I spent a brief, but satisfying few months as a vote-counter for the television show, *Chance of a Lifetime*. Sponsored by Old Gold Cigarettes, Dennis James hosted the talent show, which was a forerunner of today's *American Idol*. Each week contestants would vie for the chance to continue competing until they became a star (or not). One of the nicest people I ever met in show business was a dancer whose face was never seen by the television audience. She danced as a familiar national image, the Old Gold Cigarette Pack, yet no one knew who she really was. She was always accompanied in her routine by another masked dancer who was the matchbox. I occasionally saw both of them without masks so I learned how important was the masking since they barely broke a smile. Thus they performed with no true identity in front of the camera.

My secret wish for the cigarette lady and her matchbox colleague (a young girl less than half her age) was that they might each jump out of their boxes and do a really great tap-dancing routine across the stage. I yearned for them to give us their hearts in just one wonderful, memorable dance.

One of the more interesting guests on *Chance of a Lifetime* was singer, Al Martino. He was considered to be a sort of second or third-rate Vic Damone, and he was the star who got invited to show up and talk a bit, then sing a song and get off stage. One day, among the staff working there, rumors began to fly about Al Martino. He was owned by the mob. He was a complete product of the mob, rumor had it. He had been raised in the slums and it was later said that Francis Ford Coppola put him in the movie, *The Godfather*, to pay homage to the mob. He played the role of a singer similar to Frank Sinatra in the *Godfather* wedding scene. It was also rumored that Al Martino was difficult to record because he had trouble doing a complete song track. He could sing a third or quarter of it, but then he would hit a flat note or have trouble singing of some sort. The four kids working as vote counters and backstage at *Chance of a Lifetime* were prepared for Al Martino to fail when he appeared on the show. We were sitting around discussing his possible downfall when the front doors of the theater flew open and three big guys in camel's hair coats strolled in. They were escorting Al Martino, who also wore a camel's hair coat. He settled in, rehearsed and nothing went wrong at all. He sang half the number, took a pause, and then sang the rest of it, generally dispelling our suspicions. Even after a hiatus between rehearsal and show, Al Martino did just fine. The live audience really appreciated him, and so did we. He gave a nice interview and looked and sounded good. So much for the perception of youngsters willing to believe the worst... the rumors flew away as quickly as they were created.

Some of the vignettes of my job as a vote-counter for *Chance of a Lifetime* remain with me; I enjoyed my small role as a vote-counter. It reminded me vaguely of the days when I was keeping score as manager of the swim team at Lawrenceville. Once the audience applauded for a performer, they would be asked to raise their hands to indicate their preference. There were four of us vote-counters and it was up to each of us to count the number of votes in a specific area quickly and correctly, then communicate those numbers to the host.

In addition to counting votes for *Chance of a Lifetime*, I very briefly became the manager for a terrific pair of dancers and singers that I felt made Judy Garland and Mickey Rooney look like plodders. They were such a bright couple and they did win once, but eventually lost to a girl from New Haven who won all the time and was the nemesis of all the other acts. I thought for a while that my kids had a real chance at stardom, but they started losing and could not break the streak. I had to give them up. That's show biz!

I went from managing that talented young couple to working as assistant stage manager and then stage manager on the short-lived Broadway play *Lullaby*, which opened and closed in 1954. *Lullaby*, which starred Kay Medford, Jack Warden and Mary Boland, was a comedy set in a hotel room... a typical drawing room play of that era. Although it ran for only six weeks on Broadway, *Lullaby* provided me a wealth of experience in stage management and a depth of backstage savvy that could not be acquired in school. For instance, priceless lessons were learned when we took *Lullaby* on the road to both New Haven and Philadelphia prior to its debut at the Lyceum Theatre on Broadway.

In Philadelphia, we played at the Walnut Street Theatre which was then, and is now, the oldest theatre in the United States (built in 1809). As I watched the second act set being "flown" (hoisted) by cables into the fly space above the main stage, my breath caught in my throat. The set, weighing several tons, was to remain up there throughout the first act and then be lowered during intermission. "How many times over the past century," I mused to myself, "has the Walnut Street Theatre had the science, impetus or money to make sure that the grid holding all the equipment for raising sets into the fly space is secure?" The two aged carpenters who traveled with the set walked around to four different places and stood gazing upwards with worried expressions on their faces. Ominous pops and groans echoed throughout the theatre as the set was slowly cranked up, its sound effects diminishing as it neared its summit. What a relief when it was in place! The picture that remains in my mind is of Bob Downing (then stage manager) and I, gazing upward as we stood by the side of those two carpenters and literally willed the old, groaning stage rigging to work as the set was hauled into place.

Bob Downing had also worked in the team of actors cast by Elia Kazan for the movie, *On the Waterfront*, which had just finished shooting a few weeks before. Some of the actors, including Marlon Brando, were still hanging around New York City when *Lullaby* premiered, so Downing invited them to come see our show. I remember that Marlon Brando winked at me. We spoke briefly and Brando was pleasant, but he was obviously in a hurry to go off somewhere and have a drink with his cohorts. The show was easy for well-known actors to visit and remain anonymous, as the Lyceum Theatre is on the east side of Broadway, off by itself.

Kay Medford was, by far, my favorite actor in the cast of *Lullaby*. A former nightclub waitress and comedienne, Kay had debuted on Broadway in the 1950 musical, *Paint Your Wagon* and later received an Oscar-nomination for recreating her Broadway role as *Funny Girl*'s Rose Brice on the big screen. Kay won the Theatre World Award for her work in *Lullaby* — a well-deserved accolade on several levels. Kay's retention of lines was incredible. She knew her lines in *Lullaby* so well that she was able to walk through each scene effortlessly, whereas actress Mary Boland, at age 72, seemed to find it increasingly difficult to stay on task. When Mary flamed-out and completely forgot her lines, Kay took the older actress under her wing, exhibiting heroism of the most extreme kind by actually coaching her on-stage during performances to help her recall her lines.

Looking back, Kay Medford taught me some lessons, big and small, while we worked together on Broadway. Just before opening night, for example, she asked me to kiss her. I was expecting a big, wet, sloppy kiss but she was a very serious professional — she was kissing me to test the lipstick and make sure it didn't smear when she kissed Jack on stage.

Kay and I were invited to Patrice Munsel's apartment one night. It was for a party Patty was having for her acting friends to come over and watch a television show starring Stella Adler, the highly acclaimed acting teacher who taught such notables as Marlon Brando, Elaine Stritch, Delores del Rio, and Robert DeNiro. Two of the Gabor sisters were at the party that night with their mama, and they managed to gather directly around the front of the television set, hogging the space so that no one else could see. There were a lot of celebrities there and everybody behaved as though the Gabors had a universal right to hog the television screen. When Stella Adler came on, Kay and I allowed ourselves to get pushed aside into a back corner of the room. All was quiet and everyone was attentive to the show, even though no one but the Gabors could see the screen. The buzz of conversation began instantly at the end of the show, as though a switch had been turned on. One of the Gabor sisters tuned up very quickly and loudly with a negative-sounding statement… "I'd like to say this about Stella…" She got that far and Kay, with perfect timing from her corner of the room, said, "Well, you oughta know! You're ALL so fucking continental!" The silence was deafening. It was the first time in my life I'd ever heard the F word used in public, and Kay's remark about the central European origins of the Gabors was right on target.

Jack Warden, who went on to be a well-known character actor, playing in more than 100 movies and earning a couple of Oscar nominations, was just beginning his show business career when I met him in 1954. In *Lullaby*, Jack's role involved him changing clothes in a bathroom that was supposedly off of the hotel bedroom, but when he walked into the "bathroom" to change, the zipper on his pants came undone and he couldn't get the damn thing back up again.

This incident took place at the Lyceum, which had its dressing rooms arranged vertically — the least important actor at the very top of the tower of dressing rooms. Jack's dressing room was the third one up. I ran up and then back down the stairs, delivering his second pair of pants to him as he waited backstage in the "bathroom." The change worked, but Kay Medford had time to make some comical remarks at Jack's expense (ostensibly to herself) that kept the audience amused while he struggled with his zipper problem and finally got his pants changed.

There was a tradition on Broadway that the professional stage managers created a show using the theatre season's understudies — and everyone in the theatre came out for this annual stage manager's show on a Saturday afternoon after the Tony awards. I met Jerry Stiller and several others while rehearsing for this big one-time show. John helped by writing some of the lyrics and music, and Kay Medford sang an unforgettable rendition of the "Understudies' Prayer". Maude, John's beautiful assistant at Young & Rubicam, was in the stage managers' show. She sang a rendition of one of his songs from *Kiss the Boys Goodbye*.

After *Lullaby* closed, I went to work for Screen Gems as assistant to Technical Director Peter Keane in the Editing Department. Peter had been an assistant cameraman for the legendary *Gone with the Wind*, while working with The Technicolor Company in Hollywood. Television was moving into color at that time, and I was privileged to be working at Screen Gems with Keane at this transitional time in the history of broadcasting.

Remembering transitional times in television and show business in general, this was all at the tail-end of the McCarthy communist blacklisting era. Working for Young and Rubicam, John had been appointed as a security checker to investigate and keep an eye on a list of potentially dangerous left-wing suspects, including one David Suskind! Suskind was producing a new NBC Television dramatic show at the time called *Justice*. I attended a couple of the rehearsals and found it to be a brilliant show. John had been furnished this investigative list and he drove David Suskind nearly mad every time he came into the studio. This giant television mogul was known to be rude and loud and a bully, and generally wielded his power like a sword, but even he was subject to suspicion in those days and John had "the list."

"David, I need you," John would call in a wheedling voice across the studio during pauses in rehearsals, as he meticulously checked his list for new information about suspects. "All right, John! All right!" David would growl, helpless to rid himself of this irritating young Ivy League advertising executive. This exercise stoked John's narcissism immeasurably.

Later, when my wife, Nancy, and I talked about that era in television, she had her own horror story to tell about Suskind in the late 50s. She was working for WNET Public Television's *Play of the Week* and had a run-in with David Suskind one night when she answered the office phone. "He was a mean person," recalled Nancy. "He was known to have a terrible temper and was said to fly off the handle, cursing at the slightest provocation. Well, I found out that all of that was true. I was working late one night when he called. He wanted somebody right now — a producer or director whose office wasn't on the same floor. I asked him to hold and I'd see if the person he wanted was still there. When I came back and told him the person was gone, he ate me up one side and down the other, spouting profanities and calling me useless and incompenent."

At Screen Gems, I learned the mechanics of film editing and censorship. I also learned to appreciate light-hearted Jewish humor, particularly around the holidays where Christian and Hebrew traditions differed. Another discovery that came as a surprise to me was the proliferation of pornographic films available for viewing by our group of young film editors. The films would appear in 16 mm. format as if by magic and be periodically loaded onto projectors and greeted by a small, silent audience. No words were said as we simply shared in the fun of a forbidden experience. It was a little known perk of working in the new television industry.

My jobs at Screen Gems were multiple. In addition to editing, I assembled prints of major shows like *Ford Theatre*, *Father Knows Best* and *The Adventures of Rin Tin Tin*. For each of the shows, we would get a complete 35 mm. print and a 16 mm. print to run simultaneously. In case of breakage during the show, we could switch over to the 16 mm. I assembled the reels with possible changes that cut-in or extracted commercials and I did them three times, as they were different for each time zone and each different network — Los Angeles, Chicago and New York City. Prior to airing, each show would be viewed for final approval by our editing department staff and representatives of the National Association of Broadcasters.

One such viewing of *The Adventures of Rin Tin Tin* in which my boss and I were involved became a classic occurrence in the history of final television editing. The central scene of this particular episode showed *Rin Tin Tin* killing an eagle and throwing it off a cliff. As if the death of the eagle was not enough mayhem, the bird's body was shown hitting rocks on the way down the cliff, careening off of them and bouncing twice before landing at the bottom of a canyon.

A massive wave of shock and dismay shook the room full of viewers, including me. Telephones lit up from coast to coast. The show had been produced at Columbia Pictures Ranch in California and the idiot producer was actually proud of it, calling it a work of art and considering any editing cuts a threat to his integrity. He seemed not to care that he had turned our national symbol of fierce pride, the eagle, into a villanous potential killer of favorite U.S. pets. We were appalled, but we were also near deadline and there were millions of dollars involved. This is how early American television handled the challenge: The eagle's demise remained as filmed. Upon agreement with my boss, I cut out both of its bounces for the New York audience, cut out one bounce for the Chicago audience, and left in both bounces for the California audience. *Rin Tin Tin* and the *Eagle's Nest*, Season 1, Episode 19, aired on February 18, 1955 on ABC-TV.

Moving right up the ladder in my chosen profession, I was next hired by WCBS, the local New York television station, as a supervising editor. Less than two months after coming on board at WCBS, I received my draft notice. The Army was a rung on the ladder of success that I had not anticipated, but my perception of it was positive. At age 26, as one of the oldest draftees in basic training at Fort Dix, New Jersey, I had the advantage of knowing enough people in high places that I was able to continue pursuing my chosen field of broadcasting while serving my country.

CHAPTER 8

P. I. (Political Influence)

Pursuant to my draft notice from the U.S. Army, I reported for basic training to Fort Dix, New Jersey on 22 May 1955. Having registered for the draft in New Haven, Connecticut, I was possibly the only New York City resident required to travel to Fort Dix by way of New Haven that day. After a night in a bare barracks, we were routed early and marched in our civilian clothes to a large mess hall for breakfast. Breakfast over, we were marched into the kitchen areas open to the air on both sides of the large mess hall. KP ("Kitchen Police") was the order of the day for everyone, and I was assigned pots, pans and tableware. Of course, the wash water was near scalding, but I was capable of adjusting it, and as the morning proceeded, I found more and more surfaces upon which to display quantities of clean, shining utensils. The highpoint for inspection was a great river of shiny tableware on a wide black cloth. As the inspecting officer came closer to me, I proudly stood at attention and held up a large spoon for his admiration.

"Soldier! Never, ever pick up tableware with your bare hands! It ain't sanitary!" he shouted, adding several colorful invectives and glaring at the spoon. I had some immediate thoughts involving scalding water and this barbaric fool of an officer, but put the spoon down and gave him a hearty, "Of course, Sir — as you wish!"

Once at the barracks, the first order of business was to elect a platoon leader and assistant platoon leader. The chosen leader was Louis G. Malouf, a tall, smart New Englander who was a college graduate with a no-nonsense approach to his new command position. On the basis of my three and a half years in the Signal Corps Reserve in New York City, I was chosen as assistant platoon leader.

We were issued our uniforms, helmets and rifles and began practicing close-order drill (with some double-time) and other marching formations. During the next couple of months, physical exams followed, the last of those being oral examinations by Army dentists. As the first really hot July days smacked us hard, major tooth extractions were performed both on our platoon members and on hundreds of neighboring troops. Toward the end of that fiercely hot week, from our second floor vantage point, we (draftees spared the dentist's drill) looked down upon a scene of many, many stretcher-bearers, reminiscent of the wounded and dying Confederate Army stretched out on the railroad tracks at the Atlanta Union Depot in *Gone with the Wind*.

On a more agreeable note, during two of the more clement weekends that summer I received pleasant visits that took me momentarily away from my circumstances. One visit was from my father, who came down to the fort on a weekend, bringing with him a picnic lunch that included beer. He had been in New York on business for the National Bank of Detroit, of which he had been named one of two general vice presidents. I congratulated him for that honor and, as it sometimes happened, he and I got along very well together that weekend. I was saddened to see him depart.

The other visit was made by my "roommate" John and his pretty assistant, Maude, who was everything I had ever dreamed of in a girl. While John was aware that I had a huge crush on Maude, it was also obvious that she was interested in him. It was a beautiful job of stage managing by John, as he was certain I'd be thrilled to spend time with Maude. On that idyllic summer day, we all looked and felt great as we enjoyed many good laughs together, picnicking out in a field near the base. For a lonely soldier, the visit was a bright spot and a great relief from the Army atmosphere.

Another positive event that basic training summer was the award of a sharp shooter medal to me because of my marksmanship with my M-1 Garand Rifle.

Alternately, on one of the hottest days of basic training, I was on a combat exercise and I passed out cold from dehydration. I was given a glass of water and when I awoke an hour later, I was offered a truck ride back to our company's guardhouse by one of our sergeants, who also named me as "Charge of Quarters" for that afternoon, the evening and until 8 a.m. the following morning. Before saying goodbye, the sergeant suggested that if I wanted dinner tonight, I should name someone I trusted to substitute for me as "Charge of Quarters," for a brief time.

My period of command at the company guardhouse as "Charge of Quarters" on a Friday night was an interesting but slow-motion mix of events. I was charged with keeping detailed records of all messages received, including phone calls from individuals impossible to identify. I overheard and recorded strange sound effects that included breaking furniture, strong disagreements between two or more military policemen as to which persons, if any, were missing and why there were no reports of firearms being fired. No one could be found to claim authorship of a large puddle of vomit, so I had to locate pail, mops and other equipment to clean up that scourge. The closest equivalent to that Friday afternoon and night at Fort Dix when I was "in Charge of Quarters" was the scene from *One Flew Over the Cuckoo's Nest* when the inmates of the naval hospital began their escape with a celebration. As far as I know, at 8 a.m. the next day, no one was missing from the official roster at Fort Dix, so all of us present could consider the job well done.

The best instructors at Fort Dix were black veterans of the Korean War. Their scripts were sharp, well-crafted, effective and amusing teaching aides. My memory has dimmed since 1955-56, so I'm not sure of all the subjects they taught, but the carbine was one subject, and the bazooka, as well as map-reading. I remember most the spirit and the enthusiasm of these men. As professors of personal warfare, they were outstanding. The great thing about them was that the Korean War was the first we ever fought where black and white men regularly faced battle shoulder to shoulder.

At the end of that first six weeks of basic training, I learned I was scheduled for typing lessons and an MOS (Military Occupation Specialty) of clerk typist and probably a posting to Germany. As I had hoped for an assignment with the signal corps in television instruction, I recognized that speed for change was imperative if that hope was to be realized. Therefore, I immediately telephoned my step-father, Bill Colwes, in New Mexico and recalled his mind to a subject we had discussed briefly during my Yale graduation — that of our friendship with General Patrick Hurley and the possibility that he might pull some strings for me, should I ever need military or political help. Bill remembered that discussion. He said he would call General Hurley and propose that he act as agent for my transfer to the Signal Corps with a television production MOS. The next thing I knew, I had orders to report for duty as a television writer/director and producer at the Signal School Television Division at Fort Gordon, Georgia.

I was later to learn that the exchange between me, my step-father, the general, and the Signal Corps shared an appropriate acronym — "P.I." meaning Political Influence. And why not employ P.I.? I had grown up knowing people in high places and also knowing that no matter where that got me, I would still be expected to justify the advantage of P.I.

I arrived in Augusta, Georgia and reported to the sergeant major of Headquarters Company at the U.S. Army Signal School. He sent me quickly across a parade ground to its educational division. I walked into one of their ground-floor passageways and took a look into a working television studio. In the center of the viewing space was an instructor working on a teletype machine. Two cameras were focused on him as he made repairs on one of the machine parts. At a level of about eight feet from the floor were a series of three or four monitors which displayed teletype machine parts in other staging areas. What I was looking at for the very first time in my life was a concrete example of distance learning. The concept was to simultaneously teach 75 to 100 students how to repair communications equipment using four classrooms, three of which were remote satellites to the first. I was open-mouthed with wonder because of the breadth and multiplicity of solvable educational problems met by this system. The time, energy and money that would be saved by this new technology astounded me. I was eager to leap into this brand new distance learning phenomenon, but the U.S. Army had other plans for me. I was put in charge of an old-fashioned kind of live television show that was tedious, at best.

On the plus side, I was given the largest video screen in the state of Georgia to use for the production. Apparently, because of my experience in theater and television, it was assumed that I had the talent to add life and interest to a program about moderation on *The Chaplain's Hour*. I was the writer, director and producer of this show, which opened dramatically with a film-clip of a horrible automobile accident. This was followed by a stern reminder to the large viewing audience by the post chaplain: "Hold it! You've just seen a terrible accident in the making. We prevent such accidents by slowing down — by saying "hold it!" before we reach such a crucial point. This impending tragedy would not have occurred had there been moderation in the action of the person at the wheel. It is our purpose today to consider the subject of moderation."

The film, which featured "sermon-like" reminders from five chaplains and stock footage from several different sources, touched on achieving moderation in nearly every situation in life including eating, drinking, smoking, playing, and talking. It ended with an invitation to attend chapel services. Even looking at the script today makes me uncomfortable, but for the army in the 1950s, it was considered acceptable.

As it became obvious to me that the caliber of work I was being assigned at Fort Gordon was not on the level of either my expectations or abilities, I once again utilized my personal contacts (P.I.). I had learned that a former Secretary of the Army had become governor of the State of Michigan. My father, a former army officer and base commander, was currently a general vice president of the most important bank in Michigan, the National Bank of Detroit. Therefore, I surmised, might my father appeal to the governor for the transfer of a young man with professional experience to the Army Pictorial Center in Long Island City, New York? I hoped to finally get to the hub of where modern network shows and army documentaries were being filmed.

After some delay in obtaining the higher security clearances needed to work at the Army Pictorial Center headquarters in Long Island City, I got my orders. "Do you know what's written on your orders?" my driver (a young PFC about my age) asked, pointing belligerently to the upper left-hand corner of the document. "P.I.!" he announced, grim-faced. "That means Political Influence!" He was apparently quite nervous and resentful to be driving someone with those letters written on his orders. Being driven from one end of the base to the other was indicative of the white glove treatment and most certainly added to his wrath, but I was neither apologetic, nor proud. It was simply the way it was. He appeared to be regular Army and apparently had no access to any type of influence at all. It's interesting to contemplate how apoplectic and disgusted he might have been had he known about the equally powerful P.I. that had actually brought me to Fort Gordon in the first place! Rather than attempt to discuss it with him and appear condescending, I chose to remain silent during the drive.

When I entered the sergeant major's office at headquarters, Fort Gordon, he glanced at my orders and congratulated me. This was a welcome contrast to my driver's comments.

Upon arriving at Long Island City in the spring of 1956, I was given a series of tests in connection with my knowledge of television production, and was assigned to be Director on Traveling Field Unit #1 — the oldest traveling unit, which featured a well-experienced team of technicians. Field Unit #1 was capable of traveling from any point in the United States back and forth to the pictorial center. It was a self-contained television studio with all the equipment needed to produce Kinescope film recordings and broadcast by microwave dish. Soon after having familiarized myself with the team and the equipment, word came down that we were to go to Fort Rucker, Alabama. There, I headed up several long-distance learning productions for the Television Division, Army Pictorial Center.

On May 24, 1956, I wrote, produced and directed "How to Teach With Television," describing to personnel at the Army Aviation Center the roles of each of the field units and equipment in the new type of distance learning, and demonstrating how television might be used in the classroom.

Step-by-step weapons assembly became one of the many ways that the new distance learning technology was used by the Army, and I was involved in the writing, directing and production of many segments with titles such as "Hardware & Safety Methods," and "H-13." My involvement in the early stages of distance learning would much later provide me with the insight and experience necessary to take the concept to a new level toward the end of the 20th century.

In June of 1957, while on detached service to the Army Ballistic Missile Agency in Huntsville, Alabama, I delved into the field of invention, designing a Man-Carried TV Harness for a television camera. Working with another soldier in the Television Division, Jerry F. Colet, and a graphic designer named LaBathe, we came up with a detailed, seven page prototype model layout of the harness, including front, side and rear views, perspective, materials, and assemblage. At the time, of course, there were many similar inventions emerging to aid in television production, but Jerry F. Colet and I were firmly convinced that ours was the most innovative, efficient method by which a television camera could be easily handled by a cameraman.

Innovation was the key word for me as I transitioned from my two years in the Army back into civilian life in the fall of 1957. My steady upward mobility in the television industry had been interrupted, but now I was determined to get back on the ladder and keep climbing toward my goals. Once again, my family connections played a large role in placing me where I could use my skills to the best advantage.

At the written recommendation of a producer and banking associate of my father's, I was hired by CBS as assistant director on a brand new show called *Conquest*. It was a science documentary hosted by Eric Sevareid, premiering December 1, 1957. Working with Eric Sevareid was thrilling for me. He was the elder statesman of the television industry — a father figure for me and many of the others on the crew. *Conquest* only lasted for one season, but it was the most important television series I ever worked on, mainly because Eric Sevareid headed it up. Harry Reasoner, who was just getting started at that time, became involved late in the show. Those were glory days for broadcast television, with Edward R. Morrow, Walter Cronkite and Eric Sevareid, but you couldn't get much better than Sevareid. He was incredible. When the show debuted, Sevareid said, "A flood of discovery is sweeping down the short and narrow streambed of human history. I'd like to swim with it. '*Conquest*' itself is a try. We want to help penetrate the wall that separates the man in the laboratory and the rest of us."

In a glowing article on the day after the show's debut, titled "The Edge of Knowledge," John Crosby of the New York Herald-Tribune wrote: "Just when eggheads are back in style, CBS-TV happens to come up with '*Conquest*,' a program designed to give the public a better understanding of the scientist and his work." Right at the outset was an interview with Dr. Wendell Stanley, director of the virus laboratory at the University of California, who declared: "This may sound strange to you, but in the laboratory we look upon the virus as a potential source of great good, for it is the container of man's greatest secret — the nature of life itself... It's not unreasonable to expect that ultimately we'll control the genetic forces of life, shaping the generation of plants, animals and human beings to come."

New York Times writer Jack Gould was a bit more "mixed" in his review of the new science show. In the December 2nd edition, he wrote: "The highlight of the opening program was a filmed report of the balloon ascent of Maj. David Simonds of the Air Force, who some fifteen weeks ago rose to a height of more than nine miles. The elaborate preparations and the anxious moments when the major was trapped over a thunderstorm made an illuminating documentary film... '*Conquest*' also offered some unusual films showing laboratory study of cells and the origin of life. Another segment of the program dealt with explorations of the ocean floor by Dr. Maurice Ewing of the Lamont Observatory of Columbia University; this portion of the program, however, was marred by some soap-opera theatrics that should have been omitted."

I do not remember the specific "soap-opera theatrics" that Gould mentioned, however, I do remember the essential reasons for staging them during that segment. Dr. Ewing was a wonderful guy, but there were no laughs in him. He was pure scientist, through and through. His special machine was a coring device which drilled straight down and bored a hole in the ocean floor from which hundreds of yards of core could be extracted. What they hoped to find with all this digging was how various movements occurred, why they occurred and to what extent they occurred. This sub-Atlantic research revealed absolutely nothing of great interest at the core — no Rosetta stone, no sea monster — its purpose for a television audience was questionable. The veneer of dullness that existed in this particular segment of *Conquest* was nearly unconquerable. This is a show business challenge… when somebody is trying to "tart something up" and make a pretty bauble out of a sow's ear, there are big yawns that spread their noise all over the place. Ironically, current New York Times columnist John Tierney hit the nail directly on the head in his February 14, 2012 article titled: "What's New? Exuberance for Novelty has its Benefits." In Tierney's article, the word "neophilia" is introduced and, although it sounds contagious in a negative sort of way, as if engaging in it would make one's nether parts begin to droop, the word simply points to an important human characteristic — that spirit of adventure which prompts us to seek new vistas. *Conquest* was based on scientific novelty and discovery — neophilia. We were all fellow-neophiliacs who were attempting to convey our spirit of exuberance and discovery to the viewing audience. Thus, the segment featuring Dr. Ewing's "boring ocean coring" required some additional theatrics.

As assistant director, it was my job to perform many of the more mundane duties such as being the location guy, waking people up in the morning, arranging lunches, etc. One thing I specifically remember about Dr. Ewing's segment was that our crew managed to pour about two gallons of hydraulic oil all over the biggest rug in the doctor's study. The oil came from the dolly, which I should have ordered taken away, but didn't, because I was unaware it was leaking until far too late for repair.

We had to pay several thousand dollars to replace that rug. It wasn't the best shoot we ever did.

A technical moment where my position as assistant director made a difference was when we were filming Dr. C. Walton Lillehei, known as the "Father of Open Heart Surgery," at the University of Minnesota Hospital. Dr. Lillehei trained Dr. Christiaan Barnard, who went on to perform the world's first heart transplant. Our crew was filming Dr. Lillehei as he performed open heart surgery on small children. The operating theater at the University of Minnesota Hospital had a glass dome that consisted of upper and lower parts, with the upper part extending about 10 to 12 feet directly over the operating table. The fields of view to be photographed with long lenses from that dome made for dramatic filming, allowing the viewing audience to see nearly through the eyes of the surgeon. On the day of the first shoot, the CBS film crew was short one auxiliary cameraman and they had to hire a local man. Unfortunately, the local man turned out to be the world's clumsiest amateur. As he walked around the dome, bumping his camera into the glass and making loud thumps during the filming, I turned to our director of photography, Chic Murashnic, nodded toward the local guy and said, "I'd appreciate it if you would…" There was no need to finish my sentence. Chic took over.

While the camera angles were amazing and we were all thrilled to be filming this famous doctor performing miracles of surgery on tiny children, we were not in any way prepared when tragedy struck. The first child died following the surgery. We were all devastated. No matter how skilled you are, we found that it is nearly impossible to focus a camera with tears so thick that you cannot see. The child's death deeply affected everyone involved with the show. The deepest reason for our concern was that we had followed every step of the filming process including the interviews with the parents of the child. Now we were sharing their grief. The CBS team had become members of that child's family. I left the operating theater and didn't come back for several days. We later returned to film another surgery on another child and this one was a wonderful success, but the memory of that very first young child dying on the operating table remains with me today. It was one of the saddest and most moving moments of my life.

CHAPTER 9

New Horizons

By the early spring of 1958, the first season of *Conquest* was over. As it turned out, it was also the last season for that unique documentary science show. Through no discernible fault of anyone, the show ended meekly, simply disappearing from television screens, never to return. Everyone connected with *Conquest* seemed to have other irons in the fire, which was a good thing. The director went off to Italy and the editor had work scheduled in Hollywood, Eric Sevareid allowed himself to be simply reabsorbed back into the CBS family and there were two exciting projects on the horizon for me as well.

My first project involved the Brussels World's Fair. A French advertising firm with a New York office commissioned me to film certain aspects of the World's Fair, which was set to open in April 1958. First, though, I had some purchases to make that would facilitate the performance of all my projects as well as enhancing my advancement in the film industry.

I sailed aboard a Cunard Line ship from New York, docking in LeHavre, France. From Paris, I flew to Stuttgart, Germany, to pick up a new Mercedes-Benz 200S, and from Stuttgart, drove on to the Arriflex factory in Munich where I planned to buy a professional 16 mm Arriflex motion picture camera. I learned to my great disappointment that there were no cameras available for purchase at that time. I could order one, but there would be a long delay involved. I had a Bolex camera with all of its lenses and accessories with me, so decided regretfully to forego the purchase at that time.

My next stop was in Chesaux-sur-Lausanne, Switzerland, where the famous Polish inventor, Stefan Kudelski, designed and manufactured his world-famous Nagra portable professional audio recording device. I had already ordered one of the Nagra recorders, which were known for their precision and reliability. Kudelski would later win several Academy Awards for his recorders, as well as numerous technical awards worldwide.

Kudelski, a small man, was sitting on a stool when I walked into his office. When his assistant announced, "Mr. Scott McLucas!" the inventor leapt from his stool, grabbed a microphone and shoved it into my face. "For the news!" he shouted, grinning. It amazed me that he had invented such miraculous sound equipment — light weight, more secure, stronger and more portable than any that ever existed — and, yet, he was as stage-struck about television as the rest of the world was at that time. When I informed Kudelski that I was still in the market for an Arriflex camera, he got in touch with a friend in Zurich who had for sale every piece of Arriflex equipment anyone might want to buy. Zurich was just a one-and-three-quarter-hour drive from Lausanne, and I could have everything I ordered within a week!

Kudelski was destined to remain a good friend and business partner for many years to come. I discovered that once he had sold sound equipment to someone, he backed it up forever. A few years after I purchased the Nagra recorder, a couple of the microphones needed adjustment and I brought them back for repair by his technicians. He was charging a nominal amount for the repairs and told me that for just $15 more, I could purchase two brand new microphones that would make the others look like dinosaurs. Of course, I did so. But it wasn't long before I took them back because neither of the new ones worked properly. Kudelski then gave me three new microphones, swearing they would work. One of them worked well, but I took the two others back and asked him for the older, sturdier ones, as these new ones were more complicated and delicate. Forever the inventor and always seeking a new and better way to do things, Kudelski sadly bowed his head and said, "Maybe I should go back to the original ones." He was a man of integrity with only the highest goals, and I, for one, was proud to be testing new microphones for the Kudelski Company!

On my return to Paris from Zurich that spring of 1958, I picked up the
film stored in lockers at Orly Airport and, in April, set out for the Worlds
Fair in Brussels, Belgium with a carload of the finest film and sound
equipment known to man.

Expo 58, also known as the Brussels World's Fair or Exposition
Universelle et Internationale de Bruxelles, was held from April 17 to
October 19, 1958. It was the first major World's Fair after World War II,
and it was one of the most exciting places to be in the world at that time.
More than 41 million people strolled through the exhibits on the 500-acre
site where the last World's Fair had been held in 1935.

I was on one of about eight teams of filmmakers hired by the French
advertising company to cover the fair. We took films of everything, from
gorgeous flowers to fabulous fireworks. There were beautiful fountains
throughout the fair, and each participating country had a building or
pavilion where cultural exhibits were displayed. Living in Brussels for
about 10 days was just magnificent. We took nearly all of our meals in the
Czech Pavilion, where the food won all kinds of prizes. The Czech cuisine
was rather robust, with surprising side dishes and flavorful meat dishes.
The lamb and beef dishes were superb, and toward the end of our stay,
they served wild game such as venison and dove and quail. The Czech
wines were terrific, too — some of them as good as the French. All of the
countries competed in the matter of cuisine, and there were judges and
prizes everywhere. The weather was almost perfect for filming.

It's difficult to pinpoint why it was so dream-like to be eating delicious
meals in the Czech Pavilion, except that it made any reminiscence about
the ghastliness of war almost impossible to imagine. I remember noticing
tears in the eyes of Czechs who must surely have been at home back when
the German invasion began in 1938. I remember watching them as they
savored the delicious food and atmosphere of 1958. It was so dramatically
different now, and it seemed a joyous time, with a sense of peace and
prosperity throughout the world, despite the fact that the cold war with
Russia was dangerously heating up.

The U.N. had an enormous presence at the Brussels World's Fair, and
it was acknowledged as an assembly that had real force for peace. For me
and for many of the visiting Americans, there was a universal feeling of
great satisfaction — a rich feeling of belonging to a secure world that was
bright and shiny — modern, as it had never been before. The fair was a

delicious thrill for the senses and we filmed as much of it as we possibly could. Working as a team, with the final editing being done elsewhere, we had no say on what footage was used and what was cut, and though the final result was somewhat disappointing, I was reasonably proud of what we'd filmed.

Later, I was visiting Vienna, Austria, in 1958 when I literally bumped into one of the most famous opera singers of all time, Leontyne Price, on the street corner right behind the Great State Opera House. She and I had just arrived in Vienna simultaneously and it was easy to strike up a conversation with her because of my past friendship with Patrice Munsel.

Ms. Price invited me backstage at *Aida*, with the world-famous Herbert von Karajan conducting. The performance of *Aida* was splendid, except for that of the tenor singing Radames. He was vocally poor, and too heavy in physique. However, all other elements were perfect. Following the opera, I was invited to go out to dine with Ms. Price and Mr. von Karajan, who had just been appointed to head up the Vienna State Opera Company.

It was not until 1961 that the Vienna Opera's *Aida* production earned its highest awards. Prizes galore were awarded to the opera, von Karajan, and Leontyne Price. Internet research has shown that, by comparison, the 1958 performance was hardly worthy of mention.

Two days later, I attended the Volks Oper (People's Opera) where I witnessed the first post-war performance of *Verdi's Nabucco*, a work of art taken from the biblical story of Nebuchadnessar. *Verdi's Nabucco*, one of my favorites, is one of the greatest, most thrilling pieces of music ever written, particularly the "Pilgrim's Chorus," which describes the Israelites' being dragged out of Egypt. It is based upon Psalm 137, as follows:

1 By the rivers of Babylon we sat and wept
    when we remembered Zion.
2 There on the poplars
    we hung our harps,
3 for there our captors asked us for songs,
    our tormentors demanded songs of joy;
    they said, "Sing us one of the songs of Zion!"
4 How can we sing the songs of the LORD
    while in a foreign land?
5 If I forget you, Jerusalem,

may my right hand forget its skill.
6 May my tongue cling to the roof of my mouth
    if I do not remember you,
    if I do not consider Jerusalem
    my highest joy.
7 Remember, LORD, what the Edomites did
    on the day Jerusalem fell.
    "Tear it down," they cried,
    "tear it down to its foundations!"
8 Daughter Babylon, doomed to destruction,
    happy is the one who repays you
    according to what you have done to us.
9 Happy is the one who seizes your infants
    and dashes them against the rocks.

For the audience around me, it obviously brought back memories of the way the Nazis treated Jewish people in Austria and in other countries. It was also reminiscent of how the Viennese were made virtual slaves of the Russians from 1945 to 1956, even though they did not rule in all the quarters of Vienna. The Russians had practiced most violent lordship over the Viennese and made their lives absolutely miserable, and when the audience witnessed the performance, they must have likened it to the freedom they felt when the Russians departed from Vienna and Austria in 1956. There were people all around me, standing and crying and applauding at the end of the *Pilgrim's March* and then, an amazing thing happened. The conductor took up his baton and conducted the *Pilgrims Chorus* again! At the conclusion of the repeat performance, the joyous reception was also repeated, even more vigorously. It was one of the most dramatic audience reactions I've ever seen.

My second project involved traveling first to London and then to Germany to do extensive filming of German Shepherd dogs. When I had moved to a house in Westchester during the time I worked with *Conquest*, I had became the owner of a German Shepherd pup. I named my frisky little pup, "Hulla" because of the hilarious Bob & Ray comedy routine about Wally Ballou and his wife, "Hulla." Through a friend who was a world-renowned expert on hip dysplasia, a malady particularly affecting the German Shepherd breed, I became a member of the German Shepherd

Dog Club of America. Irving Applebaum, also a member, was the proud owner of Troll Von Richterbach, the World Champion German Shepherd for the year 1957. He contracted with me to go to Germany and seek out the finest German Shepherd dogs for a documentary on the breed. Once the other dogs had been filmed and Irving had observed them carefully, it was obviously his plan that his champion dog, Troll, would have the starring role in the final version.

Prior to leaving for Europe, I gave Hulla to the trainers for seeing-eye dogs, as her loyal manner suited that service well.

In England, I met people who were associated with the Alsatian Dog Club (their "politically sensitive" name for the German Shepherd breed). One of those people associated with the Club was a quietly brilliant woman named Iris Dummet. Iris was married to one of the luckiest heroes I've ever known in my life — an Englishman named Peter Dummet who had fought in the third and last battle of Ypres in World War I, and survived it. Having been a World War I buff all my life and carefully studied all three battles of Ypres, it was quite a privilege for me to meet Dummet and hear his reminiscences about the horrible warfare, including the enormous subterranean explosions connected to the Battles of Ypres. In addition to running the canine part of their lives, Iris Dummet was also a history buff, and when she learned of my family's interest in Napoleon Bonaparte, she presented me with a book written and personally signed by Betsy Balcom, the little English girl who became the confidant of Napoleon Bonaparte when he was exiled to St. Helena in 1815. Betsy, it turned out, was a distant relative of Iris's.

In conjunction with our film commission, Iris Dummet introduced me to a chap named Herman Bermpohl, who was my guide, on two or three separate occasions, to the entire German Shepherd Dog Fancy in Germany. I made a tour of Westphalia in July with Herman and, after a brief return to London, went back to Germany and began filming the very best dogs for what turned out to be one expensive "home movie" for Irving.

Another good friend who came to me through introduction by Iris Dummet was Julia Ward. In addition to being a member of the Alsatian Club, Julia had a passion for traveling and the money to travel often to exotic destinations like India and Africa. She wasn't the most attractive woman in the world, and it seemed she had a deep fear that men might be attracted to her only because of her money. Julia's sense of humor was hilarious and she often regaled me with stories of her various lovers, many of whom I surmised might have materialized in her rich imagination or sexually interesting dreams rather than in reality. At one time, Julia came back from her travels with two cats — one white and one gray — both of them, she said, named after lovers in India. Deciding she had too many dogs, she gave the cats to me.

Julia had an apartment in London at Onslow Square and she was interested in living part-time in Southern France. I shared many of her interests, including the show dogs, her love for travel, and her pursuit of property in Southern France. That area seemed to me to be a place of magical possibilities, and it was my dream to one day build a house there. Julia took long trips and one time when she was traveling, she loaned me her apartment at Onslow Square for nearly a year.

While in London the summer of 1958, making my connections with the Alsatian Club people and looking into filming possibilities in Germany, I had interviewed for a position at the advertising firm of Erwin, Wasey, Ruthrauf & Ryan, with a view toward long-term residence in Europe. I was hired as a senior television producer. In the meantime, John Johnson was hired by Young and Rubicam in London. Yes, he was there, too. He turned up nearly everywhere I went — even when I moved across the Atlantic. He was determined to be a permanent part of my life, and his all-encompassing obsession with me included frequent blackmail and suicide threats, as well as a perpetual need for money. I allowed myself to be intimidated by him because I was afraid of what he might do to himself and he knew it.

With the initial filming in Germany complete, and a job lined up for the fall of 1958, I sailed back to the U.S. briefly to get my affairs in order. The prospect of living abroad was exciting and inviting. Europe was known as a great and forgiving proving ground for aspiring film-makers, and that was an important part of what I wanted to do with my life.

My first residence was in a prime location in central London. It was called Ennismore Gardens Mews and was located right behind the Brompton Oratory, a Roman Catholic church in South Kensington, London, where many of those in society were married. Brompton Oratory was situated on Bromptom Road next to the Victoria and Albert Museum at the junction with Cromwell Gardens.

There was a fenced playground type area behind the Oratory in which I witnessed the biggest bonfire I'd ever seen in my life. It was staged for Guy

Fawkes Day, which is an annual English commemoration on November 5th, stemming from a day in 1605 when Guy Fawkes, a member of a group that had placed explosives beneath the House of Lords with the intent of blowing up King James I, was arrested. People lit bonfires around London to celebrate the fact that King James I had survived the attempt on his life, and Guy Fawkes Day became an annual public day of Thanksgiving for the failure of the plot.

Ennismore Gardens Mews consisted of three adjoining three-story houses which were former stable-mate dwellings. The ground floor was a garage space large enough for a car or a horse-drawn vehicle and the second and third floors were for sleeping and cooking and possibly entertaining a guest. It was a fine residence in the best part of town. The third floor had a very small balcony on which only one person could stand comfortably, and it was immediately adjoined by a similar balcony next door. Once, English actor Alec Guiness (who played Lawrence of Arabia on stage) appeared on the tiny adjoining balcony for a moment, but not a word of acknowledgment was spoken between us. It was all so very British and proper to take such encounters casually, as if they had never happened.

In 1958, Erwin, Wasey, Ruthrauf and Ryan in London was run like many other small or medium-sized agencies, with a media department buying or renting space at newspapers and magazines and buying or renting time on commercial television or radio. The main thing was that all the departments of the agency were duplicates of the same-named agency in New York. I was fortunate to have been given a comprehensive appraisal of our British advertisers by sympathetic agency people, with the exception of one, who was appraised and recognized by all as the champion practitioner of the negative in most aspects of advertising and, in fact, life itself. His name was Ron Lane and he worked for the Thomas Hedley Company (British equivalent of Proctor & Gamble, as well as its U.K. partner). Lane was most expert at analyzing television commercials and finding fault with them. He was the bane of existence for every agency's television commercial department.

In relation to Ron Lane, there was one visit to Newcastle (headquarters of the Thomas Hedley Company) that illustrated his disdain for assertive agency television producers — particularly those who hailed from the United States. I had been sent to Newcastle to monitor a special type of commercial on Tyne Tees Television, which was Newcastle's commercial network broadcasting station. It was a flower show that offered free flower seeds to buyers of Procter & Gamble's Oxydol® soaps, also represented in the U.K. by the Thomas Hedley Company. A young man, who was a Thomas Hedley employee apprenticed to their television department, sat with me in the client's booth. It was our job to watch the flower promotion show, appraise it for commercial purposes and report our appraisal back to our respective companies. Unfortunately, as the opening credits of the show began, the most awful roar I'd ever heard emanated from the television set in the client's booth. The roar completely overwhelmed the words being spoken by the announcer on the screen, and showed no signs of letting up. I rushed across the hall behind the booth to the station manager's office, complaining bitterly about the terrible soundtrack being played in the rehearsal. In my tirade, which I felt was totally justified in view of the disservice being done our client, I believe I used the words, "lousy sound," to describe the defect. The station manager told me that surely the deafening roar was an electronic problem there in the building and that the broadcast itself was unharmed and would go out under appropriate conditions. Further, he informed me that I was free to go down to the control room and listen to the show from there, which I did. I verified that the sound being developed in the studio was appropriate, after all. The sound in the client's booth continued to be poor quality, but it did not affect the quality of the Oxydol® commercial.

Soon thereafter, my boss, Paul Usher, received a three page letter from Lane, who had overheard my heated conversation with the station manager and decided to make me the target of an angry vendetta. He obviously was intent on getting me fired from the agency, but my boss knew exactly how to respond to his vitriol. He told Lane that he regretted he felt that way about me and assured him that my efforts were solely directed at making the best advertisement possible for our client as well as its agency. When I requested that I be taken off of that account, Paul Usher promptly accommodated me. In fact, I was rewarded with the Johnson Wax® account, which turned out to be infinitely more imaginative than Oxydol®.

Many years later, I got a psychological "bonus" from Paul Usher when he informed me that the insufferable egotist Ron Lane, who had made it known far and wide that he was the top expert on effective (and non-effective) television advertising, had been summarily turned down by all the best British gentlemen's clubs. His reputation for negativity had become so notorious that he was not to be welcomed into "British club land," and, therefore, was denied the respect and admiration he had so actively sought throughout his career. When others in the industry heard about his being turned down by club after club, they simply smiled. It was justice of the cruelest sort. I nearly felt sorry for him.

With the exception of Ron Lane, our agency's relationship with the Thomas Hedley Company was excellent. Much earlier in my career with the agency, I had taken my first trip to Newcastle with our top account executive, Austin Barnes. That trip stands out in my memory as a great success, with Austin touting Procter & Gamble's new Tide® detergent as the new miracle soap and the radio and television stations leaping on the bandwagon. Just as Lane was an embarrassment to the industry, Austin Barnes was a legend in British advertising. Ace salesmen like Austin were the heart and soul of advertising back then. They were great on the road, selling big chunks of advertising to radio and television stations. Austin Barnes always had a good but short supply of great new jokes on every expedition he took out of London. Some of his best jokes employed the "F" word and the shock value of that word back in those days was enough to get the attention of potential clients. In addition to jokes, Austin and these other super ad salesmen could be counted on to arrive with gifts in hand… sometimes whiskey or candy or flowers or tickets to a special show… the gifts were cunningly tailored to the personality of the receiver, and were considered an integral part of media relations.

As a senior television producer for the agency, I used to go out to work on the commercials with our various clients including The Carnation Company, Johnson's Wax and others. I remember that the U.K. advertising manager for The Carnation Company, who was a top officer in the company, used to love the idea of the cows in the field being bonked on the head with cans of Carnation milk. He thought it was the absolute ideal as far as advertising was concerned. I personally thought it was idiotic slapstick, but as I was supervising that particular set of commercials, it was my job to go with the client's instincts and not my own. The silly commercials, by the way, sold quite a lot of Carnation milk.

One of the most successful commercials I worked on while with the agency was the Johnson's Wax ad featuring a wonderful dance piece designed by David Paltenghi, formerly a ballet master and star of the Royal Ballet. In 1958, Paltenghi worked with a company called Anglo-Scottish

Films and his idea was for them to design and construct a giant book about 10 feet high, which represented a catalogue of Johnson's Wax products. The action was for a very attractive young ballerina to appear from between the pages of this book and leap into the waiting arms of a sturdy male dancer below, whereupon they would whirl away into the magical, glittering land of Johnson's Wax where everything from the floor to the furniture sparkled with a sheen that was nearly blinding. Paltenghi's flare for the dramatic, combined with his masterful knowledge of ballet, helped make the commercial such a success that it won an award at the Venice Film Festival.

As I was acquiring quite a good record of successes at the agency, Paul Usher produced a young man to be my assistant. My new assistant, Hugh Donaldson Hudson, came from English aristocracy and was the essence of English schoolboy gangliness. He was about six feet tall and somewhat awkward, all ears and eyes. He had been in the tank corps of the British Armed Forces and was by no means lazy, but it appeared to me that he had no particular focus. I took him to production meetings. We had conversations with copywriters. I went over with him what the television department wanted and needed. He was obviously capable of learning, but seemed to lack inspiration. For instance, when he could not find a chair at a pre-production meeting, he turned to me with such a helpless look that I lost patience and said, "Hugh, if you can't find a chair, you might as well go back to the agency!" I shouldn't have been so judgmental — I should simply have suggested he wait for a chair to clear at a later time, but I was intolerant and I ended up regretting it. This kid was obviously not suave or seasoned, and yet, there was genius lurking right below the surface. Imagine my shock, when years later, I saw by the credits at the end of the movie that he had produced, *Chariots of Fire*, one of the best movies ever made! Hugh Donaldson Hudson, in one fell swoop, earned his place in filmmaker's heaven and my everlasting respect.

Despite the steady progress I was making with the advertising agency, I felt there were many career opportunities still to explore, particularly in France. With the idea of moving to France always a possibility for the future, I advertised in the local press for a French tutor. Marie Rose Karpinska was one of the first responders, and I hired her on the spot. She was a gentle lady with a marvelous propensity for teaching the French language in such a way that her students also learned as much about French culture as about word pronunciation and meanings. She was married to a

Polish man named Lescheck Karpinski (in the Polish naming tradition, we learned, "ka" was female and "ki" the male version of their family name). Mr. Karpinski spoke six or eight languages and was incomprehensible in all of them. He had been a hero in World War II and was a Maquisard, fierce guerilla bands in the French resistance fighting against the Vichy French (Nazi sympathizers) and the German Army units there. He sported several medals for his heroism and I would very much have liked to discuss his war experiences with him, but it was impossible. He could not be understood. His German and French must have been passable during the war, as he survived, but he certainly did not "translate" well in London.

Marie Rose Karpinska had one wonderful expression having to do with the modern views of women and their power — "Les Dieux." (The Gods) The rights and strengths of women had grown so greatly since the 19th century that Marie Rose was in awe. The fact that women were now capable of driving an automobile was astounding to her. She especially considered women drivers to be gods.

I got along particularly well with Marie Rose because she loved history and she was an expert when it came to describing certain habits that were particular to the locale where she grew up. Her home village was Meaux, a small town on the River Marne, just beyond the northeastern corner of Paris. It was at the Battle of the Marne — one of the greatest battlefields the world has ever seen — that the French and British Armies stopped the German attack in 1914. World War I began and ended virtually in Marie Rose's back yard. Like all the Frenchmen I've met from that area, Marie Rose knew everybody's story from the Battle of the Marne.

In fact, everybody in Meaux knew everybody's story, anyway. "Le guet" (the 'get') was an integral part of that area's culture. It was the principle system for passage of communication of neighborhood news — in other words, gossip. Marie Rose explained "le guet" to me in great detail so that I would understand how structured a practice it was in France. Villagers like to use their windows and shutters in artful ways, she told me, in order to determine the exact number of times that Madame X (sometimes Y or sometimes Z) crosses the street at 2 p.m. every other day for four days every week and has done it now for the last seven months. Madame X enters the house on the other side of the street, and one happens to know who lives in that house and one must discover who this woman is visiting and why. An important relay system is put in place because this sort of information is vital, particularly among the bourgeoisie.

I found her descriptions of "le guet" both informative and amusing, but I was later to discover that Marie Rose took it very seriously. Years later, as I sat in her living room in Meaux, Marie Rose told me that she was sitting in the chair by the window where the work of watching was generally carried out. At just about that moment, another member of her family entered the room, tapped her on the shoulder, and asked, "Do you want relief?" I nearly fell out of my chair.

In musing about this French practice of "le guet," it has occurred to me that the Germans are best at this… everybody's business is theirs… but that this manner of gossipy communication has been part of small town life in just about every culture since humanity began. It's interesting that the French have put a definite structure and theatrical authority to it.

The best way to handle gossip in London, and particularly in the international advertising community, was to fly under the radar. When I began dating Elizabeth, the secretary of one of the most successful ad executives at Erwin, Wasey, Ruthrauf and Ryan, it was definitely "under the radar." As often happens in the springtime, Elizabeth and I shared a rush of hormonal desire. She was an irresistibly nubile young woman and I was a healthy young male.

The episode with Elizabeth brings to mind the lyrics of that marvelous Lerner and Loewe song from the score of *Camelot* — "The Lusty Month of May!" Lady Guenevere sang what Elizabeth and I were feeling that spring of 1960.

Tra la! It's May!
The lusty month of May!
That lovely month when ev'ryone goes
Blissfully astray…

It was, indeed, the lusty month of May. I remember sitting in the lobby one day and watching Elizabeth, absolutely mesmerized as she bounced eagerly down the stairs and headed toward the couch where I sat waiting. She had me, and she knew it.

Over the years, I had been involved in several flirtations but this was different. Elizabeth was pretty and smart, and I sensed she had her sights set on marrying me. That didn't seem like such a bad idea. She thought I was a good catch and I, in my "humble" way, agreed. I was a prosperous, upwardly mobile, eligible young bachelor… and an American citizen, to boot.

I had developed strong feelings for Elizabeth and we had been "dating" (coupling quietly at her place) for about a month when I walked out of her apartment late one night and found John Johnson sitting outside in a car. He had obviously been following me again, but even worse, the next day, he tracked Elizabeth down at our agency and threatened to kill her if she continued dating me. She was terrified, of course, and immediately reported the incident to her boss. Her boss was enraged. He picked up the phone and called John's boss at his agency to tell him that he had a psycho on his hands. It was like a soap opera — the ax fell quickly on John. Death threats were taken quite seriously in London. He was fired that same day. He was lucky the "bobbies" were not called in.

Humiliated and angry, I finally realized, without a doubt, that John was a dangerous psychotic. He began, once again, threatening suicide and begging for help, insisting that I had ruined his life by rejecting him. He had no money and no family and no future. For me, his lament was familiar. I was the lucky rich guy and he was the poor, downtrodden victim. My wealth was my barricade against the hard knocks of life, but it was also a tool that was used against me by the narcissistic John Johnson. I had established a pattern of guilt and sympathy with this man even though he was my nemesis.

As if things were not complicated enough, my mother and her husband, Bill Colwes, were scheduled to arrive in London within days of John's death threat. They were eager to meet the new girlfriend I had bragged about in my latest letters. It was a classic case of bad timing. Although Elizabeth and I had talked on the phone a few times, she was still pretty shaken up and I couldn't blame her. John was volatile. I was afraid of what he was capable of doing and I certainly did not want to put her in harm's way again.

Mother and Bill arrived knowing nothing of John's presence in London. They stayed in their usual fine room at the Connaught Hotel. As it was, Elizabeth was brave enough to come out of hiding long enough for me to introduce her to them and have dinner. She said nothing to them about the incident with John, but it became obvious later that night that our relationship had cooled. Elizabeth feared entanglement with me... a man who had a jealous psycho lurking in the background of his life. I decided, at that point, to follow my dream of building a home in the South of France.

In the spring of 1960, I gave my notice at the agency, asking them how much time they would need to replace me. Three weeks later, I headed to Paris with the intention of finding an apartment in the Seventh Arrondissement, and starting a little company called Transatlantic Films. The company was to be devoted to producing documentaries on subjects such as the sound recording of famous pipe organs throughout Europe, beginning in France.

Upon leaving Erwin, Wasey, Ruthrauf and Ryan in the early summer of 1960, I thought back over the number of great people I had met in the last three years, and looked forward to new acquaintances and creative opportunities. Before departing the U.K., I received complimentary letters from Paul Usher and from the agency's managing director, Walter Graebner. Both letters provided me hoped-for praise of the best kind, as well as a sense of being a welcome, good international ambassador from the U.S. to Europe's and other business, advertising and communication start-ups.

My only regret in all those decades when John repeatedly reappeared in my life was that I fell for his ongoing narcissistic threat that he would kill himself if I didn't acknowledge and support him. I felt I could not be responsible for the death of another human being, and I recognized the ramifications of his illness, which finally prevented him from ever being gainfully employed. I truly believed he was capable of suicide. In fact, he did attempt it a few times over the years when I refused to provide him with financial support. Looking back, I'm relieved to say that I managed to grow and advance despite John's illness. Those early decades in France, even when John showed up, were simply training periods for the fabulous years Nancy and I were to enjoy later. By focusing my life on building a house, producing documentaries, and advancing my knowledge of all that was European, I gained enough savvy about the not-for-profit television industry to eventually establish One World Foundation — my proudest accomplishment in the art world.

One of the world's greatest scholars, Kenneth Clark, published a book in 1969 about the history of art. Clark's philosophy correlates with the art connection I felt during those years. It is, truly, the best and most basic definition of art that I have ever read:

"At certain epochs man has felt conscious of something about himself — body and spirit — which was outside the day-to-day struggle for existence and the night-to-night struggle with fear; and he has felt the need to develop

these qualities of thought and feeling so that they might approach as nearly as possible to an ideal of perfection — reason, justice, physical beauty, all of them in equilibrium. He has managed to satisfy this need in various ways — through myths, through dance and song, through systems of philosophy and through the order that he has imposed on the visible world. The children of his imagination are also the expressions of an ideal."

CHAPTER 10

The First European Projects

Although I had transported to Europe adequate filming and recording equipment for a short documentary film, I lacked a vital editing tool, a flatbed editing and playback machine with magnetic sound heads. Neither Mole-Richardson Camera Equipment nor my Polish-Swiss friend, Kadelski, were able to help in finding a craftsman to build this piece of film editing equipment. I found him in Munich hanging out at a small traveling circus for which he had just completed a full-sized animated walking and talking bear. Ironically, engineer Alf Kurzader, after leaving his job as a designer and test pilot for the Messerschmitt Company located on the edge of Munich, had gone into the manufacture of life-sized toys that walked and talked.

That Munich was the birthplace of the Nazi movement as well as the location of the Messerschmitt Factory were facts known to all. It's always amazed me that Munich wasn't flattened by Allied bombers, but it had survived. In speaking to an American, Kurzader was extremely careful to explain that his war-time activities were limited to scientific work in aviation rather than combat or armament.

A gentle giant who was over six feet tall, Kurzader was a tinkerer. He really harkened back to the old "tinkerers" roots in Central Europe, where a lot of the greatest tinkerers were born. They would fiddle with little bits of metal and come up with amazing tools. He became my alchemist, turning anonymous base metal into gold by creating a modern editing machine. I had an American 16 millimeter metal viewing box and he took that and incorporated it into the editing machine. It was so well-made that it still can be used to this day — some 50 years later.

During the 1960s and '70s, I did a lot of foreign film dubbing, sometimes finding work for John, who created English translations for German-speaking actors while I oversaw dubbing of French into English. We directed actors in Paris and Italy, working with them word by word as they were actually doing the speaking. Once in a while, we'd write something for the films, but not often. There were many documentaries and school/education films that needed translating, and it paid well, although the highest prices were paid for those guys who could translate the Asian and African dialects because there were so many variations of them.

Perhaps the most productive project I undertook while first in Europe was in 1965, when construction of my "Two Bandit House" began on a hilltop in Cagnes-sur-Mer, France. It was nicknamed thusly because of the incompetence and untrustworthiness of the original architect and contractor… both of whom were eventually dismissed. The house was built on three levels, encompassing approximately 4,000 square feet including the pool and the pool house. There were three bedrooms, not including the pool house (which acted as a fourth bedroom), four baths, and two garages — one above and another on a third level underneath the house. On the surface, it was a magnificent home, but due to the lack of competence of the architect and builder, as well as the costliness of completion, the interior of the house remained unfinished for a very long time.

I designed the house to fit the hilltop on a piece of property that measured 7,000 square meters, the top level sharing the edge of the neighbor's land, with a part of the northern fence row and about seven or eight feet width of sloping garden land. The main base for the house and lower garage was a peninsula about 50 or 60 meters wide, which contained three sides of a patio, with the fourth side open to a panoramic view of the sea and Cap d'Antibes. Beyond the patio was a rectangular pool with a pool house to the left. The neighboring property of about 20,000 square meters was used for farming and eventually had a handsome stone house on it. My house used cinder block, stucco and cement. The patio and pool were well-designed and the house provided two levels of living — the top level had a fabulous driveway that went all the way around the building, with a certain amount of lawn along the way.

Above the main garage was the guestroom with its own terrace that afforded a fabulous view of the Mediterranean, the Cap d' Antibes, and the Alps behind. One guest who particularly enjoyed that room was a lady named Dorothy Matzner, an attractive woman that I met in a motel swimming pool in the Florida Keys. Dorothy was smart and stylish and enjoyed having a male escort while in Florida. We became friends and I later learned that she and her husband, Harold, had been personally involved in one of the longest and most notorious murder trials in the history of New Jersey. Dorothy wrote a book about it entitled *Victims of Justice*. In addition to being an author, Dorothy was a devoted dog person. She owned two of the most magnificent standard poodles I've ever seen. In fact, she showed them at Westminster Dog Show and associated with other dog people like the wife of my dad's friend, Henry Kaiser (Kaiser-Permanente), who also owned standard poodles.

When she came to visit me in France, Dorothy came alone, sans dogs and husband, and had a great time seeing all the sights. She was quite impressed with the house, especially the guestroom, where she spent a great deal of time on the balcony enjoying the view. One funny moment occurred as we were driving up the beautiful top ridge of my road on the way to the house. Dorothy and I were having a conversation about "controlled response," and she said, "Oh yes, that's like Pavolova's dogs!" Excuse me?

The main thing about the house that pleased me was the site planning, which I facilitated. It turned out well. I was proud of having designed the house, but unfortunately, the first workmanship on it was so bad that it was nearly necessary to tear it down and start over. As it was, there was a pile of rubble in the kitchen for several years. I had moved into the ruins of the worksite within a year after construction began, because the roof was up and the shell of the house was complete.

At one point, my friends from Germany, Hermann and Emma Bermpohl, showed up at the house and worked with me diligently for 10 or 11 days, laboring to build exterior walls because it was nearly impossible to get workers to come to work for this strange foreigner. Nobody wants to take over someone else's mistakes. Once you stop work and pay off your workers at any time, then you have difficulty getting them back… that is a universal rule that has nothing to do with locale.

Later on, I was advised by a lawyer that in order to hire a new contractor, I needed an official record called a "réferé" of all the bad parts of my house construction. This réferé was to be created by an official inspector and served as a good guide for the future work. I was also proud that our English word, "referee," was thus borrowed from the French by sports officials and those concerned with justice everywhere. Unfortunately it took over a year to find and engage a new team of masons.

So, during that time I did some of my own masonry and some planting around the property with the help of my gardener, Le Clerc. Now there's another story!

Guy LeClerc presented himself as having worked in the greenhouses of the City of Nice — taking the horticultural courses there. He even gave the name of one of the teachers there as a reference. Most impressive, he looked exactly like a French Legionnaire in his white, safari-type clothing. He turned out to be far less experienced than he was supposed to be. I would take long trips to the U.S. and Guy was supposed to be taking care of the garden areas in my absence, but he did not do a good job of it. On top of that, he was suspected of being a member of a secret French band of refugees from North Africa — a bunch of guerilla fighters in the Algerian wars that had crossed the Mediterranean and become professional criminals — robbing banks and armored cars and homes, etc. This group of hard-bitten former French colonials were united with all non-criminal former colonials in being called Les Pieds Noirs (black feet) meaning that their feet were so deep in the sands of Africa they carried their private opposition to French authority wherever they were.

During one of my absences, LeClerc got a second job as a night watchman at a newly completed house on my road. He kept the job for only about a week and soon thereafter, the house was robbed of a very fine collection of firearms, this despite the fact that the house was guarded by German Shepherd dogs. One of the dogs was killed during the robbery. It appeared that LeClerc had taken the job just long enough to earn the trust of one of the guard dogs so that a robbery could be carried out.

I fired LeClerc and he was angry at being let go. Knowing what he was capable of, and having heard enough rumors about his association with the secret French band of guerilla fighters, I consulted with a lawyer about what I should do to protect myself from LeClerc. The lawyer advised me to tell LeClerc that his wages owed would be made available to him at the offices of the lawyer and that he could collect them there. He never collected his wages. He obviously thought it was a trap. It was also suggested that I take advantage of an old French law — placing a criminal charge against LeClerc by going to a Notaire (Notary Public) and officially making a statement that if my property was attacked in any way — thievery, fire, or other destruction — LeClerc would be the first person investigated. This was a completely secret procedure. I never saw him again.

Despite the challenges with the gardener, the vegetable garden, especially the green beans and asparagus, produced some wonderful meals using homegrown vegetables. I also had apricot trees and clementine trees planted, but another gardening challenge put an end to planting anything else. It was those damned nematodes that destroyed nearly everything in the garden. Much later, when Dana Ivey came to visit Nancy and me, and I complained bitterly about the destruction wrought by the damn nematodes, she was intrigued. She had never heard of nematodes (which are one of the most numerous parasitic life forms... microscopic worms... known to live on earth), and for ever after, she kidded me mercilessly about our "nematode problem," which in truth, did little to detract from the beauty of my property.

I certainly enjoyed entertaining guests over the years, but the main reason I decided to finish the home right away was that I became tired of paying rent to my landlady, Madame Vassie Lemberger. When first arriving in France, I had lived for five years in her house, "Cassa Lami" on the Moyenne Corniche, which was one of the three roads running parallel to each other along the southern coast of France, delineating the French Riviera. It's difficult to describe how fabulously rich it was... you could almost smell the money just by driving past the homes there. Madame Lemberger lived in an upscale apartment in Monaco. The country of Monaco contains just one city — Monte Carlo. Living so near Monte Carlo was marvelous. I had the privilege of hearing great singing stars in the opera house, which was located on the western side of the casino. The opera house had its own special entrance for residents of the Royal Palace. The weather in Monte Carlo was spectacular during the summer. There was a superb restaurant that was partially outdoors right next to the palace with a view up a mountain range to the northwest, which also afforded a bit of a view of Madame Lemberger's house where I lived.

Madame Lemberger was an English woman who had grown up in

Ireland and in the U.K. in very easy circumstances, learned all the right things that a young lady is supposed to learn, and ended up living in the northern French Riviera — just across the English Channel — where she met her husband. It was in a resort area where the English came to gamble, near the French towns of Deauville and Trouville, an easy trip from England. After her husband died, she had built the Casa by herself.

Monte Carlo was exciting all year round, but especially during the summer months when celebrities from all over the world gathered there. I met Prince Rainier himself one day and found him to be a very pleasant man. The prince's father had a friendship with an Olympic swimmer, Brenda Helser de Morelos, with whom I nearly had an affair. Brenda was married to a French count. Through her, I also met Grace Kelly's brother, Jack, who was quite an athlete — a great oarsman, like his father, and a damn nice guy. I never did meet Princess Grace face to face, but did have the privilege of attending her birthday party at the Monaco Opera House. Princess Grace had invited Gene Kelly and his dance partner, Juliet Prowse, to perform a short history of ballroom dancing in honor of her birthday. I was in the audience, sitting far above and behind Princess Grace in the "pie in the sky" seats, but it was magnificent to watch those two great stars dance together.

There was another, somewhat less famous show, but nearly equal in entertainment that I saw at the Monte Carlo Opera House. It was Danny Kaye conducting the orchestra and he had a very famous routine in which he named all of the Russian composers in a hilarious singsong voice. I remember that when Danny Kaye performed, my cousin Ellen was visiting. She was just beautiful — a terrific dancer — and she was wearing a kind of springtime, rose-petal dress. Her simplicity was quite a contrast to the extravagant evening gowns worn by Monaco's present and former ladies of the evening. She was even favored by the spotlight a couple of times during intermission. The dress was pale pink — hardly any color to it at all — and she really knew how to wear it. I was always proud to contribute to the evening's drama and scenery by escorting my beautiful cousin to it.

It was generally fun to be in Monte Carlo, a comfortable haven for rich people. It was fascinating just to walk around in the casino and imagine the money being won and lost. Gambling was never one of my vices, fortunately, but it was great fun just to be there.

One night I went to dinner at the Hotel de Paris with Madame Lemberger and there, at his own special table, was Winston Churchill. He visited there often during a period of time not long before he died. It was well after he had retired. He was accompanied by an attractive female nurse at whom he snapped often, and he had a military escort — an officer he obviously admired, probably because of all the medals on his chest, having been in famous battles in World War II.

The thing that distinguished Mr. Churchill from the others in the dining room was the great fuss he made when his companions attempted to make him leave and go up to bed. He was not about to do that. He loudly protested that he wanted to smoke the rest of his cigar and have more coffee, more brandy, more this, more that — he made quite a scene. It was obvious to me that he was aware of the attention he was attracting. This was the last part of his last act, and he wasn't going to have many more times to perform it. He certainly managed to get everyone's attention that night, and it seems to me that he died soon thereafter back in England. Mr. Churchill did love the Mediterranean, and I can't blame him. He enjoyed the pure beauty of being in Monte Carlo and had the opportunity to go out on yachts like that of Mr. Ari Onassis, the Greek magnate who married Jackie Kennedy. Onassis was said to have one of the largest yachts in the world at the time, and Churchill enjoyed that type of opulence.

Monte Carlo was actually more accessible and affordable back in the 1960's and 70's than most people realized. For about 100 Francs ($25) I could rent a small pavilion for the whole day very near the royal family's pavilion. In addition to the beach there was a large fresh water swimming pool to enjoy. It all belonged to the Societe des Bains de Mer in Monaco. It owned the casino and all that went on in and around it, the restaurant, the opera house, the Hotel de Paris, the beach hotel, everything.

The most exclusive and attractive of the outdoor arrangements in Monte Carlo were the ones where Princess Grace had her pavilion. Her summertime habits were such that she had the pavilion nearest the doorways to this arrangement of buildings. You could pass right next to them, but never see them, as she had her children protected there.

There was a child — a little girl — who played a large role in my life in the late 1960s, when I spent about three years creating a 13-minute documentary called Christmas Journey that centered on the world-famous Wies Church in Bavaria. The reason we took so long was that we could only film in the wintertime on the property of the church, due to the great number of summer visitors and the fact that we had a snow scene to film. *Christmas Journey* was about a little German girl, Bettina, who traveled by sleigh to the church with her aunt to celebrate the little girl's birthday and the birth of Christ. I allowed John to join me on the project, as he needed the work.

The Wies Church has been a pilgrimage site since June 14, 1738, when a wooden statue called the "Scourged Savior in the Wies" was seen to have tears falling from its eyes. The miracle drew pilgrimages from throughout the world to the little village of Wies and the small wooden church there. It was soon recognized that a larger structure was needed to accommodate the pilgrims and the current Wies Church was created by architects and brothers Dominikus and Johann Baptist Zimmerman of Wessobrunn, Germany. The rococo style of the interior is so beautiful and graceful that the church has been named a cultural site on the World Heritage List.

In order to properly film the interior of the Wies Church, we needed special lighting equipment, and I looked in the Munich phone book and found a professional British lighting company, Mole-Richardson, Inc. that I recognized. Mole-Richardson, Inc. had branches in New York, Hollywood and Chicago, and, as Munich was a film capital in Europe at the time, had offices there as well. I went to the company in Munich and spoke to a tall lady wearing an I.D. card that read "Schneeberger"... that name seemed familiar to me, and it began to work on me as I explained our project to Frau Schneeberger. "You're going to be filming in Die Wies and I can offer you the best advice on lighting free of charge. My husband, Hans Schneeberger, will help you." The tumbling blocks of memory started to fall... Frau Schneeberger was about to introduce me to one of the greatest cinematographers in the world! Hans Schneeberger had worked with most of Hollywood's brightest stars as well as European stars, such as Marlene Dietrich. He had done the lighting for *The Blue Angel*, one of Dietrich's most famous films, and for many other popular films.

Hans Schneeberger, at his wife's request, came out from a back room and got on his overcoat so that he could ride to the Wies Church and advise me on the lighting needed to film the interior. He was about five feet tall and his wife, at a height of nearly six feet, towered over him. He was friendly and helpful as he pointed out what lighting was needed, but unfortunately, I didn't have the kind of money to pay for the lighting he advised. I did get some good ideas, though, and I was simply thrilled to be in his company.

He was an icon in the movie industry.

During World War II, Schneeberger, a Jew, had worked closely with German filmmaker Leni Riefenstahl, who was infamous for making *Triumph des Willens*, a propaganda film for Hitler's Third Reich. Rumor had it that Leni had been Schneeberger's lover and protector during the war, but had run out of patience with him and thrown him out in 1945, when the war was over. His big wife, Gertrude, had obviously come to his rescue. My chance meeting with the famous cinematographer seemed to be a lucky augury for our film. It was one of those moments of grace that happen in the midst of ungraceful times.

During the years spent filming *Christmas Journey*, I had the privilege of meeting and getting to know the prelate, Father Alfons Satszger, who served there from 1946 until 1978. Father Satszger had served as a high ranking German Army Chaplain at Stalingrad during World War II. He was quite learned, a great speaker and bastion of Christianity who was well-known and highly respected in Germany before the war broke out. When he refused to join the Nazi party, citing his Christian beliefs as the reason, Satszger and Hitler clashed mightily. His faith and reputation ultimately saved his life, getting him out of Stalingrad before its surrender. If the Russians had captured Satszger, it is certain they would have falsely made him an example of extreme Nazi complicity, claiming him as a vicious torturer and muderer of all enemies of the German Reich. Such was claimed of other German military priests who were captured during World War II. In effect, Satszger won his private war with Nazidom and spent the rest of his life at one of the most beautiful churches in Europe.

In the meantime, the little girl, Bettina, was a good pesrformer. She was easy to train as an actress because she reacted very readily to bribery and loved sweets. Along with her "Tante," the little girl experienced a gorgeous birthday celebration in the film, accompanied by some splendid musical selections such as La Creation by Joseph Haydn and Bach's B Minor Mass.

It had originally been Lord Kenneth Clark's enthusiasm about the Wies Church as a great example of the rococo in architecture that inspired me to produce a documentary about it. Once completed, I invited Lord Clark to view the documentary and he graciously accepted my invitation to a screening of it quite near his London home at the "Albany," which has been the epicenter of English culture for over a century. Lord Kenneth Clark and his wife greatly enjoyed the film and were highly complimentary about it.

They later wrote a note to me saying that they found the film to be charming.

In conjunction with a later documentary that I filmed about wine, I was taken through the wine cellar of the Rothschild castle by the chap in charge, the Maitre de Chais, chief of storage of wine barrels. He explained in great detail about the workings of the wine according to temperature changes and other factors. At one point, I asked him who I should speak to about acquiring a small bottle or two of Chateau Lafite Rothschild wine. "You, sir, must go to the bank in Paris," he explained, with a somewhat haughty air.

I duly made an appointment to purchase the wine, dealing with the sales department of the bank in Paris. I was met at the bank with grim, unsmiling faces — archetypical banking types — and I was escorted to the inner sanctum, located on an entire floor of one of the upper levels. The atmosphere on this floor was carefully dignified... all dark, gleaming wood and hushed voices. As the buyer, I was made to realize how very privileged I was to be in this exclusive place, and how important, secret and masterful this business of buying Lafitte Rothschild wine truly was. Finally, I was admitted into the office of a surprisingly delightful, cooperative, cheerful lady who happily showed me catalogues and price lists. As I was explaining apologetically to her that I was only a meager film maker with few funds to dispense for luxury and planning to make only a minimal order, the door opened behind me and a youngish man shot out of an inner office, paused in front of the desk, turned to the lady and, in a cheerful sing-song shout delivered "Vendez! Vendez! Vendez!" ("Sell! Sell! Sell!") I enjoyed the irony tremendously.

Another banking irony occurred when I asked Jean Paul Getty if he had ever met the banker W. Scott McLucas, my grandfather. Both men were pioneers in the oil business almost simultaneously and had much in common, I thought. Mr. Getty responded that he had not met my grandfather personally, but he sure had heard of him! That conversation between Mr. Getty and me occurred at Sutton Place, Getty's legendary home outside of London. Built in the 16th century, it was a gorgeous Tudor manor on 700 acres. There giant Alsatian dogs ran around, and there were two caged lions, Nero and Teresa, in addition to incredible gardens and rare works of art. To me, however, the most memorable feature was the tall statue of Eros, the Greek God of Love and Lust, on a central hilltop above the castle.

Speaking of love and lust, one of Jean Paul Getty's many mistresses,

Marie Tessier, had extended me the invitation to a luncheon at Sutton Place with the famous man. Marie was one of the most flamboyant women I've ever known. She was a fiercely loyal member of Russian royalty — a real Romanov. During World War II, she had married a man who bought or built her a house in Versailles. In 1945, Marie Tessier had been known as one of the most beautiful women in the world. She was the "first face" of the Parisian press, and was one of a coterie of lovely ladies known to Jean Paul Getty. In fact, Mr. Getty had bought her a house in the South of France, one of several homes he had for his various female friends. This house was outside of Grasse and had formerly been restored by Fragonard.

Marie knew that I wanted to do a documentary on the Getty Museum in Los Angeles, and this luncheon was an opportunity to speak to Mr. Getty about getting the rights to interview him for such a documentary. In fact, I remember Marie's exact words: "Scott, I think Paul needs a film about his new museum." Mr. Getty was receptive to the idea, and informed me that a New Jersey woman named Elizabeth Bryant had been given the rights to a personal interview with him in regard to his museum. He suggested that I contact her. He talked of her "qualifications" for these rights by describing her first appearance at Sutton Place. Elizabeth Bryant had written to Mr. Getty, introducing herself as a publisher and complimenting him extravagantly on his patriotism by listing the wonderful things he had done for his country. Flattered, Getty invited her to visit him at Sutton Place. His words, as I remember, were: "Elizabeth walked into this house dressed from head to toe in red, white and blue! She was a vision of America standing right here in the castle of Anne Boleyn. It was great!" As to my contacting her in New Jersey, where she "published" grocery coupon booklets and related items, Mr. Getty advised that she would probably be grateful for a partnership as she had no funds available for a documentary and knew very little about art.

My luncheon at Sutton Place was brief, ending quite abruptly when Getty announced he was going upstairs to take a nap, rose from the table and led an entourage of five fawning women up the stairs, including my friend, Marie Tessier, and another shapely guest who was simply known in the tabloids as "The Fucking Duchess."

Getty was in his early eighties when we met and he was still a magnificent man. In my opinion, he was more than the equivalent of any man who ever drilled for oil.

Jean Paul Getty was extremely proud of his father, George Franklin Getty, who taught Paul everything he knew about the oil business. His father had done a lot of surveying in the oil fields — locating oil underground was his specialty — and his passion was trains — train engines and train whistles. Many of the oil deposits that Getty acquired at that time were in California, not far from railroad tracks. They were near Bakersfield one day when Getty, Sr. said to his son, "I think there's a possibility of the beginning of a good drilling spot nearby." The fact was that he'd heard trains passing over a certain spot and the trains had a tendency to strain when they reached this point in the early evening in a northbound direction. They drilled two or three test wells in that area and came up with a good and long-producing well right next to where the train engineer had geared down in order to get over the hillock. It came a gusher! The railroad loved the idea, of course.

When I contacted Elizabeth Bryant, it was just as Mr. Getty had predicted. She was thrilled to be partnering with me in the production of a documentary on the Getty Museum in Los Angeles. The Getty Museum in Brentwood is one of the most visited museums in the U.S., and in 1974, J. Paul Getty opened his second museum, with a replication of the famed Villa of the Papyri at Herculaneum (southern Italy, near Pompeii) on his property in Pacific Palisades, California. It was in the early 1970s when we visited him at Sutton Place, and although I had gathered all the film footage needed for a documentary on the Getty Museum in Los Angeles, we were still attempting to get a filmed interview with the man himself when he died at age 83 on June 6, 1976.

Despite the fact that I had an exclusive contract signed by J. Paul Getty, giving me complete access to film the documentary, it was not long after Getty died that *The Sunday Show*, one of the big television network productions, did a huge panoramic show of the Getty museum. It was a major breach of contract on the part of the museum curator to allow the television broadcast, and we sued the museum and the estate of J. Paul Getty immediately. Unfortunately, the lawsuit went all the way to the courtroom and even though I won, the lawyers were the only ones who profited. In fact, I had to sue twice even to get some of my money back for the production of the documentary. It had been in the space of time between finishing the filming of the museum and beginning the interview with Mr. Getty that the trouble lay. We had three different prominent announcers lined up, each one of whom would have been a marvelous interviewer, but they all canceled out at crucial moments. This wasted a great deal of time that, unfortunately, we did not have, as the old man was ailing throughout the entire filming process. And, speaking of filming process, that was complicated by the fact that the curator of the museum suspected us of being "Sutton Place Spies," there to film and report back to the big man any irregularities or incompetencies of the new museum's staff. All in all, the documentary on the J. Paul Getty Museum proved to be an expensive but quite interesting exercise in futility.

One thing I can say, without reservation, is that Elizabeth Bryant appeared in court looking like a million dollars, wearing some beautiful new clothing (not red, white and blue) that we had purchased for her. She looked great, but the lawsuit was a bust. We created absolutely no tremors whatsoever in the legal community with either of the lawsuits against the Getty Museum.

Meanwhile, back in France, my house was a work in progress, being completed little by little as time and finances would allow. The "Revolution of 1968" had slowed down the progress of house building, due to bank closings and general unrest in France. The banks being closed was not a major inconvenience for me, as I had plenty of French francs, due to my relationship with Madame Lemberger and her connections across the border in Italy, but gas stations were often closed and workers were otherwise occupied. France was in stasis during May of 1968 and into June.

There was a day late in May when I drove to Nice for an appointment with my attorney, having no idea what I would encounter when I arrived. I had parked my car and set out for his office when I heard a sound I'd never heard before. Tramp, tramp, tramp... the sound of marching got louder and louder until, as I stood at a crossroad with Nice's main avenue, I could see marching toward me, to my right, 40 or 50 policemen wearing raincoats loaded with lead. They were wearing the same coats the Paris police wore for crowd control and they also wore helmets. They carried their guns at port arms. Soon, they were trotting in formation directly past me, and I saw a second barrier of policemen up ahead to my left on the avenue, and beyond them, the approaching rabble of students and workers. There were thousands of them. Although I saw no visible pushing or shoving on the part of the demonstrators, their yelling and screaming was deafening and they angrily waved the black and red flags of anarchy and revolution. No French flags were visible as they regrouped in the Place Massena (central square of Nice).

Within a day or two of witnessing this encounter between the police and the demonstrators, I heard that General DeGaulle had made a desperate flight to a French base in Germany to marshal his troops and had been informed by his top generals that they would do everything they could to maintain and preserve the power of his government, except fire upon students or workers (which, ironically, accounted for the majority of the demonstrators). It didn't take him long to return to Paris by helicopter to give a speech about the "menace of revolutionary forces from the exterior of France" and plead for the support of French citizens everywhere. Amazingly, that age-old ploy worked, and within hours, the 1968 revolution was finished.

I drove down to the Place Massena on the day of DeGaulle's declaration. The citizens of Nice were celebrating the end of the revolution just as vigorously as it was being celebrated in Paris, and I felt a part of the excitement as people drove around the Place in open cars, waving the French flag, tears streaming down their faces as they sang "La Marseillaise" (the French National Anthem).

An amusing moment that occurred during the first days of the revolution was when my Italian iron monger (ferronnier) expressed his deep concern that the border between Italy and France would be closed. Wringing his hands and extremely agitated, the little fence builder, whose iron shop was in Saint Laurent du Var, about eight minutes from my house, was terrified by the prospect of being unable to get back into Italy. No, I assured him, closing the borders was not an option. That would be an act of war and I was certain it would not happen. He was quite relieved to be assured by a "smart, rich American," and I acted as if I was absolutely certain about something that I was not really sure about.

It was during the bank closures and the gas shortages of that brief revolution that I discovered the Vaucluse, a department in the south of France named after the famous spring, the Fontaine de Vaucluse. For centuries, poets have been inspired by the power of the natural springs, and I understood why one day when the resulting waters flooded a nearby town, coursing down the streets and bubbling out of the earth in pumpkin-sized bubbles. It was an unforgettable sight. Several villages surrounded the Vaucluse and in those villages were some interesting salvage operations that the French called "Récupérations." In the salvage yards there were some incredible finds — various relics from various wars, including much wreckage from World War II. Dedicated treasure hunters could come upon true treasures like the wonderful oaken beams that I found for the patio area.

There were nearly a dozen of these beams — about 50 years old, a foot in diameter and 12 to 15 feet in length — some of them carved in very interesting designs. I had them transported by truck and hired a couple of craftsmen, led by a talented worker and artist named Michel Natale, to install them over the patio area. I was so impressed by Michel's workmanship that I ended up hiring him as the caretaker for my home. Later, his son, Fred, came on my staff as well.

At one point, there were four of us working on those magnificent beams, as they were very heavy and difficult to handle. I also found a great many slabs of stone flooring for the patio and terraces. The slabs were about three inches thick and about 20 by 24 inches on a side. I had them laid by a professional on two different levels — the covered walkway around the patio, as well as the main patio level a few inches below the walkway.

My pool was beautiful and was one of the few things that went together well for me. The engineer who designed my pool had just recently designed a pool for Gregory Peck, who had a villa just outside of Monte Carlo in Cap Ferrat. I was well pleased with the design of my pool.

One of my great finds in the Vaucluse was a large stone bowl, about four feet in diameter and nearly two feet in depth. It was placed in the center of the patio and I brought in a plumber, Mr. Toutain, to turn it into a fountain. Mr. Toutain was an amusing local character who was, he admitted, a plumber by circumstance rather than training. His favorite story was that he was a soldier in the Ligne Maginot, a line of concrete fortifications, tank obstacles, artillery casements, machine gun posts and other defenses which France constructed along its borders with Germany before World War II. The Maginot Line was supposed to keep the enemy out but it failed miserably because it ended in Belgium and the forces simply invaded around the end of it. As one of the soldiers building the Maginot Line, Mr. Toutain had been asked which trade was his specialty — carpentry, electricity, plumbing, etc. — and he had chosen plumbing.

Despite his lack of real training in the specialty, Toutain made it clear that he considered himself superior, particularly in the company of "lamentably ignorant foreigners" like me. His arrogance, which was consistently amusing, came out in his favorite conversation starter, "Vous allez le comprendre comme moi," (Let me explain because then you will understand as I do). Somehow, Toutain managed to perform various complicated plumbing jobs around the house, including a water softener in the basement that had a very strange appearance, and functioned for only a few weeks. It was a complete "washout," pardon the pun.

He also installed a very tall water storage tank which was modified oddly. It involved a floating cork to test the water level and, at one point, Toutain had to tilt the tank about one-half inch by putting cement under one side of it (the tilt facilitated draining during cleaning). The tilted water tank was just one of many idiosyncratic features that lent color and character to the house… or so I later explained to my wife, Nancy.

Mr. Toutain enjoyed life and he particularly enjoyed installing an automatic sprinkling system and the fountain system in the patio, because he got to play hide and seek with two wily young lion cubs named Scarlett and Lily. Yes, I had been inspired and intrigued by Getty's lions, and this led to me bringing several pairs of lion cubs back to the house over a two-year period in the 1970s.

Young lions were often seen being trotted around in the central square of Nice, where tourists were allowed to touch them and hold them. Brindille,

Grisby and Scott

a lady who had formerly been a lion tamer at the Marseilles Zoo and now had her own smallish zoo about 50 to 60 kilometers to the west in the Var department, was the keeper of the baby lions, and presented Scarlett and Lily to me.

One of my lions came with me from Switzerland, and when I stopped at a famous restaurant and chateau, the Auberge du Père Bise, nestled in the mountains on the eastern side of Lake Annecy in Savoy, the restaurant staff spotted the lion cub in its cage in the car. They asked me all kinds of questions, but I knew as little about lions as they did at the time. A few summers later, Nancy and I visited the Chateau on Lake Annecy and the restaurant staff recognized me and asked immediately if we had a lion with us. Many years passed, and yet, when Nancy and her sister-in-law, Mary Doyle, and I stopped at that same beautiful place to enjoy dinner and spend the night, they still remembered the lions and again inquired whether we had a lion cub with us.

Scarlett and Lily were rambunctious cubs and delighted Mr. Toutain to the point where I had to put them back in their cage in the pool house in

Scott and Mao

order to get him to finish the job. I had added bars and a metal door to the pool house when I began bringing them there, a pair at a time. The lions were a passion for me. I started out with small lion cubs gradually bringing home larger lion cubs.

I named the first large cub Grisby, which was a French underground expression for swag (what criminals steal). He was beautiful but handicapped, crippled with a bad leg. The neighbors saw us out walking one day and realized he was not dangerous as he limped along. They enjoyed him without being afraid. Then one day, when I was away, Grisby got out and attracted attention by falling off of a ledge. Michele was in charge at the time and was mortified that he was not watching the lion closely enough. Luckily, he got him to a veterinarian quickly and all was well, but the newspapers picked up the news that a lion was out and there was an article written about Grisby. Fortunately, no gendarmes visited as a result of the article.

The final lion I kept for any length of time was a robust, healthy male named Mao after the Chinese leader. He was quite prepossessing, with great authority. Mao was getting large when I took him back to Brindille and he became the king of lions at the Marseilles Zoo. A few years later, I went to visit him. I had been warned that I should be prepared for a mighty rush of affection because lions are family-oriented animals and I was his first family.

Mao was enclosed in a wooden pen with a strong wooden gate and as I approached the hill, it was obvious he was listening. He stopped and cocked his head and you could almost watch the memory clicks working on him. He was hearing a voice he hadn't heard in years — the voice of his first father. He gathered himself together at the end of this large, open field, and as I arrived at the gate, he hurled himself across that space with such a force that I was afraid he would crash through the gate. He was a huge lion and he hit that gate with great strength. As I stroked him and talked to him, he mewed and hummed and sang to me — purring like a huge cat in remembrance. One thing I know for sure, elephants don't have anything on lions. He never forgot me.

In fact, lions are so familial and affectionate about their keepers/parents that they can actually die of loneliness if they feel abandoned by family. I discovered this, to my great sorrow, when I was asked to provide temporary foster-care to a lion cub who bonded with me in just one night. When

I took him to the place where he was supposed to be kept until his new owners came for him, I reluctantly left him alone as instructed. I tried to say a kind goodbye, but I could tell he was suffering terribly as I left. The lion died that night. I never took in another lion cub.

CHAPTER 11

Life & Death

During the more than 20 years that she was married to Bill Colwes, my mother was a devoted wife, supporting his many business ventures and helping him raise his son and daughter. It was around 1970 that she divorced Bill, after his kids, Billy and Sissy (Carol) Colwes, had graduated from college and gone off to live on their own. Mother and Bill had moved to Los Angeles, where she had loaned him the money for one more unsuccessful car dealership, and when he approached her for yet another loan, she decided that enough was enough. She even told me, at the time, that she wanted to have something left to leave to me and if she remained with Bill, she would run out of money.

By the time mother decided to divorce Bill, Carol Colwes had married and divorced a professional Canadian football player. Carol knew the ropes. Because she and my mother had remained close, she actually helped mother get a quickie divorce from Bill by filing as a resident of St. Thomas in the Virgin Islands. Mother remained in the Virgin Islands for nearly a decade.

In her later years, despite struggling with alcohol addiction, mother retained her beauty, intelligence and general enjoyment of life. She and I remained very close and I visited her annually during the Christmas season in St. Thomas. This was my tropical vacation time and, in addition to spending time with mother, I would occasionally indulge in carefree love affairs.

For some years while she was living in St. Thomas, she had a young gay boyfriend named Paul, who made a living as a teacher. Despite the fact that he was gay and less than 10 years older than her own son, Mother and Paul seemed to have a good relationship. Paul loved to give Christmas parties and she would sometimes loan him some of her good silver for those gatherings. A lot of drinking went on at the affairs, and she talked of the difficulty of rounding up all the silver following the holidays. I ended up inheriting a full set of silver, which Nancy and I use to this day, and I'm grateful to Mother for rescuing it each Christmas after Paul borrowed it.

Mother had many fine possessions, including her silver and jewelry, and that may have been the catalyst for one of the most traumatic things that ever happened to her. Her home in St. Thomas was burglarized one night, and Mother was robbed at gunpoint and locked in a basement room. She managed to escape by breaking a window and crawling out, but she would never discuss what happened during the robbery with the exception of the fact that she lost some cash and jewelry. My mother's home was always sacrosanct to her, and this event affected her deeply.

Paul eventually moved to San Juan, Puerto Rico and went into the real estate business. He wanted Mother to come live with him there and help manage a property, but what he really had in mind, and she knew it, was the use of her assets. She was a great deal older than he was and her health was not good. She severed the relationship with him when he asked her to join him because she rightly did not trust the situation.

While in St. Thomas, Mother made many good friends, as she did throughout her life. One of her friends was the mother of a young man who ran the major jewelry store in St. Thomas, which is saying a lot because the town catered to wealthy passengers from cruise ships that docked there, and featured a row of silver and jewelry shops on its main street. At any rate, this young man who owned the most important jewelry store in town lived with his mother and was known to be gay. He took full advantage of the decadence of the island when he threw his annual New Years Eve party. The entertainment at this party — dancers, singers and performers of all sorts — were also models for his jewelry, and about 95% of them wore nothing else except the jewelry. Mother always joked that each year, his mother (who was as middle-western as anyone I ever knew in Kansas City,

Missouri) would confide in her that she was so proud of her son's success, as evidenced by this elaborate holiday party, and that her only wish was that he would marry well. She would sit there at that decadent party filled with bejeweled nudes and be completely oblivious to the fact that her son had no interest in anyone of the opposite sex.

I, on the other hand, had a great deal of interest in women and was generally involved in an affair throughout my tropical flings.

Mother had exploratory surgery in Miami in 1978 and I came down to spend a couple of days with her. My cousin, Ellen, came down, too. Mother's doctors determined at that time that she had pancreatic cancer. I went over to St. Thomas and supervised the loading of her furniture and clothes to be shipped to Los Angeles, and moved her into an apartment building in Santa Monica that was filled with wealthy Iranians. She was bedridden most of the time after I got her to California, although she'd be able to go out to a nice restaurant once in a while.

Hammie, my beloved mother, died in the spring of 1981. There was much sorrow in my family when she passed away. She had been so close to her sister, Dorothea and her niece, Dee. They were nearly inconsolable. As for me, I was grieved but felt relief at the same time. I knew my mother was ready to go. She had always been an advocate of usefulness and had long felt it was definitely behind her. She hated waste, and passed that emotion down to me, along with the determination to do no harm. Mother had been ill for some time, and the dying process involved a lot of waste, in her opinion. Mother was in charge right up to the end. When she died, I was there at the St. Johns Hospital with a small group of others who loved her. There was an intimate church service for her in Kansas City and, true to her plan, she did manage to leave a small inheritance for me.

I took the money she left me and founded the Hamilton Theatre Company which, within a few years, became the One World Arts Foundation with offices in New York City., the heart of the theater in America. It had always been the mecca for new converts to the professional theater. It was a great launching pad location for One World Arts Foundation and, I hoped, for my career. It was also destined to be the launch pad for my future as the husband of a special woman named Nancy. How we happened to meet still amazes me, as we were introduced by Betsy Crawford, a woman who somehow had a way of getting things done despite having an abrasive personality that irritated me no end.

Betsy, now deceased, was the wife of Donald Crawford, who had been in the Yale Dramat with John and me. Donald, also deceased now, had gone on to become a successful theatrical stage designer in New York City.

During the years when I lived in France and traveled back and forth to the U.S., I engaged Betsy to oversee the little walk-up apartment I kept in New York (rent-frozen at $66 a month). Betsy was a natural-born manager and, in 1983, she thoroughly enjoyed managing my introduction to Nancy McQuiggan, sister of actor, producer and director Jack McQuiggan. I was instantly attracted to Nancy for several reasons, the least personal of them being an interest in collaborating with her brother. In the meantime, Betsy Crawford (our chubby, conniving cupid) instantly sensed the chemistry between Nancy and me and found it wickedly delicious. Betsy was to become a truly subterranean messenger/matchmaker in our relationship.

Nancy is charming. Born in Detroit, Michigan, the daughter of a doctor, Nancy learned to adjust to new places and new faces during the five years of World War II that her father served as a physician in the military, being transferred from base to base. The family had eventually settled in Xenia, Ohio, with her parents later retiring in Ponte Vedra Beach, Florida. Nancy was well educated, well-spoken and well-traveled when we met, and, in addition to being quite attractive, she had a wonderful sense of humor. She had much the same private-boarding-school education that I had experienced, and we found that we had much in common. Nancy had lived in Paris, as had I, and loved it. She had worked with the Peace Corps in Washington, D.C. and in Senegal, West Africa, and had many of my basic values. She even had a background in theatre and television. While in Paris, she'd worked as a stage manager for an English-speaking theatre company and as an assistant to script and comedy writers at CBS Television in New York. Through her brother, Jack, and through her own contacts, Nancy was familiar with many of the top actors in the American theatre, including Arthur Lithgow and his son, John, as well as the English actress Rosemary Harris, and actress Nancy Marshand, who more recently played Tony Soprano's mother in the HBO Series.

Nancy and I shared many of the same views on human rights, even though we ran in different circles back then. In 1963, she had joined in the "I Have a Dream" march on the American Embassy in Paris, marching shoulder to shoulder with her friend, "Buttercup," a black woman who lived a bohemian life, cooking gumbo on a hotplate at the Hotel Louisianne

Nancy and Scott on cruise

on the Rue de Seine and entertaining an eclectic group of activists, artists and musicians. Buttercup had a child by jazz piano player Bud Powell, and knew everyone in Paris.

When we met in 1983, Nancy was a young divorcee working in New York City and traveling back and forth from there to her mother's home in Ponte Vedra Beach, Florida.

For the first time in my life, I was so completely infatuated with a woman that I truly did not care what John thought about it. I warned Nancy that he had been the bane of my life for three decades and had even made a death threat to the last woman with whom I'd fallen in love. Nancy was stoic and unruffled. She was as attracted to me as I was to her and felt, as I did, that nothing could stand in our way.

Acting on an irresistible impulse, I invited her to come over to Europe with me in the summer of 1983 for a ten-day vacation. Later, when John learned of it, he hated her like fire, but there was nothing he could do. She was my lady love — the woman I'd been seeking all my life. We went on a romantic, rambunctious and hilarious driving trip together through France during the hottest summer in memory. I had made the unfortunate decision to rent a black, non-air conditioned car that intensified the heat enormously, but we laughed our way from one scenic place to the next, seeking cool moments of respite and enjoying delicious French cuisine. We saw glorious vistas in the French Alps. It was there that I first rowed Nancy across the beautiful Lake Annecy in Savoy, rowing all the way out to a magical peninsula where we could see a gorgeous gothic castle close up. Later, we stayed and dined at the famous Auberge du Père Bise Restaurant. I had advised Nancy that one of that restaurant's specialties was a delicious fish (an Omble Chevalier) caught in the ice cold lake and prepared to perfection by the chef, but when we inquired about that dish, we were regretfully informed that there had been no fish caught in the lake during the heat wave. The fish had all gone to the cold bottom of the lake to avoid the heat.

Unfortunately, it wasn't long after our beautiful summer holiday that John was diagnosed with cancer and my guilty obligation to take care of him kicked in. This caused me to treat Nancy unfairly for the next two years until John died on April 26, 1986. Why I allowed John to have the power over me that his narcissism demanded is still beyond my comprehension, but even with my love, Nancy, in the wings, I felt trapped by his threats until the day he died.

In the meantime, Nancy's brother, Jack McQuiggan, became an integral player in the success of the One World Arts Foundation. Jack was a thoroughly integrated theater person who had a great, comprehensive knowledge of all that was good in the theatre. It didn't stop him from making mistakes, but nevertheless, his advice was invaluable.

Dana Ivey
Photo Courtesy Shevett Studios

Just prior to the time that Jack and Nancy came into my life, Jack's production of *Quartermaine's Terms*, a play by Simon Gray, was performed at the 91st Street Playhouse. The play garnered eight Obie Awards and was named one of the Ten Best Plays of 1983 by over a dozen major publications. Actress Dana Ivey had a role in *Quartermaine's Terms*, and we became good friends. Some of Jack's later productions, as well as readings and musical performances by visiting groups from England and Ireland, were funded in part by One World Arts Foundation.

During the winter of 1983, John Johnson and I explored the Parisian Theatre with a view toward emulating the French habit of successfully running the same play at the same theater for three or four fall/winter seasons. During those explorations we had the great good fortune of spending an entire afternoon drinking champagne with iconic French actor and director Georges Wilson. Wilson, who had served from 1963 to 1972 as the Director of the Theatre National de Chaillot in Paris (formerly known as the Theatre National Populaire), was in great form that day, and talked in detail about his past triumphs as well as his current projects. One project that interested me greatly was Wilson's unique adaptation of a play, *Memoir*, written by Canadian playwright John Murrell. The play, based on the later life of actress Sarah Bernhardt, had been a monumental flop, but Georges Wilson's French adaptation of it, which he called *Sarah et le cri de la Langouste (Sarah and the cry of the Lobster)* was acclaimed as brilliant. Wilson's scrupulous script writing and his casting of himself in all the male roles and French actress Delphine Seyrig in the role of Sarah was monumental. The cry of the lobster (a faint squeak of protest just before death) had a forceful, dramatic correlation to the last torturous days of Sarah Bernhardt, and the chemistry between the two actors on stage was sensational.

I was entranced by the play and enjoyed Wilson's company. When the show was in Edinburgh, I was there, too, and One World Arts Foundation funded a portion of it. I remember that it was so well received in Edinburgh that people clamored to come backstage. Among the backstage guests one night were Eli Wallach and Anne Jackson, two American actors who often did plays of a similar vein. They would have been damned good in *"Sarah's"* two main roles. I introduced them to Georges and Delphine and it was very interesting to watch the interaction. Eli and Anne were so intrigued by the play and the evening that they lost their actor's ability to use their imaginations. They were also burdened to understand or penetrate French dialogue.

While in Edinburgh, I got to know Delphine, who was lauded as one of France's finest actresses. I'd often go to lunch with Georges, Delphine, and her handsome, sharp boyfriend, French actor Sami Frey. Those were golden days, as I thoroughly enjoyed being associated with these creative, talented icons of the theatre and I hoped that we would be able to bring the production to American audiences, but it wasn't to be.

Having been diagnosed with colon cancer, John Johnson was quite downtrodden by it, and more determined than ever to make one big last splash with the play adaptation by Wilson, but our plans to bring Wilson and Seyrig to the United States to perform in an English-language version of *Sarah et le cri de la Langouste* were soon dashed. When we went on an information gathering trip back to New York City and met with John Murrell, we were not well received. We discovered this was not the ideal moment for mentioning further adaptations of Murrell's original play.

As an ironic aside, several years later, in the early 1990s, actress Mary Doyle starred in that play in Wilmington, Delaware, to good reviews. She was the former wife of Jack McQuiggan. Small world.

By 1985, John's illness had become advanced, and I was bent on resolving my pent-up feelings of resentment toward this dying man.

Back in the mid-1970s, when John and I decided to make a base in Southern California for the filming of the Getty Museum, we also observed that the cultural and intellectual atmosphere in Los Angeles would prove advantageous on many levels, and now, several years later, we found that to be true. The medical facilities were there to serve John's needs and both of us were still seeking solutions to personal psychological problems as well. In that respect, we began seeing Dr. Zanwil Sperber, a psychologist with offices in town and out at Santa Monica Beach. Dr. Sperber challenged us, asking pointedly for information on our latest body of work as a team involved in the field of arts and education. In the midst of our sessions with the very insightful Dr. Sperber, my One World Arts Foundation did go ahead and provide the funding for the commissioning of *Hamlet's Ghost*, to be written by a young Englishman named Jeremy Childers, a playwright known to us from previous visits to the U.K. We brought this play back to Los Angeles to be directed as a staged reading by a talented friend, Jeremiah Morris. We then invited an audience to attend the play in rehearsal, filling the theater and enjoying the production, despite John's rapidly deteriorating condition. The play's lessons about the conflicts of power, kingship, and fatherhood produced tragic family drama, but certainly did not improve on Shakespeare's version; however, it did help us in working through personal psychological issues, just as Dr. Sperber had hoped it would.

Dr. Sperber worked with us right up to the end, and was one of the regular visitors to John's hospital room during his last illness. The work we did with Dr. Sperber was some of the most valuable therapy I had ever experienced. Dr. Sperber seemed to know both of us, inside and out, and he dug deep into my reservoir of bitterness, making it almost possible for me to forgive John prior to his death for his years of torturous threats.

I remember one weekend day in particular when John and I met Dr. Sperber at his Santa Monica Beach office. He had brought his kids with him that day and let them play in the next room while he was meeting with us. Obviously, some sort of excursion had been planned because as we sat there, little notes began to appear under the door of the office. It was a touching interruption — a charming reminder of family ties that brought tears to my eyes. I was at a fragile time in my life, touched by little things, and very much in need of the counseling that Dr. Sperber provided so well.

As it was, John's cancer took him pretty quickly once I got him to Los Angeles. At the end, he spent about a month in the hospital in the spring of 1986, and died on April 26 (ironically, on the historic day of the catastrophic Chernobyl Nuclear Power Plant explosion in the Ukraine).

During John's hospitalization, only a few people came to see him regularly, including Dr. Sperber, and another psychologist friend who gave him massages. A lady from Kansas City, who had been married to a Kemper and had a house in Malibu, came to the hospital to see him toward the end. The only thing left to do was reduce his pain level as much as possible with morphine. I had his Power of Attorney, and when he was hospitalized, I called an uncle of his in North Carolina, where the majority of his relatives lived. It was then that the bleakness of his relations with his family became painfully evident. They had his phone number and no one contacted him. I later got a request for his death certificate — something to do with an insurance policy. It was cold, indeed.

Day by day, as John drifted closer to death, I began to have the sensation of being lighter and able to shed the heavy burden of responsibility I had carried for so long. Never had I felt free from his narcissistic threats of attacks and suicide. The gut-wrenching fear instilled in me by his death threat against Elizabeth was unforgettable and indelible. During his last days, I felt he was still my responsibility, but I began to see a light at the end of the tunnel.

John asked to be cremated and have his ashes scattered in the garden of the Good Samaritan Hospital where he died; I later did this, but first things first. On the day he died, I walked out of the hospital a free man, unburdened by guilt for the first time in 35 years. Within an hour of his death, I was standing on the sidewalk in the sunshine and making arrangements to purchase tickets for a trip to London to attend the grand opening of the Royal Shakespeare Company's new Swan Theatre at Stratford-Upon-Avon.

I invited three lovely ladies to accompany me — Dana Ivey, Polly Warfield (head of the Drama Division of LA Publication, Drama Log) and Polly's daughter. They were thrilled to be invited to this historic event. I was thrilled, too, not only to have such pleasant company, but because I had absolutely no designs on any of the ladies except to provide each of them with a wonderful trip and a beautiful, innocent memory. I felt I needed to cleanse my soul before I made the big move to get down on my knees and ask Nancy for her hand in marriage.

The new Swan Theatre at Stratford-Upon-Avon was a success for audiences that were interested in theatrical performance and those also interested in theatrical architecture. The new theatre boasted one of the most lighthearted, simple and elegant three-dimensional theatre designs I'd ever seen in my life. The openness of the play space combined with the dramatic and versatile points of view offered to audience members, added a full sense of theatricality — both for the listener and the viewer. It was pure theatrical magic, and my three lady companions thoroughly enjoyed the unique setting and the new version of Shakespeare's play, *The Two Noble Kinsmen*, on May 8, 1986, directed by Barry Kyle.

Although the opening of the new Stratford-Upon-Avon Swan Theatre was not a startling theatrical global event, it was a damn good one because of the design of the theatre. For me, it was historic indeed, because of the weight that had been removed from my shoulders and the great promise of a new life. My delightfully innocent holiday with three lady friends gave me a vast relief from guilt and an exciting new view of a creative, secure and untroubled future.

CHAPTER 12

New Life with Nancy

I spent the summer of 1986 reveling in the fact that I was a free man and moving back and forth among projects in California, France, New York City and London.

In September 1986, Nancy flew over to London to join me for a brief vacation. My father and stepmother were also in London and I was proud to introduce her to them. She liked them and they liked Nancy. They were obviously happy that I had found such a fine lady with whom to share my international life.

I wanted Nancy to see my house in France, and we had a great trip there. She always says that she remembers having early dreams about such a place, and as we drove up the hill and she saw the large wooden gate, she knew her dreams had come true. As for me, I was frankly proud of my design and had described it to her as shaped like the bow of a ship poised on a hill. On the starboard side toward its point were cypress trees, with the swimming pool forming a support for its tip. The trees framed the view of the sea beautifully, and on the portside of the "ship" was the pool house, which was never really completed, but was certainly not an eyesore. In fact, it had been used as a "lion's den" for wild feline visitors over the years and did not become a functional pool house until it received its first coat of

LYRIC STUDIO Hammersmith
01 741 2311 • 15 January - 7 February

MILK WOOD BLUES BY BRIAN ABBOTT

The Cast:
Michael Bertenshaw
Allan Corduner
Bob Critchley
Marian McLoughlin
Peter Robert Scott
David Shaw Parker
Reginald Tsiboe

Director:
Keith Boak

Designer and
Lighting Designer:
Paul Dart

Musical Director:
Jonathan Whitehead

Produced in Association with
One World Foundation, Inc.

paint when we sold the house in 2006. On our first sharing of the house in 1986, Nancy and I glowed as we enjoyed the realization that we would spend many happy days there in our new life together.

One of the delightful things about Nancy has always been her beautiful grasp of the French language. She not only speaks French, but does so very well. Her friendliness and ease with the language endeared her to the local French citizens and other Europeans, who loved her. It was clear to me, and to all, that she felt comfortable in her new surroundings.

Furthermore, when we've wanted to share something private, we have enjoyed the fact that we can always veer off into French or English, depending on the language of those nearby. Eavesdropping on us was never easy and we have experienced a marvelously intimate camaraderie throughout our relationship. All married couples have their own private language, but ours was uniquely wonderful. Love, longevity, learning and respect — our relationship is based on everything good! When I think of the other women I've known in the past, none of them ever came to the level of completion that Nancy and I have achieved. We still wake up each day ready and eager to begin a new conversation.

It was on a Christmas cruise to the Caribbean in 1986 that Nancy and I became engaged. I eventually gave her my mother's emerald-cut diamond ring as a symbol of that engagement. We had both suffered in our former relationships, and it was thrilling to be laughing again and thoroughly enjoying life.

In addition to cementing a new and permanent relationship with Nancy, I had also begun to explore some new creative avenues for One World Arts Foundation, and one of those was the production in London of a play entitled *Milk Wood Blues*. I had the luck of a connection with attorney Laurence Harbottle, one of Great Britain's most brilliant people in the theatrical community. Laurence, who represented nearly everyone who was anyone in the London theatre, including Sir Lawrence Olivier, advised me to choose the Lyric Hammersmith as co-producer of *Milk Wood Blues*. The play was actually a play about a play entitled *Under Milk Wood*, written by Welsh poet Dylan Thomas as a radio drama that had later become a movie starring Richard Burton and Elizabeth Taylor. The premise of the play was that Dylan Thomas and a drinking buddy (said to actually be his good friend Richard Burton) were out at a local pub, and Thomas had lost the original script of the play just prior to leaving for America, where it was scheduled for its premiere. Thus, the title, *Milk Wood Blues*. Keith Boak directed our play, with the cast being led by well-known British actor Michael Bertenshaw (later in the movie, *Da Vinci Code*). Actors Allan Corduner (movie, *Gilbert & Sullivan*), Bob Critchley, Marian McLoughlin, Peter Robert Scott, David Shaw Parker and Reginald Tsiboe completed the cast, with Paul Dart the stage and lighting designer and Jonathan Whitehead the musical director.

Milk Wood Blues ran at the Lyric Hammersmith from January 15 through February 7, with a full house nearly every night. This, despite an exceptionally cold spell (said to be the coldest since 1740) that lasted nearly the entire run of the play. The heavy, cold snowfalls in and near London caused transport to be gridlocked and were even blamed for affecting Big Ben's chiming hammer. Best of all, The London Telegraph welcomed One World Arts Foundation as one of its producers.

At the time of the play, Nancy was still working for the New York branch of a French champagne company, Laurent Perrier Champagne, and had promised her boss that she would work two more months until he found a replacement. Naturally, for the opening night *Milk Wood Blues* cast party in London, I ordered champagne from Nancy, but due to raging snowstorms, the roads were closed and the champagne could not be transported to the hotel. At the last moment, I had to order the more expensive, but not as fine, champagne the hotel had on hand. What was amazing to me was that the professional cast and crew of *Milk Wood Blues* did not allow severe weather conditions to keep them from the theatre, nor were theatre-goers absent because of the weather.

As a result of the successful run of *Milk Wood Blues*, I discovered on the day it closed that I had acquired a good reputation around town as a successful foreign producer. Good enough, it seemed, for a British producer well-known to me in London to get me on the phone to ask to use my name as a foil to fire the director of a play that had flopped on the fringe of the fringe of the West End. One of England's greatest musical comedy stars, Finella Fielding, had been stuck in this rather poor production and the producer needed a reason to fire the director. It was a strange compliment to be asked to wield my full weight as a producer for negative purposes, but I was pleased to do anything to help Miss Fielding.

One of the great reasons for the success of *Milk Wood Blues* was Robert Cogo-Fawcett, the artistic director of the Lyric Hammersmith. In addition to being a talented artistic director, Robert was quite adept with languages and could speak several fluently, including English, French, German, Italian and Spanish, and he was learning Hungarian. When Nancy and I first met him, he was married to Margaret, who was a generous, spirited lady we enjoyed immensely. Margaret was very certain that the human animal was filled with flaws and that some of them were absolutely delightful. We agreed wholeheartedly. Robert and Margaret later separated and divorced and she remarried. In the meantime, Robert was greatly responsible for the excellent presentation of the play and also helped us find Jo Benjamin for *Milk Wood Blues*. She was a great business manager who had worked with several of the biggest hits including *Les Miserables*. All in all, my first big solo project with the One World Arts Foundation was successful and my new quest for creativity was launched. In London, after producing *Milkwood Blues*, we went on to produce, with Theatre Royal Productions, *A Woman Destroyed* by Simone de Beauvoir, translated and performed by Diana Quick.

With the end of the plays in London, I escaped the snow, returned to the United States, driving my 1985 Peugeot out from California to meet Nancy at the airport in Albuquerque to go on to Santa Fe, New Mexico. It was spring in the Southwest, and Nancy had expected the weather to be warm, but it turned out to be quite cold enough for her to be forced to buy warm clothing. We were, after all, at 7,000 feet of elevation most of the time. We were in Santa Fe to pick up some paintings my mother had purchased from two well-known Southwest artists, Fremont Ellis and Randall Davies. One of Ellis's paintings needed some restoration work done on it and we found the painter's daughter, Bambi Ellis, who put us in touch with a craftsman who could restore the painting. We enjoyed Bambi's company and ended up doing a few things with her. She took us to her father's original, old-fashioned Hispanic ranch house, which was wistful and charming.

We had finished our business and were heading back to California when we ran into some difficulties. Somewhere along the way, some bad gas was put into the tank of my car and we broke down on a major highway not far from Joseph City, Arizona. One of the best things about our relationship was that we have always been able to find the humor in most situations, even when in car trouble on a desert road near a place like Joseph City (that we wryly agreed was anything but biblical). Laughter was to carry us through as we rode in the cab of a huge tow truck to Winslow, Arizona, with an 18-year-old simpleton and his drunken boss. We later found out that they had even attached our car on the back… backwards! The motel where we chose to stay in Winslow had a French name, Entrée, which boded well, but it turned out to be bogus. It was an old motel with rusty fixtures, thick orange shag carpet and a Magic Fingers bed that would vibrate when you put a quarter in the slot. There were no phones in the room, and the switchboard phone system was totally occupied by a talkative traveling salesman, so we had to find a phone booth to make a call. There was a Chinese-American restaurant attached to the motel, but it was obvious that Chinese fare was not in great demand. In fact, they appeared a bit concerned when we inquired regarding the Chinese food on the menu, and we most assuredly ordered the only bottle of wine they had ever sold in that restaurant. As I said, laughter carried us through.

Nancy still has a marvelous red t-shirt with a martini glass and the words Entrée Motel, Chinese-American Cuisine emblazoned on the front. Yes, we enjoyed many good laughs on that road trip and on the myriad trips to follow.

Our next adventure was our wedding in New York City, which we repeated just to make sure we were officially married. The first wedding was at the city hall on May 22, where the judge signed our marriage license and Donald and Betsy Crawford witnessed the short ceremony. The next day, we had our small family wedding at the chapel at the Regis High School, which was part of St. Ignatius Loyola Church on Manhattan's Upper East Side.

The announcement of our wedding was very important for both of our families and although neither of our parents was able to attend, they were proud to join in announcing the nuptials. The very proper wedding announcement was sent out to all of our friends, many of whom, I'm certain, were surprised and pleased at the same time.

Our wedding announcement read as follows:

Mrs. Paul Frederick McQuiggan
and
Mr. and Mrs. John Nichols McLucas
Announce the marriage of

Nancy McQuiggan Devitt
and
Walter Scott McLucas II

Saturday, the twenty-third of May
One thousand nine hundred and eighty-seven
New York City

Enclosed was the following "At Home" card, inviting friends and family to celebrate by visiting us and also describing in a very few words the delicious international lifestyle we would enjoy as a married couple.

At Home
415 East 85th Street, Apt. 9-F
New York, New York 10028
Chemin de la Maure
06800 Cagnes Sur Mer, France
Nancy and Scott McLucas

The wedding ceremony took place in the little chapel. Nancy's brother, Jack, walked her up the aisle and his former wife, Mary Doyle, stood up with her at the altar. Donald Crawford was my best man. Father Ed Lavin, a good friend of Mary's, performed the ceremony and his final blessing was eloquent and prophetic. It is a blessing that has been fulfilled for Nancy and me and one I wish for every married couple:

> *May almighty God, with His words of blessing, unite your hearts in the never-ending bond of love. (Amen.)*
> *May the peace of Christ live always in your hearts and in your home.*
> *May you have true friends to stand by you, in joy and in sorrow.*
> *May you be ready and willing to help and comfort all who come to you in need.*
> *And may the blessings promised to the compassionate be yours in abundance. (Amen.)*
> *May the Lord bless you with many happy years together, so that you may enjoy the rewards of a good life.*
> *And after a long and happy life on earth, may he welcome you to His eternal kingdom in Heaven. (Amen.)*

Wedding Party

Following the wedding, Nancy and I and our guests — Jack and his daughter, Ruth A. McQuiggan, Mary Doyle (Ruth A's mother and Jack's former wife), Donald and Betsy Crawford and their son, Andrew, my cousin, Ellen and her husband, Harvey, and Father Ed Lavin — celebrated with a special luncheon at Le Bernadin. The menu was splendid, with toast and Nova Scotia spread, green salad, salmon with sorrel sauce, a variety of raspberry and dark chocolate desserts, coffee with chocolate truffles and coconut cakes — all enhanced by generous portions of Perrier-Jouët Grand Brut Champagne!

Jack McQuiggan and his daughter, Ruth A.

The first leg of our honeymoon involved a trip to California, where we stayed at the Beverly Hills Hotel for a few days while clearing out my Los Angeles apartment and selling the car. Then we rented a car and drove to San Francisco, taking the coast road and stopping at the Hearst Castle on the way. We enjoyed a great visit with my cousin, Dee, and her husband, Bud, near San Francisco, and then drove further up the Northern California coast to Eugene, Oregon, where we stopped to see my dear friend, Judith Meltzoff, a psychologist from California. Judith had helped John and me a great deal when we lived in California, and she became a special friend to Nancy and me, even coming to visit us in France early in our marriage. Unfortunately, Judith contracted cancer of the eye and passed away a few years later, but I'm glad Nancy and I were able to share some of our happiness with her.

From Oregon, we traveled to Washington, stopping in Seattle to see Cousin Dee's son, Ross Morris, and his wife, Heidi. They had an infant son, Winston, who they told us had been fussy and crying all day long, but they were so proud of him they invited us to quietly tippy-toe into his room and peek into his crib, even though they had just gotten him to sleep. The baby's eyes popped open instantly when we leaned over the crib, and he began to scream at the top of his lungs. He would not stop. Nancy joked that this would make a fine childhood memory for the boy — the time we came for a visit and scared him half to death. My joke is that it only took one loud, seemingly endless visit with one baby to convince Nancy and me that we were not cut out to be parents.

The next time we saw Winston, he was about fifteen years old, had a younger sister, Amanda, and was staying at a rented house in the South of France with his parents and their best friends, Chef Thierry Rautureau and his wife, Kathy. Thierry is a James Beard award-winning chef and over the years, has owned two Seattle restaurants, "Rovers" and "Luc." He is from the Muscadet region of France and is known worldwide as "The Chef in the Hat." People traveled from everywhere to taste his wonderful, fresh cuisine, and, would you believe it, he actually took a "busman's holiday" and cooked an elaborate meal for us when Nancy and I drove over to visit them on a Sunday afternoon. I remember all kinds of fresh vegetables and much olive oil. The meal was fabulous. I especially enjoyed the roasted potatoes, which were delicious.

Meanwhile, back to our honeymoon trip, we drove from Washington State to Vancouver and then flew back to Los Angeles and on to New York, where we stayed in Nancy's apartment on East 85th Street for a short time. Then, it was on to our home in France. That began a beautiful pattern that lasted for many years, with us dividing our time between France and New York and thoroughly enjoying our life in both places. Later, we added sunny Florida to the mix. Nancy's parents had retired in Ponte Vedra Beach. Her father had passed away, and we visited Nancy's mother often, later doing some major caregiving as she aged and needed assistance. For more than a decade, from the early 1990s on, we maintained homes in France, New York and Florida, but since 2006, we've lived permanently in Florida, with occasional visits to France and New York.

Returning to my home in France in 1987 with a fine lady and great companion by my side was intensely satisfying. Nancy's ease with the language and the people made her an instant hit with everyone she met there, and my caretakers/gardeners/all-around handymen, Michel and Fred Natale, adored her. Soon after we got home to France, Fred had to go off to do his military duty as all young Frenchmen do, and while he was away, we had a man from across the street trimming the hedges. There was still much to be done to the house and we seemed to be working on it constantly, but from the beginning, it was destined to be a work in progress. There were just so many other exciting ventures in which to invest money, and the house was perfectly charming and presentable enough for entertaining friends and visitors from near and far.

Chef Jean Stephane Poinard

Nancy and I did venture to make certain improvements and, in conjunction with those, we contacted Andrée Poinard, a woman in the restoration business who lived in a little town next to Cannes and owned a small hotel there. She had just restored her hotel and was very helpful to us. We needed bedspreads, curtains and other special fabrics, and she put us in touch with the proper vendors. In fact, we became close friends and had many adventures with Andrée, whose son, Chef Jean Stephane Poinard, has since moved to St. Augustine and opened a restaurant, Bistro de Lyon. Partially sponsored by One World Foundation, Chef Poinard was invited, in 2011, to cook a meal at the James Beard House in New York City. He has since appeared in several television newscasts and local publications. We are confident that great things are in store for Chef Poinard, as he is not only a fine chef but a charming man who sincerely cherishes his family tradition of creating the finest French cuisine.

We were at a restaurant near our home in Cagnes-Sur-Mer when we were introduced to NALL by our Canadian friend Pat Huyduk, who was taking courses in art and running tours of artists' homes and studios on the French Riviera. Her introduction of us to NALL was one of those moments of destiny in my life. I consider NALL one of the finest artists in the world and am honored to call him my friend.

NALL invited Nancy and me to his studio in Vence, which had belonged to artist Jean Dubuffet. We found the studio to be extremely attractive… it looked directly across a small valley to the enchanting Matisse Chapel; however, walking into NALL's place was also a shocking experience. On the right was an open sarcophagus and in it was a symbol of a life-size human figure with the inimitable features of the late James Baldwin, who had been a personal friend of NALL's. Baldwin had lived in Vence during the last years of his life and had died about six months before we met NALL. NALL's memorial of him was striking. Baldwin was an ugly black man with distinct features — there was no doubt that Baldwin's big eyes were staring out at us from that casket, which was six-sided and open for full viewing effect. As if that weren't enough, there was a second, similar, casket placed end to end with the first one. I'm fairly certain that NALL eventually gave the caskets to the Birmingham, Alabama, Black History Museum.

An excerpt from NALL's biography on his website reads as follows:

A native of Troy, Alabama, NALL (Fred Nall Hollis) received a degree in Art, Political Science and Psychology at the University of Alabama in Tuscaloosa. He was mentored by Spanish Surrealist, Salvador Dali. In 1986, when he bought Jean Dubuffet's studio in Vence, NALL began publishing his own line engraving and having apprentices. Later, with his wife, Tuscia, he purchased the Karoly Foundation, a seven acre estate in a small valley between Vence and Saint Paul de Vence, France. He rechristened it the N.A.L.L. Art Association. NALL's

NALL

diverse, multi-media works (paintings, sculptures and porcelain) are featured permanently in galleries, museums, cathedrals and homes around the globe including the Boston Museum of Fine Arts, the Cathedral of Saint-Paul de Vence, France, Beaux Arts Museum in Nice, and the town square in Pietrasanta, Italy. NALL's monumental 15 foot high white injured dove with a wounded face and missing toes, entitled "Violata Pax Dove," stands near

NALL, Nancy and Scott

for y dear friend and supporter through thick
and thins....
Scott M-Lu45 All love /all ♡

the Kennedy Monument and Freedom Tower on the Miami Dade Downtown Campus in Florida and another Violata Pax Dove, along with several smaller doves greet visitors to the Pisa, Italy International Airport.

Since our first meeting with NALL in 1988, Nancy and I have gathered a collection of his art and an equally marvelous collection of enjoyable memories of time spent with him. Through One World Foundation, we have been privileged to help fund a few of his projects, and through our close friendship, we have been privy to many of the personal aspects of his life. In August of 2011, for instance, I was called to give a deposition on

NALL's behalf in his divorce from his wife, Tuscia. My testimony during an hour-long deposition in Birmingham, Alabama, was all about whether or not NALL had ever had a homosexual relationship with a man named Jean Pierre in Vence. The attorney hinted to me about sexual blackmail, which naturally harkened me back to the 35 years of emotional blackmail perpetrated upon me by a narcissist named John M. Johnson. Apparently, in NALL's case, Tuscia was making accusations that NALL blackmailed her into spending excess money by threatening to bring back his former lover, Jean Pierre. The deposition was interesting, but Jean Pierre has never resurfaced in NALL's home in France or in Alabama, rendering the accusation of blackmail pointless.

NALL's pen and ink sketch of me, which graces the cover of this book, is one of my most treasured possessions. His art and friendship have become, and always will be, integral in our lives.

When Nancy and I stood at NALL's house and looked across the valley at the Matisse Chapel on the hillside opposite Vence, we wished ourselves there… and soon we arranged to visit the famous landmark.

Matisse lived in Nice and designed the chapel. It is such a simple, delicate structure with a tall, almost fragile-looking 8-foot cross on top. Inside the chapel is an astounding 8-10 foot black and white painting of Christ, dressed in a robe with cassock. It is not gender-specific and it is one of the most spectacular paintings by Matisse. There are small circular Stations of the Cross marked with paintings in black ink. The tiny white chapel will hold only about 50 people. There are exquisite stained glass windows arranged so that a kaleidoscope of light shines into the chapel every day of the year. When we were "at home" in France, Nancy and I enjoyed taking our guests to Vence, Monte Carlo, Nice, and other stunning points but the Matisse Chapel stood above most art anywhere.

When "at home" in either New York City or Vence, France, our lives revolved around the theatre and the productions we sponsored through One World Arts Foundation. Ours was a marriage of love, laughter and mutual respect that transcended the ordinary. Never had I lived with such a supportive and insightful partner. She saw my vision and encouraged it. As the foundation grew, we were delighted to help launch some spectacular artists and productions.

CHAPTER 13

One World Arts Foundation

It was in the late 1980's that One World Arts Foundation truly became the catalyst for the artistic excellence I had envisioned. Several factors combined to allow me the exploration of exciting new avenues of creativity in the performing arts.

The prime factor was my marriage to Nancy. I now approached life with a real enthusiasm as a result of her encouraging presence by my side. Another factor that helped me go forward toward achieving many of my long-term goals was an inheritance from a skip-generation trust passed down through my father from my grandfather.

When he was on his deathbed in 1989, my father called and asked me to share some of my inheritance with his wife, Kitty. She deserved it, as she had taken wonderful care of him when his health was failing in his last years, and I gladly gave her a generous gift from my inheritance. Dad had gone into a retirement home near San Diego. He had always harbored the fear that his demise would happen quickly if he ever went into an elder care facility. It was a death house for him. He died the day after he arrived there.

Poor Kitty had put up with a great deal during her marriage to my father. First, despite the fact that she was smart and attractive, my grandfather had despised her for not being my mother, Hamilton Simpson McLucas, whom he admired without reservation. He never got over the fact that my mother had a right to seek a different life companion than my father. In my grandfather's eyes, Kitty was absolutely no match for my mother, and, therefore, he never gave her a chance. I never knew what exactly transpired between my grandfather and Kitty, but I do know it was serious enough that my father had to beg her on bended knee to stay with him. She had to be strong to live with my father. For instance, there was the notoriously bad business decision he made after a few highballs at a dinner party, when he actually approached a very high ranking bank executive and asked him if he would like to dance to Swan Lake with him. "I knew then it was time for us to take early retirement," Kitty later commented to me.

Although the inheritance eased the way a bit and helped give me the freedom to do more than I had been able to do before, it was not the deciding factor in one of the best career decisions I ever made —— taking a lease out on the South Street Theatre on West 42nd Street in New York City. Marriage to Nancy had proved to be a daily celebration, and my new brother-in-law, John A. (Jack) McQuiggan, was a new and dynamic partner for One World Arts Foundation. Jack was the one who suggested that we consider taking out the lease on the South Street Theatre. It was a fairly small theatre with a capacity for an audience of 99 people, but it was perfect for its purposes. Jack also introduced me to Ciaran O'Reilly and Charlotte Moore, founders of the Irish Repertory Theatre, who said goodbye to the temporary homes they'd had in the past when they adopted the South Street Theatre as their own in 1988.

Providing the first real home for the Irish Repertory Theatre was thrilling for me and a great catalyst for the reputation of One World Arts Foundation. The foundation co-produced eight plays during the time the Irish Rep headquartered at the South Street Theatre. In 1995, they moved to a former warehouse in Chelsea on West 22nd Street, with three completely renovated floors. The larger space allows for both a Main Stage Theatre and a smaller space, the W. Scott McLucas Studio, of which I am inordinately proud.

The Irish Rep's 1988-1989 season included a revival of *A Whistle in the Dark* by playwright Tom Murphy, that was directed by Charlotte Moore, with Ciaran O'Reilly in one of the lead roles. The play centers on the brawling, street-fighting family of Carneys of County Mayo. In a long and predominantly positive review of the play, New York Times

THE IRISH REPERTORY THEATRE
presents

A WHISTLE IN THE DARK

critic Mel Gussow wrote: "The play is a worthy example of the company's announced intention to establish an American home for classical and contemporary Irish theatre."

Brian Friel's *Philadelphia, Here I Come!* was directed in the 1989-1990 Season by Paul Weidner and starred Pauline Flanagan, Patrick Fitzgerald and Ciaran O'Reilly. It was set in 1962 in the small village of Ballybeg, Ireland.

During the 1990-1991 Season, the Irish Repertory Theatre and One World Arts Foundation, Inc. partnered to co-produce *The Playboy of the Western World*, written by J. M. Synge and directed by Charlotte Moore. The setting was in a village on a wild coast in Mayo, Ireland in 1900. *Making History* by Brian Friel was the second play of the Season, also directed by Charlotte Moore.

The Irish Rep's 1991-1992 Season was completely consumed by the exciting production of Harold Prince's original play, *Grandchild of Kings*. The play was adapted from the autobiography of Irish playwright Sean O'Casey – a panoramic script spanning a transitional period from the 19th and 20th centuries at the beginning of the Irish struggle for freedom from Great Britain when Sean O'Casey was just beginning to write plays.

All Nancy and I knew about *Grandchild of Kings* prior to its production was that Charlotte Moore and Ciaran O'Reilly came by our house in France on their way to visit Harold Prince in Italy, with contract in mind. The first thing they asked was to borrow our typewriter so that they could type up a contract for the play. Unfortunately for Charlotte and Ciaran, our Olivetti Electric typewriter had a French keyboard. The two of them burned the midnight oil for several nights in a row struggling to create a legal-looking document for presentation.

Nancy and I, through our One World Arts Foundation, ended up co-producing Prince's play, along with the Irish Rep., the Shuberts and a host of other enthusiastic supporters. It was performed at the Theater for the New City, a black box theater that would accommodate a larger audience than our small proscenium stage on 42nd Street. Although there were some musical numbers, it was a drama, overall, and the writing was so well-done that I actually found myself wiping away tears a couple of times. Young Patrick Fitzgerald did such a marvelous job of portraying Sean O'Casey that he won the coveted Clarence Derwent Award for Acting, an award which is more treasured among actors than the Emmy.

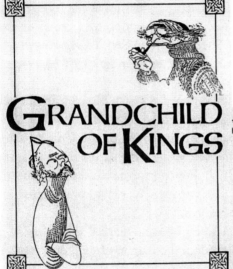

He was breathtaking in his role, and Harold Prince did a glorious job of writing and directing the play.

In the 1992-1993 season, the Irish Rep partnered with the Actor's Playhouse and One World Arts Foundation, Inc. to produce Thomas Kilroy's *The Madame MacAdam Travelling Theatre*, and my cousin, Ellen Adamson, had top billing in the play, along with W. J. Brydon, Denise duMaurier, Rosemary Fine, Michael Judd and Charles O'Reilly. I was listed in the playbill as executive director.

Seconds Out was a Very Special Arts production at the Joseph Papp Public Theater/LoEsther Hall. The play was written by a group of Irish youth and won the 1991 Very Special Arts (VSA) Young Playwrights Program Award in Ireland. It was brought to New York by VSA Founder Jean Kennedy Smith.

On opening night, in honor of our special guest, Mrs. Smith, the play was preceded by a one-man show performed by Irish Rep Actor Chris O'Neill called *My Oedipus Complex* by Frank O'Connor. Unfortunately, Ms. Jean Kennedy Smith and her entourage arrived for the welcoming ceremony, exited during the Irish Rep performance, and reappeared just in time to watch the VSA performance. It was an unexpected and somewhat disappointing turn of events.

In the 1994-1995 Season, Rosaleen Linehan starred in *Mother of all the Behans*. Adapted by Peter Sheridan, the play was based on a book by Brian Behan.

Yeats on Broadway! was a benefit performance at The Helen Hayes Theatre on June 6, 1994, with supper following at Sardi's. The playbill/brochure reads: "The Irish Repertory Theatre Company's performance of *Yeats: A Celebration of poetry and songs* and the play *Cathleen ni Houlihan* performed by the Company and celebrity guests including Claire Bloom, Susan Bloom, W. B. Brydon, Deirdre Danaher, Geraldine Fitzgerald, Patrick Fitzgerald, Pauline Flanagan, Peter Gallagher, Daisy Prince, Kitty Sullivan, Milo O'Shea. Miss Katharine Hepburn will introduce the evening."

On the back of the playbill/brochure for the benefit, there is chronicled a brief description of the Irish Repertory Theatre Company's progress to that date (just prior to moving to the much larger space that they now occupy):

THE IRISH REPERTORY THEATRE COMPANY was founded in 1988

by Ciaran O'Reilly and Charlotte Moore. They have produced such critical
successes as Sean O'Casey's THE PLOUGH AND THE STARS, SECONDS
OUT, the winning entry in Ambassador Jean Kennedy Smith's VERY
SPECIAL ARTS, IRELAND project, and Harold Prince's GRANDCHILD
OF KINGS for which they received three Outer Critic's Circle nominations
and the Drama Desk Award for "Excellence in Presenting Distinguished
Irish Drama." THE IRISH REPERTORY THEATRE receives support from
the National Endowment for The Arts, The New York State Council on the
Arts and One World Arts Foundation which has produced several plays
with the IRISH REPERTORY THEATRE COMPANY.

The Irish Repertory Theatre has featured the best of Irish and Irish-
American writers over the past 24 years, and was recognized with
the 2007 Jujamcyn Theatres Award, a special Drama Desk Award for
"Excellence in Presenting Distinguished Irish drama," and the Lucille
Lortel Award for "Outstanding Body of Work." I'm very proud to have
been instrumental in their success and, to have had a theatre in New York
City named after me is a high honor, indeed.

In addition to providing a home for the Irish Repertory Theatre
Company for seven years, One World Arts Foundation used the South
Street Theatre for some other productions including *Magical Circles*, by
Carman Moore and the Skymusic Ensemble, with three performances
in 1989, on December 28, 29, and 30th. New York Times Reviewer
James R. Oestreich, wrote on December 30, 1989, the following glowing
description of Moore's performance:

Many composers defy categories, but Carman Moore simply treats them
with disdain... Mr. Moore has a lot of music in his head, the product of
his upbringing in black culture, his classical training and his voracious
curiosity, and in his multi-media extravaganzas he finds some distinctly
odd and wonderful places for it.

The York Theatre revival of *Carnival!* ran at St. Peters Church from March
31- May 2, 1993. This production was directed/choreographed by Pamela
Hunt and featured Glory Crampton (Lili), Robert Michael Baker (Paul
Berthalet), Paul Schoeffler (Marco), Karen Mason (Rosalie), Robert Lydiard
(Jacquot) and William Linton (Schlegel).

I was honored to receive the Outer Critic's Circle Award for the production.

Outer Critics Circle
AWARD

Presented to

One World Arts Foundation
W. Scott McLucas
EXECUTIVE DIRECTOR

Producer of
"Carnival"
The Outstanding Revival of a Musical
of
1992-1993

Since we were dividing our time and resources between New York City and France, it occurred to me to capitalize on that international connection through One World Arts Foundation. Just a day's drive away from where we lived in France, the best dance festival in the world, Biennale de la Danse de Lyon, took place every two years in Lyon. Having begun in 1984, the Biennale consisted of nearly two months of marvelously talented celebration. Nancy and I agreed that One World Arts Foundation should be part of this remarkable event. When I called Anna Kisselgoff, the dance critic for the New York Times, and asked her to introduce me to Guy Darmet, the brilliant founder and director of the Biennale, Anna simply said, "Call him." Thereupon, Nancy and I drove to Lyon in 1988 and met Guy Darmet, who flipped through his huge catalogue of talent and asked us which of the dance companies we would like to sponsor. I recognized Bill T. Jones, having known of him through the Arnie Zane Dance Company in New York City. Thus, the New York/

France connection was cemented by One World Arts Foundation when we helped produce Bill T. Jones' Last Supper at Uncle Tom's Cabin in 1990. We later became first commissioner and co-presenter of the world premiere of Bill T. Jones' award-winning ballet, Still/Here, which was reviewed by Anna Kisselgoff in the New York Times. Excerpts of her review follow:

... "Still/Here," a major and often startling new mixed-media piece by the experimental choreographer Bill T. Jones, is a singularly American work.

For a year and a half, young to elderly volunteers articulated their thoughts about their life-threatening illnesses in "Survival Workshops" led by Mr. Jones in 10 American cities. From this potentially awkward raw material, Mr. Jones and a particularly outstanding mix of collaborators have fashioned a true work of art, both sensitive and original.

"Still/Here," which had its local premiere on Wednesday night with the Bill T. Jones/Arnie Zane Dance Company at the Brooklyn Academy of Music (30 Lafayette Avenue, at Ashland Place, Fort Greene), may not tell you anything you don't already know. But the experiences transmitted by the way of live dance, video and commissioned music that is integrated with the voices of the workshop participants, will stand out in unexpected ways.

... Mr. Jones succeeds as deeply as he does most of the time because he has realized the paradox of giving immediacy to emotion by distancing himself from it.

...The choreography is genuinely abstract, focused on the heightened distillation of gesture that is Mr. Jones's dance signature. Every aspect of the piece is integrated to the point of refinement."

From New York to the Orient, Nancy and I savored and supported the arts far and wide. In 1992, we took a Yale University Wanderlust cruise to Vietnam. This was important because international groups and those interested in our nation's international future wanted our government and our merchants to sign a new commercial agreement with Vietnam. The reason, over and above economics, was simple: with good commerce comes good healing. It took our countries until 1992 (more than a decade after the Vietnam conflict) to begin making peaceful overtures to one another. Realistically, American women wanted those beautiful silks of Vietnam, and Vietnamese businesses wanted modern American technology.

We traveled from Hong Kong, China to Vietnam, starting with Hai Phong and then on to Hanoi, the capital of Vietnam, one of the main reasons for our visit there being that this town was the worksite of a Yale graduate, a young news editor who was living and working in Vietnam. Seeing this fine example of American enterprise coming out of Yale University made us all joyful. There were a number of historians from Yale and Harvard Universities among the many intellectuals that came together on the Wanderlust Cruise to Vietnam, the first such visit of discovery since the end of the conflict. We visited tomb sites, temples and other structures that were still being repaired, and we enjoyed eight magnificently prepared meals. Danang was one of the ports for the cruise ship and there was a big American beach which had served as a landing place — a piece of history for those of us now landing there. In Danang, we were entertained and charmed by a Vietnamese flute player who was a skilled and imaginative player of the local wooden flutes and other native musical instruments. His name was Man Hung and I asked to meet with him after the performance. Through a translator, I proposed a European itinerary to introduce this unique type of music, with One World Arts Foundation partnership, to European audiences. I was astounded that it took nearly a year to complete the preparations and get permits necessary to arrange this sponsorship of Man Hung, due to bureaucracy on both sides because no formal treaties or other accords existed between the nations involved.

The route to success was circuitous indeed. We were led to the French Embassy in New York City. They pointed us to the Colonial Records Department of the French Government in Brittany. In the National City Bank in New York City's China town, the banking industry of America had its own wire service between the U.S. and Vietnam. At one point I had to pose as Man Hung's father in order to get funds past some artificial barrier posed by one of the governments, both of them somewhat obtuse. Communication for the project was mainly between an English-speaking agent representing Man Hung and myself. It was more than a year after our first meeting with Man Hung that Nancy and I learned about the enormous value of the French Colonial system which, even today, keeps its records going back more than a century. What they had on record was everything about Man Hung and his family going back five generations, which gave him legitimacy in the eyes of the French government and allowed us to sponsor him, moving him in and out of France and back to his native Vietnam. Had it not been for the colonial services extraordinary record-keeping, this roundtrip journey wouldn't have been possible. It was a magnificent opportunity for Man Hung, a 40 year old man who had once been a young musician in a North Vietnamese Army Band. This was quite a departure for him.

We arranged several concerts for Man Hung across France, and his performances were extremely well received, in fact, often greeted with wild applause. We put him in a magnificent concert in our cathedral in Vence along with a harpsichordist playing Bach and a beautifully dressed Laotian lady reciting poetry in Vietnamese. He also performed with the Syrinx Orchestra, another of One World Arts Foundation's creations.

Man Hung was quartered in a bungalow on the NALL Art Association's grounds a few miles away from our house. NALL also had a large open space for entertainment and we presented Man Hung in one or two other venues in the area as well. The point of this sponsorship was a personal attempt by me to compensate Vietnam partially for what I considered an invasion of their country. I did it for the sake of all the Vietnamese who were under attack and disrespected and hated. Our country had not been invaded at that time since the war of 1812, and yet we have felt the need to invade other countries repeatedly. By sponsoring Man Hung, I felt well satisfied that we had done our part, which happened to be unique, in respecting both the people of Vietnam and their culture.

During his third month in France, a group of Vietnamese citizens who were teachers and musicians living in a fairly poor section of Nice, approached Man Hung to be a tutor for their children. This was based on his connection with the traditional musical instruments of Vietnam. I managed to explain in French to the family leaders of this group that Man Hung was obligated throughout his stay in France to remain under the supervision of his sponsors, who included NALL and his wife, Tuscia, Nancy and me. We were responsible for him until he returned to Vietnam and it would have been breaking our contract if we allowed him, unsupervised, to risk breaking his contract. Thus, we kept him in view, thanked him affectionately, and successfully delivered him to the Nice Airport for his return trip to Vietnam, without ever losing sight of him.

George Rondo and Man Hung

One of the funniest memories Nancy and I have of the time Man Hung spent with us was when he and George Rondo, our One World Arts Foundation Artistic Director, accompanied us to a performance of Mozart's *The Magic Flute* in Aix-en-Provence. It was a thrilling occasion to provide this privilege for our Vietnamese flute-playing guest; George Rondo, who sat in the back of the car with Man Hung on the way to the performance, wanted to make sure he understood what a wonderful opportunity he had in store. Talking non-stop to Man Hung, George waxed eloquent as Man Hung (who understood not one word of English) literally "hung" on every word, torn between watching George's mouth move and glancing repeatedly at George's rather unusual socks. A friendly, loquacious man who never met a stranger and was a fabulous networker, George was wearing his Mickey Mouse socks that evening. Man Hung found him equally as fascinating as he did the opera!

George Rondo's main assignment with the Foundation was to research dramatic artistic projects of all kinds to add to our repertoire of New York and European ballet and theatre. In 1992, George was able to obtain an invitation for us to the Jackson Hole, Wyoming Film Festival, where independent film projects were presented and promoted by their authors, directors and producers. There, George found a subject of great interest to me: the production of a documentary concerning the careers of Olaus and Mardy Murie, researchers of the great elk herds in the northern reaches of Alaska and Canada. Film producer Bonnie Kreps was doing the documentary and she felt we could work very well together, especially after she heard about my work on the CBS television show, *Conquest*.

Bonnie had a sister in New York City and many friends there, so she suggested that she come to me and we could work together in our New York apartment on final editing, which we did. We agreed on a modest investment by One World Arts Foundation in the production of the film. Bonnie and I spent a fruitful four weeks working on final editing of the film and it was made easier by her high degree of film editing talent. A further detail is that she was always prepared with appropriate filmic material to cover all aspects of narration and action in this film, and she showed possession of a great sense of humor. I recall that we invested an initial $10,000 in the Margaret Murie film, and then the same again at a later point in the production.

One of the most delightful things about the Murie family was Olaus's enthusiasm for dancing, so I thought the film should be named reflecting Olaus's dancing in the Arctic. Thus, the documentary was entitled *Arctic Dance*.

Arctic Dance featured several impressive participants, including famous wild-life photographer and cinematographer Charlie Craighead. John Denver, who was a great fan of Mardy Murie's, appeared in the film, and Harrison Ford narrated it. Production credit for One World Arts Foundation would depend on the size of its support and creative input. We were listed as a sponsor in the production when they showed the documentary on PBS.

There were a couple of occurrences in relation to *Arctic Dance* that were amusing and embarrassing in equal measure. These were my attempts to interest Bonnie in Wagnerian and Northern European music backgrounds for the epic drama of nature in the film. There was, for instance, a gathering of elk — one of the largest herds in the world — in

Jackson Hole, Wyoming each Christmas. Imagine the power of Wagner and the elk combined! As forceful and filled with imagery as I was, Bonnie's interest in my operatic leanings remained nil.

Most embarrassing was my imagined scenario where Mardy Murie and Harrison Ford were to work their way by horse drawn carriage through the elk herd for a triumphal Christmas meeting. Then, there was the bride on a dogsled, which actually happened on the Murie's honeymoon.

Arctic Dance premiered in Jackson Hole, Wyoming and it is still in demand to this day. In fact, with the current emphasis on green building and green living, the documentary is even more in demand now than then. We wouldn't have had an environmental policy in Northern America if it weren't for Olaus and Mardy and their good work. They were among the environmentalists who helped found the Sierra Club.

I heard that the play, *Nagasaki Dust*, had been optioned by the owner of the Helen Hayes Theatre in New York. The name of the play intrigued me and I called the owner of the Helen Hayes Theatre and asked him if I could get a copy of the script and possibly back the play. *Nagasaki Dust* premiered at the Philadelphia Theatre Company in February of 1992. I wasn't aware of the real magic in the play until I saw it performed. The play deserved to be seen by much larger audiences. It was a dramatic depiction of the conflict between Japan and America in World War II, seen through the eyes of a young American-born Japanese man who happened to be visiting his relatives when war broke out and remained in Japan through the American bombings of Hiroshima and Nagasaki.

In addition to the well-written story of a Japanese-American who was overseas at precisely the wrong moment, the staging and oriental flavor of the music punctuated the action. The lone kodo drummer and the tiny Japanese dancer who slowly descended from above and swirled about the stage in the ancient Butoh style dance; the low stage lighting and the expectation of adventure made the opening scene unforgettable. The second act was just as memorable when a procession of Japanese mourning boats rowed across the stage in a curving pattern that resembled an ancient funeral procession. It was one life blending into another; one culture blending into another... and the transition was neither easy nor dull. I found it fascinating, and it was well-received, but we were unable to take it to larger audiences due to lack of funds.

We wanted to have it performed at the Kennedy Center. After the play

Scott with Claude & Pete Tannahill - Italy

ran to its conclusion in Philadelphia, we had several meetings in New York with the investors and came up with some great artistic changes that would have made it even more powerful, but even though the playwright, W. Colin McKay, was willing to make whatever changes would enhance the play, there was no promise of additional financing. It was one of those enigmas of show business — a great play that was probably ahead of its time, despite the fact that the war with Japan had been over for several decades. Nancy and I attended opening night with a friend, Doug Robinson, and his wife. Doug was a former writer with the New York Times and was city and state editor of the Philadelphia Enquirer in 1992. We'd met the Robinsons on a trip to Australia and were glad to be back in their company. Doug enjoyed the play. Everybody did. It is still a unique, important and timeless play that should be performed.

In addition to working with national and local producers in New York

City, I had a great opportunity in 1992 to pursue my interest in distance learning when Pete Tannahill, an executive with IBM and a board member of One World Arts Foundation, made it possible for our foundation to share in a project involving the Gertrude Stein Repertory Theatre, IBM, and some of the biggest telephone companies on the planet. Pete and his wife, Claude, have always prided themselves on being proactive in the arts.

The distance learning scenario worked like this: We had a stage director borrowed from another production currently on the Riviera; in New York, the production team included set and lighting designers, actors, stage managers and so forth; and in Chicago, we found a costume designer eager to participate in this particular task. All of the elements in all of the locations were able to communicate over digital data lines. They were to create a live, theater-size working model of our stage production and this involved making changes which were shown in detail to our audience in La Napoule, France. Our audience in La Napoule consisted of 70 or more executives of the major telephone companies in the world,

Cheryl Faver - Gertrude Stein Rep

all fascinated with the implications of this new technology.

According to Cheryl Faver, the founder and artistic director of the Gertrude Stein Repertory Theatre, "We wanted to avoid (or at least ameliorate) that dual nightmare of American theater, the four-week rehearsal and the three-day tech...In the digital world, we can (if we want) strip theater of its physical components."

In my opinion, the most exciting part of this project was our ability to make a video copy to guide us in rehearsal and, later, full video versions of our project. The digital world allows us to create and employ distance collaboration. One World Arts Foundation partnered with IBM and the Gertrude Stein Repertory Theatre in funding this project. We were introduced to IBM's Person to Person software, which combined video conferencing with a suite of real-time collaborative tools. It produced a vision such as a conversation showing your collaborator, the sharing of graphics, the sending of files back and forth and the running of applications (3D set modeling program). Because it was created on video, and made from scenes and other sources located in various different global sites, it all seemed quite amazing.

In conjunction with the IBM/Gertrude Stein Repertory Theater collaboration, we produced a bi-coastal music performance with musicians in L.A., New York and Paris, and audiences in all three places. We envisioned eventually having the ultimate multi-site performance, a 24-hour play running continuously at 12 sites around the world, two hours each, to which anyone could dial in anytime and see a dramatic element in action. The viewing possibilities were called streaming. This was in 1993, nearly 20 years ago, and today that vision is a reality in more ways than one.

Cheryl Faver called it "a multimedia feeding frenzy," with the world of art being presented an incredible opportunity — a new means of communication and expression. "Experimentation yields its own rewards," she said. Every new distance learning project we worked with from that moment on shed new light on the essential nature of dance, drama, theater or narrative. Working with the Gertrude Stein Repertory Theater and IBM to establish new communication technology in the field of the arts was exciting and rewarding for One World Arts Foundation, and for me personally.

In 1993, I was honored to receive the special medal of the Writers Society of the United Nations in New York for innovative work in developing international artistic exchange. This recognition stemmed from many years of cooperative work with the Eugene O'Neill Foundation in New York City and a project with a group of theater professionals in Moscow who became known as the reborn Russian Theatre (or Russia's New Spring).

One of the things people in the Russian Theatre liked to do in both America and Russia from the early 1900's onward was to juxtapose language. American writers such as James Fennimore Cooper, Mark Twain, Jack London, Ernest Hemingway, Thomas Wolfe, and, later, Stephen King, earned great affection from the Russian population, while Chekov, Pushkin, and Tolstoy were favorites here in America. Eugene O'Neill (the first American playwright to win the Pulitzer Prize for drama) was welcomed and respected in Russia, bceause the working man was a frequent subject of O'Neill's plays. At the same time, Chekov, author of *The Cherry Orchard*, and other plays about aristocracy, its disappointments, and failures, was an author whom we Americans found fascinating. The Russians would feature Eugene O'Neill plays in the Russian language, and in America, we wanted to present Chekov in English. A festival of exchanges between the two theatre groups occurred when the Berlin Wall fell. One World Arts Foundation organized and facilitated this exchange.

In addition to reaching out around the globe, One World Arts Foundation became involved in co-producing several successful plays with the York Theatre Company during the early 1990's. The York Theatre Company was located in the Midtown Arts Common at Saint Peter's Church, Inc. at Lexington and 54th Street in New York City. Working with York's Director, Janet Hayes Walker, was a delight. The first play we co-produced at the York Theatre was *Noel & Gertie*, with words and music by Noel Coward. The play premiered on November 24, 1992 and starred Jane Summerhays and Michael Zaslow in the leading roles. *Down by the Ocean*, a comedy by P. J. Barry, was next, and then we co-produced *Booth*, by Austin Pendleton, starring actor Frank Langella.

We were proud to be associated with York's excellent plays and musicals, the most triumphant of all being our production together of Stephen Sondheim's *Merrily We Roll Along* in May of 1994. Based on the book by George Furth and directed by Susan H. Schulman, the Sondheim musical was originally directed on Broadway by Harold Prince. Reviving the 1981 play at the York Theatre in 1994 was one of the most exciting and gratifying moments in all of my years of co-producing plays. Here is what Patrick Healy of the New York Times wrote about the most recent production of *Merrily We Roll Along* (September 4, 2013):

"*Merrily We Roll Along* to be Screened – An acclaimed London production of the Stephen Sondheim-George Furth musical, *Merrily We Roll Along*, which Mr. Sondheim said was the best one he had ever seen, will be screened in movie theatres in New York and worldwide on October 23, the producers and the film distributors announced on Tuesday. The production received rave reviews last fall after opening at the Menier Chocolate Factory, then transferred to the West End, where the run ended in late July....

Several Broadway producers went to London to see *Merrily*, and privately expressed high regard for it, but no plans have been announced to bring the show to Broadway. The story of three close friends, *Merrily*

We Roll Along, is best known for its unusual narrative framework - the plot unfolds backward, with the main characters first appearing onstage with their relationship in tatters, and their falling out is then told in reverse chronology over 20 years. The original Broadway production opened in 1981 to mixed reviews and closed quickly; the show has since been revised but has yet to return to Broadway." - PATRICK HEALY

Our 1994 production of *Merrily We Roll Along* was extended at New York's York Theater and almost transferred to a commercial off-Broadway theater. Unfortunately, expensive royalty requirements prevented that final step forward. Theater folk and numerous critics who saw our York Theater - One World Arts Foundation production of *Merrily* in 1994 have been lavish with their praise – "a lovely production" and "unequalled" were frequent remarks up to the present day. Thus, we veterans of American Musical Comedy battles will be ready to cheer loudly on October 23, 2013, when we see the unique film version of *Merrily We Roll Along*.

In early 1994, I heard rumors of a play script entitled *Night Seasons* by the playright Horton Foote (possessor of a great reputation for the play, *Trip to Bountiful*, and Academy Awards for screenplays for *To Kill a Mockingbird* and *Tender Mercies*). After research on *Night Seasons*, I met Mr. Foote and acquired rights to his play, negotiated a co-production agreement with a promising new theater company in New Jersey, and enjoyed the great news that Jean Stapleton and Mr. Foote's daughter, Hallie, had agreed to appear in the play, which would also be directed by Mr. Foote. *Night Seasons* opened successfully in New Jersey, but its production was but a prelude to much greater success for Mr. Foote, our foundation, and another innovative production company, the Signature Theater Co. of New York. Our not-for-profit One World Arts Foundation was attracted in the early '90s by Signature Theater's program of production of an entire season of plays by a single playwright, and we made important contributions to several seasons of their productions.

Late in the summer of 1994, our artistic director, George Rondo, gave us news that Signature Theatre's 1994-95 season would consist of plays by Horton Foote. Further, our foundation was invited to contribute to the production of any one of the four plays to be produced. We chose to contribute to a new play, *The Young Man from Atlanta*. Our handsome contribution for it earned gracious thanks from Horton Foote and in addition, he praised me with the statement that "the American theatre-going public owed me a great deal of gratitude." Thus, we all shared in glory when the 1995 Pulitzer Prize for Drama was awarded to Horton Foote for *The Young Man from Atlanta*, produced by Signature Theater with sponsorship by New York theatre organizations such as the newly named One World Foundation, Inc.

It was also in 1995 that Nancy and I became permanent residents of Ponte Vedra Beach, Florida, and with the newly-created One World Foundation, Inc. as a private, operating Florida foundation creating 21st century initiatives in art and education around the globe. Once again, we were able to expand our vision and our outreach. During the next two decades, our foundation would fund imaginative and exciting projects for the world stage and for the enrichment of each of the three communities Nancy and I called home.

CHAPTER 14

One World Foundation, Inc.

One of the many perks of living in Cagnes-sur-Mer and heading One World Foundation, Inc. was my time as president of the Syrinx Orchestra, beginning in 1995.

In classical mythology, Syrinx (Greek Συρινξ) was a nymph and a follower of Artemis, known for her chastity. Pursued by the amorous Greek god Pan, she ran to a river's edge and asked for assistance from the river nymphs. In answer, she was transformed into hollow water reeds that made a haunting sound when the god's frustrated breath blew across them. Pan cut the reeds to fashion the first set of pan pipes, which were thenceforth known as syrinx.[1] The word syringe was derived from this word.

At one point during those first years after establishing the orchestra, we invited the finest music critic from Nice Matin newspapers to a private Syrinx concert. The review was fantastic. "Any music lover can go to listen to members of the Syrinx Orchestra play in Cannes, Nice or other small communities here in the Alpes Maritime, but they won't hear the same thing they will hear at a Syrinx Concert," the critic wrote. "The difference is one man — their conductor Errol Girdlestone."

Implying that Errol was the finest conductor of classical music in our part of France, the critic was correct, but we had to wait more than a decade... until February 2006... to have this fact confirmed by an outside musical expert.

It was in February of 2006, soon after our orchestra's tenth anniversary year, that a representative of the Vienna Philharmonic Orchestra attended a Syrinx concert, and at the conclusion, asked if he might have a word with the manager of our orchestra. Errol was subsequently asked to conduct a French tour by the Vienna Concert-Verein (chamber music division of the Vienna Philharmonic Orchestra). He was also asked to conduct the same orchestra playing at the Festival of Bregence in 2006, and again, in the Concert-Verein Hall in Vienna. What a magnificent acoustic! There is one giant space for the entire philharmonic orchestra and there are three smaller spaces, each about half as large as the big hall… and the quality of sound throughout the building is breathtaking.

Errol Girdlestone is a magnificent conductor. The music is in his blood. He has a very fine bass voice and his trueness of voice translates to a talent in the musical arena that is rare. A singer, pianist, composer, conductor and musicologist, Errol also has a passion for mentoring young performers. One of the most outstanding musicians Errol brought along early on was violinist Pieter Schoeman, now the concertmaster with the London Philharmonic — an amazing position to have achieved at such a young age, and one that might never have occurred had not Errol seen and nurtured his considerable talent.

Errol Girdlestone Conducting

Looking back at the year-long tenth anniversary season of Syrinx, which involved chamber music, recitals and choirs as well as the full orchestra, Pieter Shoeman had gone on to London by then, but sent a message to us summing up what made the Syrinx orchestra just about the best between Lyon and Turin.

"It was all thanks to Scott, whose generosity and prescience inspired all our achievements," Errol wrote recently as he was reminiscing about those grand days when Syrinx was in full swing. He continued, "During the fifteen years of our existence, we performed so many memorable concerts that it is difficult to pick any of them out. For me, the most important ones were those whose programming drew forth the best and most committed playing from the orchestra and gave it its unique sense of identity. I cherish souvenirs of some particularly proud moments: a Sibelius 5th Symphony, a Brahms Requiem in Saint Maximin, the virtually unknown Konzertstück of von Dohnanyi with that fabulous cellist, Maria Kliegel, Chopin and Beethoven piano concertos with François-René Duchâble, and Bach's St. Matthew Passion in the Monaco Cathedral — a work I had never conducted before. I remember having to steel myself to bring the orchestra in for the final chorus, so reluctant was I for the evening to be over!"

In celebration of our tenth year, I wrote a message to Syrinx from my heart and I'm incorporating that message into this book because it truly describes the rewards of having contributed to the beauty of the world of music through sponsoring this wonderful orchestra:

A Humanist Discovers His Happiness

The 23rd of May 1987 I had the joy to marry Mademoiselle Nancy McQuiggan in New York. A few weeks later, in France, my wife and I had the great pleasure to listen to a chorus of children sing in the Cathedral in Vence. The church had marvelous acoustics. What a wonderful musical experience. What an extraordinary synthesis of history, representing Christian spirituality since the 11th century and now, in this modern age, presenting an exceptional musical concert of children's voices. I turned to Nancy when we were there and I said, "Wouldn't this be a great place for us to produce concerts?" It was a prophetic statement.

During the course of the six following years, One World Foundation, of which I'm the President, earned an important reputation collaborating with other producers in the New York theater as well as a new reputation in distance learning by its work cooperating with Shakespeare's Globe Theatre in London, England. An international reputation in the arts was completed by our sponsorship of two prize-winning ballets entitled "The Last Supper at Uncle Tom's Cabin" and "Still Here," both by choreographer Bill T. Jones, produced during Dances Bienalles in Lyon, France in 1992 and 1994.

In 1993, I made the acquaintance of Errol Girdlestone and Ingeliese Fichtl, who were introduced to me by my friend, the artist NALL. One World Foundation, with the additional support of NALL, the City of Vence and the first President of Syrinx Concerts, Pierrette Carion, enabled Errol Girdlestone to gather together the best musicians in the Alpes Maritimes to form the Syrinx Orchestra. Ingeliese came from the Syrinx Vocal Ensemble and eventually became the business manager for the orchestra.

Fortunately, we were welcomed by the Curate of the Cathedral of Vence, Father Antoine Costa, from then on and most of our concerts were presented in that fabulous venue.

Our first program introduced Man Hung, who interpreted the folk music of Vietnam on his wooden flute; we had a rising pianist named Egan Minailovic, who played pieces by C. P. E. Bach, and Schubert, with the Syrinx Vocal Ensemble; and the professional musicians brought together by Errol Girdlestone who directed the ensemble. For me, a remarkable event that evening was the applause welcoming Nancy and me. Joy ruled that evening over this strange but beautiful assemblage. This was the announcing preamble of concerts which followed, with the creation of Syrinx Concerts Vence.

Syrinx's first official concert was presented the 9th of February 1995 with the music of composers Gounod, Gouvy, and Char. Fraincaix, interpreted by an ensemble of 10 wind instruments, under the direction of conductor Errol Girdlestone. That was the first of more than 100 concerts by Syrinx Concerts Vence.

Nancy and I share many happy memories with Errol and his wife, Susie, in the Vence Cathedral, at our home in Cagnes-sur-Mer sitting on the verandah having dinner, and during our many visits to the festival in Aix. Errol had worked in Aix as chorus director in 1991 before we started Syrinx and he always said it was delightful to be "on the other side of the curtain," enjoying the atmosphere and surroundings in the company of friends and loved ones.

One incident I'll never forget is the time someone misplaced the key to the monastery that was attached to magnificent historic St. Maximin Cathedral near Aix-en-Provence, where our Syrinx Orchestra had the privilege of playing regularly. Syrinx guest soloists and the stage crew usually stayed at the monastery the night before a concert, as did Nancy and I. The priest was very upset about the lost key, wringing his hands and searching everywhere. Trying to soothe him, I suggested that possibly we could get in touch with the gendarmes in Toulon and they might be able to help us find the key. "Toulon! Never!" was his adamant reply. The lost key was his responsibility and he did not want police brought in or gossip about his lack of control in this situation. By midnight, with everyone exhausted from waiting in the dark to get into the locked monastery, the key was found in a statue in the courtyard of the cathedral, where it had been hidden all along.

In further reminiscing about those years, Errol wrote: "I shall never forget surprising Scott in his garden with the orchestra playing Handel's *Water Music* in his honour to celebrate his 70th birthday. Well, I don't think we really surprised him — he's much too smart, and although we got rid of him fetching somebody from the airport I know he smelt something fishy. It's not easy smuggling a whole symphony orchestra into someone's home without them knowing!"

Yes, our days in France were idyllic. Nancy and I truly surrounded ourselves with the arts in Vence (the City of the Arts), and did all we could, through One World Foundation, to promote artists of different disciplines.

When I became vice-president of the Renoir Museum Association in 1996, my role was to develop new exhibitions and international programs emanating from the late painter's last home in Cagnes-sur-Mer. Living and working in one of the most beautiful places on the globe had obviously been inspiring for Renoir, and that inspiration was certainly not lost on Nancy and me either. We considered one of the highlights of spring to be the Museum's fabulous bi-annual exhibit among the ancient olive groves that Renoir painted so beautifully.

For several years we enjoyed the Renoir Museum grounds from an insider's point of view, often basking beneath the shade of a huge tree in the garden that cast cool shade in the hot, dry months of summer. We invited our friend, sculptor Aprille Best Glover, to exhibit her work at a bi-annual event in 2000. Aprille is a Florida native who lives in a picturesque cave in

"Aprille's Equilibrium" photograph by Jacques Renoir

France with her husband, Bill, also a Floridian by birth. The cosmic forces were definitely with Aprille during that exhibit, as her stunning duo of life-size plaster, wood and stone angels were photographed brilliantly by the great grandson of Auguste Renoir, Jacques Renoir.

The statues were carefully placed, presenting a memorable view from all sides. Set on a hillside in the Renoir gardens, the 11th century Chateau of Cagnes-sur-Mer provided a spectacular backdrop from one angle and viewed from a different perspective, one can see the house Renoir built for his family when he lived there.

Aprille's dramatic and meaningful description of her Équilibre at the Musée Renoir sculptures follows:

"A paired set of figures aligned along the north-south axis to take advantage of the natural lighting conditions around the autumnal equinox. The figure

facing west holds smooth stones with individual English words. The figure facing east holds stones with French words. Each word has a matching word in the other language. In some cases the word pairs have the same meanings. In other cases the word pairs will have opposite meaning. The work explores how balance comes from both similarity and the tension between opposing forces.

The shadows are as important as the work itself. At dawn the eastern figure's shadow touches the western figure and as morning progresses the shadows move slowly apart. At noon the light divides the forms completely as though by a blade. But as the afternoon sun arcs, the western figure's shadow reaches towards the east. Night falls and both are enveloped by shadow."

Bill Glover wrote a weekly internet column on French life entitled "Tales from the Loir" and his column of October 4, 2000 chronicled a delightful visit that he and Aprille had at our villa. Excerpts from that column bring back special memories of those idyllic days:

"We were invited to stay at the villa of our friends, Scott and Nancy McLucas in Cagnes-sur-Mer. Cagnes means "an inhabited place on a rounded hill" and is a name of Ligurian origin…Scott's villa sits on the top of a ridge with a view of the sea to the south and a view of the Alps to the north. To the southwest, you can see Cagnes' XIVth century chateau. The villa is at the end of a beautifully landscaped, tree lined path about 300 meters long. As one enters the gate, tall, stately cedar trees lines the left side of the path while terraced flower beds line the right side. The villa itself is "U" shaped with a courtyard full of flowers and a fountain in the center. A red tile roof covers the open veranda where you enjoy the sea view from morning until late at night. This is a perfect venue for sipping a 1964 Chateau La Tour but I'm getting ahead of myself. Scott also has a passion for France and its wines. Fortunately for us, he has been collecting wine for quite some time. When Scott asked me if I wanted to see his cellar, I didn't expect a room in the basement to be anything new. After all, I live in a cave and my neighbors have caves that contain thousands of bottles. Even I have about 500 bottles in my cellar. A man's cave says a lot about who he is and quality is the word for Scott's cave. As we walk into an air-conditioned room in the basement, I see bottles of Chateau Margaux, Chateau La Tour and some of the great houses of Burgundy.

These bottles are labeled from 60s, 70s and 80s. This is a completely new experience for me. In my little corner of France, we are always looking for the wines in bulk that you can buy for seven francs (90 cents) per liter. A bottle is three quarters of a liter. We are generally pushing the envelope to find a wine for less than 75 cents a bottle. Of course my neighbor, Maurice Cheron, will sometimes pull out his foot long brass key to unlock his secret chamber and disappear in the depths of our mountain to pull out a prized bottle but even Maurice cannot match Scott's collection.

Later in his article, Bill Glover noted that I presented Aprille with two bottles dated 1964 (Chateau La Tour and a Chambolle-Musigny) in honor of the year of her birth and her successful show at the Renoir Museum. Bill also talked of the passion that Aprille and I share for art, commenting, "Aprille and Scott have a passion for the arts and can talk for hours about things that few people can follow. I am not one of the few who can follow those conversations but that is no problem. Nancy and I have our own animated conversations but the subject is different. We talk about la vie en rose. All I have to do is bring up a topic like wine or food to get Nancy started. She is like a sunflower at noon. She stands up squarely and her face lifts like a soprano delivering her music. Her eyes sparkle and she sways slightly from side to side as she rushes to express her enthusiasm. It is mesmerizing to watch but I understand her clearly."

Later, Bill incorporated many of his Noir columns into his book, *Cave Life in France*, including the one in which he described the 1964 vintage wine gift to Aprille, my villa, my wine cellar, Nancy, and my friend, Michel Natale and his son, Frederic, who worked for me and could fix anything.

Looking back and reviewing his October 2000 column, it is obvious that Bill Glover was as captivated by the lives Nancy and I were leading as we were.

Bill also described, in great detail, our bouillabaisse "dining adventure" at Cros de Cagnes, one of my favorite restaurants, where the dramatic presentation of the bouillabaisse is as important as the delicious flavor. The wine, the cuisine, the art and the friendship we share with Bill and Aprille Glover has enriched our lives. We've enjoyed many fabulous evenings in their cave and it was our great pleasure to entertain them at our villa in Cagnes-sur-Mer.

In addition to our memorable moments spent with Bill and Aprille and other artists and performers in France, Nancy and I returned to New York City often, continuing our global quest for excellence and innovation in the arts. After having worked with the Gertrude Stein Repertory Theatre and IBM in the distance learning project of the early 1990s, I again leapt into this phenomenally time-saving and efficient mode of communication in 1996, bringing a landmark interactive learning experience to students gathered at the Kennedy Center, at a New York location and at a university in Japan. This was accomplished by bringing together World Stages (a division of the Gertrude Stein Repertory Theatre) and Ladysmith Black Mombasa, a South African all-male a cappella singing group.

One World Foundation's journey into the technological world of interactive distance learning continued in 1997 through PROJECT DISCOVERY. Partnering with Unity Theatre *Television* Film Co., Inc. in New York City in a joint initiative to provide highly professional film and television instruction for high school students, the course consisted of two phases, each with a ten-week, tuition-free, extracurricular summer course of virtual classes. It was interactively taught over the internet using Lucent Technologies Montage; the multipoint digital video-conferencing system. Phase I featured a live digital video and audio connection between Professor Janet Neipris, Chair of the Dramatic Writing Program at New York University's Tisch School of the Arts, with 30 11th and 12th grade writing students in the TV studio at the University of North Florida in Jacksonville. These students, selected from the nine-county Jacksonville region, had the enviable assignment of creating a finished, workable teleplay for Phase II of PROJECT DISCOVERY in the summer of 1999 when their script would be produced and telecast.

After Nancy's brother, Jack McQuiggan, conducted extensive talks in Jacksonville and Boston with Media One and in New York with Lucent Technologies/Bell Labs, they agreed to be major sponsors of PROJECT DISCOVERY in 1997, along with BRAVO, The Independent Film Channel and HBO.

The Florida expenses at PROJECT DISCOVERY were financed entirely by One World Foundation. PROJECT DISCOVERY was co-produced by Nancy's brother, Jack McQuiggan, and Producer Daniel Rosenbloom, co-founders and partners in the Unity Theater *Television* Film Co., Inc., and special consultant Winnie Holzman (writer-producer of *Thirty Something* and creator-writer of *My So-Called Life* and *Wicked*).

The regional coordinator in Jacksonville was Beth Voils, associate producer of *Education is Everybody's Business*, a monthly television series highlighting projects of Jacksonville's Duval Public Education Foundation. Once again, the Gertrude Stein Repertory Theatre was involved in this inspiring next generation project, having provided technical assistance in the transmission to students.

Another distance learning experience that was initiated and sponsored by One World Foundation in those years was the Globelink between the New Globe Theatre (the reconstituted birthplace of Shakespearean drama) in London and the rest of the world. Globelink, a new internet capability, allowed the Globe Theatre to broadcast its extraordinary cultural riches worldwide.

In the meantime, our One World Foundation artistic director, George Rondo, ever vigilant for an opportunity to support the arts, got us to the White House in 1997. It was through George's contact with Frankie Hewett, the manager of Ford's Theatre, Nancy and I found ourselves at the White House. It was the annual meeting and theatre event at Ford's Theatre in Washington, D.C. (better known as The President's Theatre, where Lincoln was assassinated), and the weekend-long event began with an evening at Ford's Theatre, with Little Richard and Whoopi Goldberg performing. Later, on that same stage, Frankie Hewett enumerated the number of important personages present in the audience, including President Bill Clinton, first lady Hillary, and later mentioned Nancy and me and our One World Foundation. We were present because of OWF's $10,000 contribution to a Ford Theater Production. It was quite an honor.

The next evening we attended a beautiful dinner under the Capitol Dome. Frankie Hewett had arranged the evening with Tip O'Neill and it was an evening to acknowledge contributors to Ford's Theatre. The final evening was when we attended a reception at the White House and as we were standing in line, we ran into Sam Waterston (*Law & Order*), who was very pleasant and seemed quite impressed by One World Foundation's accomplishments.

Those were golden years for us, as Nancy and I divided our time between two beautiful homes... our comfortable condo in Ponte Vedra Beach, Florida, and our villa in Cagnes-sur-Mer, France.

In 1997, Nancy and I celebrated our 10th wedding anniversary in Paris with our friends, Laird Koenig and Mary Jo Connealy, at the reopening of famous chef Joel Robuchon's restaurant. Sadly, Mary Jo has since passed away, but we will never forget the sound of her bell-like laughter. It seemed we spent the entire night laughing. Laird was at his height of comic wordplay and satire, and we, his audience, were at our height of appreciation. Humor was king that evening in Paris. We celebrated life with good friends. It doesn't get better than that.

CHAPTER 15

Mistral, Wind of Change

In the late 1990s and early 2000s, One World Foundation continued to support the wonderful Syrinx Orchestra and also began to support several worthwhile arts endeavors in North Florida.

In 2000, I was elected to the Board of Trustees of the Museum of Contemporary Art (MOCA) Jacksonville, Florida, after several years of actively being involved with art exhibits there. Nancy and I brought Israeli artist Rivka Rosenthal to Jacksonville in 1999 to exhibit her work at MOCA. Back in 1996, at the annual international art festival in Cagnes-sur-Mer, we met Rivka, and were so taken with her paintings that we bought four of them. What struck me was the heart that I saw in her paintings. I saw by her dramatic strokes and brilliant color schemes, all in plain wooden frames, that Rivka had both passion and talent. "Rivka Rosenthal… Luminosity," was the name of the exhibit, which featured 40 of her paintings. The titles of her paintings were taken from the Old Testament of the Bible, Ecclesiastes, and feature many colorful scenes of Israel, both realistic and abstract. In some of her paintings, fanciful three-dimensional flowers adorn the canvas; in others, she uses lace in three-dimensional patterns. Rivka considers cloth and canvas "family," and creates her paintings accordingly. It was an extremely successful exhibit.

Nancy and I enjoyed both of our homes equally, traveling back and forth to "winter" in Ponte Vedra Beach and "summer" in France, and supporting the arts in both communities in every way we could.

The summer of 2003 in Europe required additional strength of body and of character. In France the highest temperatures of the century caused over 10,000 deaths but our friends, Aprille and Bill Glover proved their courage that summer nonetheless. They completed a roundtrip Paris — Santiago de Compostello, Spain pilgrimage (About 1,000 miles doubled). The Glovers were even accompanied by a live burro for a few weeks of their pilgrimage. They kept us informed of their progress by internet.

During that long hot summer, we benefitted at night from a strong cross-draft across our patio and separate air-conditioning in kitchen and bedroom. We spent many long, cool hours during the day in our pool, enjoying good wine and our magnificent view.

For daytime cooling, our pool was quite sufficient; however, a distant neighbor's inattention to his overturned gas-fire grill cost us and hundreds of neighbors thousands of Euros in repairs and lost property value due to the resulting fire.

The famous western wind, called the Mistral, came at us with added force that August, blowing east from the Rhone River, and spreading

Pool and Patio – Cagnes-sur-Mer

numerous small fires throughout the hills of the Alps Maritime, Marseilles, and the Department of the Var. We found out later, in talking to other citizens of Cagnes-sur-Mer, that a grill had overturned on a tree-lined hill and caused numerous small fires.

Our initial warning came from tiny streaks of fire topping two ranges of hills to the west of us. The fire continued its movement down our closest hills toward the valley between us, so we gathered a few belongings and prepared for exit by car to the east and then down to the bordering Mediterranean coast. When we reached the junction of our driveway and the road south, we stopped for a look back at our house and the neighboring forest. Suddenly, we spied an official looking jean-clad man where our neighbor's property met ours. Apparently (to me) this man had authority over fire endangered areas in this emergency, and I thought we should go to him to learn the best refugee action at that moment. We jumped out of the car and ran to join him. He was, indeed, a volunteer fireman and the authority over the last moment before flight. He continued to concentrate on watching the advancing fire as I grabbed a watering hose and asked Nancy to turn on an outside faucet. No water resulted as the pump had already failed. Thus, Nancy, I, and our blue-jean clad fireman trotted up our private road on foot exactly parallel with the advancing fire that was devouring the neighbor's grass on our left.

Once on the town road, we moved our car 50 yards down so that we could continue to watch our property, which we hoped would benefit from the aerial water bombers promised to our neighborhood. Also visible from the town road at that moment was a 65-yard row of our beautiful blue cypress trees (over 16 feet in height), which were beginning to be attacked by wildfire. One helicopter tried to drop about 400 gallons of water on some of the blue cypresses, but this was dramatically unsuccessful because of the wind and inadequate space for a helicopter to maneuver closely enough to the trees.

Our house was designed somewhat like an expanded tower — wide at the bottom and narrow at the top — and fortunately, this unique design kept the Mistral constantly in motion around it so that it was saved inadvertently by a design factor. However, there were heroes involved in its salvation as well, and the first was Etienne Ciarlo. He had been hired by Michel Natale only three weeks previously as an apprentice mason and all-around helper. That Sunday, Etienne was enjoying the company of his girlfriend and other friends in the neighboring town of Villeneuve Loubet and happened to look east in the direction of Cagnes-sur-Mer, which was at a much greater height than his vantage point below. He spotted a regular line of fire which led directly to our property, and immediately took the initiative, hopping on his motorbike and speeding off in the direction of our home. As he arrived on the road above our house, he noticed a thin column of smoke rising from the edge of our patio. Etienne argued with a fireman on the road, convincing him to make an inspection of the house and they descended on our property together. They found that a burning chaise lounge had been blown against a wall under a portion of wooden roof support. With water from the swimming pool, that fire was quickly extinguished, and the damage did not represent the threat to the roof that might have been had Etienne not acted so quickly.

Other heroes of the fire were Michel and Fred Natale, who had to haul away from their places of storage on our property three of their automobiles, a trailer and a boat. They had parked these vehicles against walls beneath a big tree so that they were unobtrusive. Their possessions were simply burned out by the fire.

Fred and Michel were subsequently called on to work long hours on helping us repair, refurbish and replant. They were absolutely essential to our recovery and we rewarded them accordingly.

On the Monday following the fire, we had a general assembly of workers on the property, including Michel and Fred, and discovered that the damage was light and generally superficial The stone wall which bound the swimming pool to the patio had only suffered scorch marks and was easily repaired. New paint on a few other areas would cover any hint of fire damage. Much replanting was necessary, but the house itself remained nearly unscathed. Of course, it was even more apparent to us than ever before that the property was still a work in progress and had needed some work even prior to the fire.

The fire and the expenses involved in even the slight refurbishing that resulted turned out to be the catalyst that Nancy and I needed to make a decision that had been lurking in the background for some time. We needed to schedule a departure from our French home and take up permanent residence in Florida. We'd known, prior to the fire, that the cost of maintaining two homes was becoming too much and we would eventually have to sell the house in France, but our schedule was suddenly accelerated. We had to get the repairs and replanting done before the insurance company would even consider reimbursing us, and it was in 2005 that we finally made the transition.

In order to sell the house, it was my thought that every trace of the fire had to be obliterated, also the sooner we got out of there, the more money we would realize from the sale of the property. We had been lucky. We needed to get out while our luck still held.

Our neighbor on the hill above ours had not been fortunate. The fire had come through their kitchen windows, straight through their stone house, which had been completely gutted by the fire. It was ghastly.

Possibly the most important hero having to do with the aftermath of the fire was Mr. Sicsic, who was a former highly positioned official in charge of real estate procedures in the area of Cagnes-sur-Mer. He liked us and knew he would be paid well for his services. He found us a buyer for our house and also dealt with the insurance company, using every bit of influence he could gather to get us the right price. We were paid a wonderful price, considering that Cagnes is not well known to people who live the high life. The couple who bought our house fell in love with it. Alain and Francine Verger du Quene are old nobility — a romantic Parisian couple who felt that our house was the perfect place to continue that romance. It was a wonderful find for them and a terrific outcome for Nancy and me. Alain and Francine continue to love the house in Cagnes-sur-Mer, and Nancy and I delight in our home in Ponte Vedra Beach.

One final irony of the Mistral of 2003... we had escaped to a hotel in the small town of St. Laurent du Var, checking in with no luggage. To say we were feeling displaced is an understatement. As was my habit upon first entering any hotel room, I walked over to the large picture window and drew back the drapes. Unfortunately, the panoramic vista was one that nearly brought tears to my eyes. Three big water bombers (Canadaires) were heading directly toward us from the direction of our hill after having exhausted their water supply. The sight of those water bombers returning so majestically from their task, regardless of the fact that it had been accomplished too late to save our beautiful blue cypress trees, seemed to be a strange salute... a dramatic farewell that left no doubt in my mind it was time for us to move on.

CHAPTER 16

Looking Back...
Looking Forward

During my time spent living in both Europe and the United States from 1958 through 2006, I had the privilege of earning several positions of significance in the art world, including recognition by the Writers Society of the United Nations, New York City, and involvement through One World Foundation participation in the Pulitzer Prize-winning production, *The Young Man from Atlanta*, by Horton Foote, and as First Commissioner of the Bill T. Jones Ballet, *Still Here*.

From 2000 to 2008, I was on the Board of Trustees for Jacksonville's Museum of Contemporary Art (MOCA). The main task of One World Foundation at MOCA was to provide all equipment for the MOCA Theater, including projectors and sound system as well as assuring permanent contact between the stage and the sound booth. MOCA also benefitted from the free loans of a considerable amount of additional motion picture and sound equipment as needed in the theater for its operations. Contributions from One World Foundation paid the salary of the engineer in charge of the theater, Carlos Rodriguez, for the eight years I was on the Board of Trustees. At about the same time that my eligibility as a Trustee ended, MOCA became a partner of the University of North Florida. Today, in recognition of the excellent service it provides to the community, One World Foundation continues to contribute support to MOCA.

Later, as vice president of the Cultural Center of Ponte Vedra, I was given valuable knowledge of staging of fashion shows and similar events, plus the honor of working beside Mary Marx, one of the most brilliant executives I've ever known anywhere. I have recently renewed my membership in that worthy organization.

During the first years of the 21st century, Nancy and I maintained our New York connections, continuing to contribute to productions of the Irish Repertory Theatre and, occasionally, the York Theatre. Recently, the W. Scott McLucas Studio Theater, which is located on the Irish Rep property, achieved renewed fame when producer Charlotte Moore presented a landmark production of Harold Pinter's thoughts and writings directed by John Malkovich and performed by British actor Julian Sands.

In Cagnes-sur-Mer, I was elected vice president of the Renoir Museum, a unique honor that gave me great pleasure and allowed One World Foundation to help provide some of the museum's most exciting exhibitions, including the exhibit in 2000 of Aprille Glover's dramatic sculptures that were so beautifully photographed by our friend, Jacques Renoir. In 2003, Jacques wrote a book about his great-grandfather Pierre-Auguste Renoir, titled *Le tableau amoureux* (*The Painting of Lovers*) and inscribed one of his books to Nancy and me with the following words: "For Scott and Nancy – who do so much for the Renoir Museum, with devotion and affection; with all my sincere friendship. La Gaude, June 1, 2003. Renoir." Coincidentally, coinciding with the 2013 publication of my book, the book written by Jacques Renoir was reprinted in response to interest inspired by a new movie titled *Renoir*. Based loosely on Jacques' book and directed by Gilles Bourdos, the French-language movie is billed by New York Times movie critic Stephen Holden, "a compassionate late-life portrait of this French Impressionist painter..." It is still exciting to recall the enjoyable days Nancy and I spent at Renoir's home, Les Collettes, at Cagnes-sur-Mer on the Cote d'Azur (now the museum).

As founder and President of the Syrinx Orchestra and Chorus, conducted by Errol Girdlestone, I am gratified to say that I spent many good years working vigorously with wonderful musicians and enjoying some of the finest musical entertainment on the face of the earth. The name Syrinx, Pipes of Pan (Greek: One for many) was serendipitous.

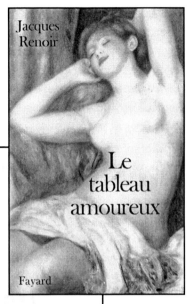

LE TABLEAU AMOUREUX

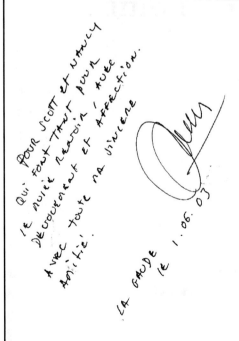

The leader of that marvelous group of musicians, Errol Girdlestone, is of Welsh descent, which explains a great deal about his excellent character. If you are a Scotch-Irish American as I am, the Welshman is likely to like you and give you a fair chance to become his friend and equal, and so it happened with Errol and me.

The friendship that developed between Errol and me has been greatly enhanced by the relationship Nancy and I share with his beautiful wife, Sue. A former professional ballerina who is strong, loyal, and has a delightful sense of humor, we have enjoyed many memorable and thrilling musical moments with the Girdlestones. Sue is wonderfully supportive of Errols' career.

Errol is a discoverer of new music and new aspects of music which he loves to develop. He also enjoys the historic aspects of music and loves planning the ideal music program. As for me, Errol discovered that I knew a few things about music and its place in the theater, plus opera, and, incidentally, that I also understand how a fire extinguisher works. He also learned that I knew how to judge the playing of an orchestra and what the solo instruments should sound like. His choice of singing soloists did not bother me but both Errol and I became concerned when a famed jungle expert (my choice, alone) played his array of flutes and pipes

Sue and Errol Girdlestone

one night as entertainment in the Vence Cathedral. On that opening night our audience answered our concerns by judging this soloist magnificent and unique. From then on, Errol Girdlestone and I trusted each other without doubt.

Season after season, Errol rolled out splendid examples of great music. One could hear in a season pieces of great spirit such as the Rossini Overture of the Opera The Italian in Algiers, the Mozart Symphonia Concertante, K364, Dvorak's Romance Opus 11 in F Minor, and Mozart for the Syrinx vocal ensemble plus the full orchestra, and the opening of the Opera La Clemenza di Tito, and Beethoven's Fantasie for Piano, Chorus and Orchestra, Opus 80 with the Ensemble of the Syrinx Orchestra, one of the world's greatest pianists, Francois Rene DuChable, and the Syrinx Vocal Ensemble.

Going back to really early days, we played music in the glorious venue of the Great Cathedral of St. Maximin (dedicated to Mary Magdalene who is said to be buried in the crypt of the church). At St. Maximin, we played several wonderful pieces of music, including the Mozart Requiem, with its score displayed in the Luck's sheet music version. (Luck's was our supplier of sheet music throughout the years of Syrinx.) This score intrigued and excited Errol. He later researched the piece and wrote a fascinating essay on the history of the Requiem, as follows:

"Originally written in answer to a commission from Count Franz von Walsegg, the requiem was far from complete before Mozart died. Only the opening movement was fully completed. However, he had fully indicated a large amount of the choral parts for much more of the work and sketched in some orchestration to go with them, mostly the bass and some string passages.

In order for his widow, Constanze, to benefit financially from the commission, the work had to be completed – not as insuperable a task as it might seem because in the course of composition Mozart had already handed out pages to be completed according to his instructions by a couple of amanuenses: Süssmayr and Eybler.

Eybler had the first shot at posthumous completion but soon gave up and handed the manuscript back to Mozart's wife, who then turned to Süssmayr. He completed the job, claiming probably more than his fair share of credit, having pillaged from some of Mozart's other works (and possibly even some by other composers) and recycling the first two movements as the last two, so the final work is in a kind of sandwich form.

The beauty of the edition you sent me [Luck's Music] is that it shows what is in Mozart's hand and what is not, plus the uncompleted Eybler version which was handed back to Constanze, as well as Süssmayr's completion.

In any event, the skullduggery didn't stop there. The Count himself was well known for commissioning works from known composers, having them performed et soirees chez lui and passing them off as his own compositions with a smile that nobody dared question. The only innocent parties (who received not a sou between them) were Mozart and Eybler – everybody else, including Mozart's widow, was to some extent a crook!"

Our connection with Conductor Errol Girdlestone continues to be strong today, although the Syrinx Orchestra has greatly reduced the number of its concerts in recent years. Errol is currently involved in formation of an exciting new chorus that is traveling throughout France to perform at various venues.

Early in his career, Errol Girdlestone worked with Brian Dickie, former Artistic Director of the Wexford Festival in Ireland and General Administrator of the Glyndbourne Festival Opera where many leading British singers began their careers. In the summer of 1998, when Brian was adviser to the International Youth Foundation during the establishment of the European Union Opera, he asked Errol to assist him by being in charge of full musical preparation for an opera at the Baden-Baden Festspielhaus - Tchaikovsky's "Eugene Onegin," in Russian.

Although Errol would have other duties during the run of "Eugene Onegin," his main work was to rehearse the chorus, the soloists, the orchestra, and then the ensemble in preparation for the full dress rehearsal and the performances. The performances were under the baton of the eminent Russian conductor Gennadi Rozhdestvensky who had a summer absolutely packed with other major conducting assignments, with no time to rehearse "Eugene Onegin." Thus he depended on the broad experience of Errol Girdlestone and the great value of his recommendation by Brian Dickie. Indeed, Errol had spent many summers preparing

singers and musicians for opera performances from South and Central America to northern Europe, as well as England, etc. So he knew what had to be done! All the tasks ahead of him were wrapped in the language of Pyotr Illyich Tchaikovsky! The only solution for Errol was "back to school," building rapidly on any earlier knowledge he may have had of the Russian language.

The rehearsals went very well. An extremely successful dress rehearsal guaranteed a great performance on opening night. Maestro Rozhdestvensky arrived in Baden-Baden to take over the conductor's baton from Errol who joined his fellow artists backstage and awaited the conductor's downstroke to bring dramatic and musical life to Eugene Onegin. When Brian Dickie came to share the jubilation of the cast and orchestra after the opening night performance, one could sense how content he was to have matched Errol's great ability exactly with that of the masterful Russian conductor. Thus, once again a producer demonstrated his great skill for the artistic benefit of the cast and audience. In the theatrical world, we look to our producers to make the best choices and Brian Dickie showed us how, once again, that

Certificate of Appreciation

presented to

Mr. Walter S. McLucas

In recognition of your important contribution to the ongoing fight against hatred and intolerance in America.

The name shown above will be added to the Wall of Tolerance in Montgomery, Alabama, to provide inspiration to all those who choose to take a stand against hatred.

Thank you for taking a stand.

MORRIS DEES, FOUNDER
SOUTHERN POVERTY LAW CENTER

Stetson Kennedy with Nancy & Scott at Beluthahatchee - 2011

September night in Baden-Baden.

Later, when Dickie was appointed General Director of the Chicago Opera Theater (COT), he called on Errol regularly to come to Chicago as a guest conductor and chorus master. During Dickie's tenure with COT, he produced 20 Chicago premieres and was honored many times, including being twice named "Chicagoan of the Year" by the Chicago Tribune Newspaper. Our One World Foundation was honored, in April of 2012, to sponsor the season opener of Dickie's last year as General Director of COT.

Opening at the Harris Theater to excellent reviews was Dmitri Shostakovich's Moscow Cheryomushki, conducted by Alexander Platt with assistance by our own Errol Girdlestone. Nancy and I had the pleasure of being there for that splendid performance.

Today, the focus of One World Foundation is to support several art forms such as fabulous painting and sculpture created by our longtime friend, NALL, as well as the works created later by Aprille Glover and other artists. We are also supporters of the annual *Christ Church Nutcracker*, which is performed only once a year at the University of North Florida's Lazzara Theatre before an audience of 1,500, and benefits an orphanage, the pediatric hospice and other charitable health programs. The educational arm of One World Foundation is reaching out to help the Cultural Center at Ponte Vedra with its outreach program to elementary school students.

Our dedication to social justice, equality and the environment is carried on by support of the Stetson Kennedy Foundation in its determination to provide a tranquil place of peace at his home, Beluthahatchee, now a Florida hertiage park and wildlife sancturary where activists, artists and environmentalists come to study Florida's flora and fauna.

In conjunction with our support of the Stetson Kennedy Foundation, Nancy and I attended a Jacksonville NAACP dinner at Stetson's invitation in the spring of 2011. Morris Dees was the keynote speaker that night. Coincidentally, I recently discovered that one of my treating physicians is the son of the same Morris Dees who founded the Southern Poverty Law Center.

Sadly, our new friend, Stetson Kennedy, passed away on August 7, 2011, but it was our privilege to know him, if even for a short time. Nancy and Stetson had several memories of Paris in common, both of them having been there in the same era, and Kennedy was a supporter, as are we, of the Southern Poverty Law Center.

Stetson Kennedy was a man who studied the animal kingdom from the time he was a boy growing up on and near the St. Johns River and deep in the woods of Mandarin at his beloved Beluthahatchee. He decided, as a boy, to become a zoologist of his own species – humanity, and he would have been thrilled to read a 2013 New York Times article entitled "Hope in the Age of Man" written by an impressive group of like-minded scientists: Emma Marris (author of Rambunctious Garden: Saving Nature in a Post-Wild World), Peter Kareiva (Chief Scientist for the Nature Conservancy), Joseph Mascaro (Carnegie Institution for Science and the Smithsonian Tropical Research Institute), and Erie C. Ellis (Associate Professor of Geography and Environmental Systems at the University of Maryland, Baltimore County). These scientists have named the current transformation occurring on planet Earth the "Anthropocene" (Age of Man), and assert that humanity cannot simply give up in despair regarding the damage that has been done to the natural environment, but instead, must consider actively moving species at risk of extinction from climate change, designing ecosystems to maintain wildlife, filter water and sequester carbon, thereby restoring the once magnificent ecosystems like Yellowstone and the Gulf of Mexico. "We can fight sprawl and mindless development even as we cherish the exuberant nature that can increasingly be found in our own cities, from native gardens to green roofs," the scientists wrote, "and we can do this even as we continue to fight for international agreements on limiting the greenhouse gases that are warming the planet." They concluded that the Anthropocene does not represent the failure of environmentalism, but is instead, a stage on which a new, more positive and forward-looking environmentalism can be built. One World Foundation wants to be a part of that positive construction!

Our ongoing support of the theater arts is more exciting than ever before! I am inspired and overwhelmed with memories whenever I hear the lyrics to the song, "The Eyes of Texas," written in 1903 by John Sinclair and now the alma mater of the University of Texas at Austin:

"The Eyes of Texas are upon you, all the live long day.
The Eyes of Texas are upon you, you cannot get away.
Do not think you can escape them, at night or early in the morn.
The Eyes of Texas are upon you, 'til Gabriel blows his horn."

It has been my honor to have befriended a Texas family, well-known in our American culture and admired by all. The head of that family was a great playwright, screenwriter and theatrical director named Horton Foote. Horton's Texas eyes were as sharp as those of an eagle and his courage and pride were unequaled. This memoir was inspired by Horton's works. As a master of style, he had few equals, and I have attempted herein to emulate him. Horton's influence and also that of his daughter, Hallie, have been pivotal in helping me

Hallie Foote and Scott McLucas pose at Players by the Sea Theater, 2011
(Horton Foote Portrait painted by Barbara Sarvis)

Scott & Nancy McLucas, 2012
Photo by Maggie Fitzroy

Henry, Ruth A., Molly and Danny Rosenbloom

formulate this memoir.

In 2009 and 2010, I became enthusiastic about the professionalism of a nearby community theater, "Players by the Sea," in Jacksonville Beach, Florida. The quality of the performances produced by the local professional equity theater often suffered by comparison with those produced by Players by the Sea. In 2010, I noticed that a play by my friend, Horton Foote, *Dividing the Estate*, was scheduled for production in May 2011, at Players by the Sea. Pursuing an idea about providing professional assistance to that community theater, I sought an introduction to Joseph Schwarz, executive director of Players by the Sea. Upon meeting Joe, it was clear to me that we had much in common and shared a vision for the future of a Horton Foote Memorial, so I suggested that One World Foundation become involved by first requesting that Horton's daughter, Hallie Foote, come to spend two or three weeks working with and assisting the cast of *Dividing the Estate*. Hallie was nominated for an Emmy Award for her Broadway performance in the play in 2009. We had known Hallie since her 1994 off-Broadway performance in *Night Seasons* (also authored by Horton Foote), which our foundation had co-produced. Things went well with the Players by the Sea and One World Foundation co-production of *Dividing the Estate*. However, during rehearsals, the play's artistic director had difficulties with some cast members, so Joe Schwarz asked Hallie to step in and help. By opening night, the cast had learned much from Hallie's extensive experience and familiarity with her father's work, and they all gave heartwarming performances which resulted in sold-out houses for the entire run of the play.

Before her arrival, Joe and I also asked Hallie if we could add to her accountabilities by having her do some readings from her father's works before a guest audience at the Jacksonville Main Library.

We, of course, were pleased to provide Hallie's usual professional compensation for this in addition to her stipend and expenses for helping with *Dividing the Estate*.

Equally important during that springtime set of weeks with Hallie Foote, Joe and I began discussing with her and her brother, Horton Foote, Jr., the future of a major monument to Horton's genius as well as storage of documents and other elements of his cultural legacy. The Foote family home is in Wharton, Texas, and one or two of its buildings will be used for lodging award-winning playwrights working on new grants.

We are looking forward to a bright blooming of new theater works and reproductions of older works under serious professional management. We also hope we can include public and private support for Horton Foote's legacy so that it will remain under "The Eyes of Texas," and the world, well past Gabriel's last trumpet blast.

At this writing, the first playwright to benefit from the writer's program of the Horton Foote Legacy Foundation has already begun work in Wharton, even before the official announcement of the commencement of that Foundation. David Lindsay-Abaire has agreed to be our inaugural playwright-in-residence at the Horton Foote home in February of 2013.

"David's resume is beyond impressive and I am very pleased that he is as excited about being in Wharton as we are to be hosting him," said Joe Schwarz. "He was the recent winner of the 2012 Horton Foote Prize for Outstanding New American Play, *Good People*."

Also coming in the spring of 2013 is One World Foundation's co-production at Players by the Sea of Horton Foote's play, *Trip to Bountiful*, starring Gayle Fotheringill and directed by Joe Schwarz. It promises as successful a run as *Dividing the Estate* in 2011, and the title, *Trip to Bountiful* is fitting in that it can be applied to the long-term vision we share for the Horton Foote Legacy Foundation.

As I near the end of this writing project, I feel a sense of pleasure at completing a broad act of creation: writing about my life, some of which I enjoyed and some of which I managed well, despite challenges. The most critical 35-year period from Spring 1951 through Spring 1986, I have always considered largely wasted because I devoted so much of that time to saving the life of a very selfish and undeserving person. However, having reflected more on that time, I realize that I actually did make the better choice. Despite the deep resentment bubbling constantly just beneath the surface, I chose the path of least resistance and avoided cruelty. Whether or not this was cowardice is a matter of opinion and is now immaterial. John M. Johnson died a natural death through no fault of mine and I, thank God, was given the great privilege of spending all my remaining days with the most wonderful woman in the world.

Nancy and I are one. Our One World Foundation, Inc. has made a positive difference in many lives over the past three decades and we have reached out to personally help friends and family as well. We continue to feel the same love and respect for one another as we felt when we said our marital vows. Life is good, and it has always been so for us.

When Nancy and I were married, her brother Jack McQuiggan, and his family became my family, too. Jack is deceased now and so is his late wife, Mary Doyle, but their beautiful progeny, Ruth A. McQuiggan, her husband, Danny Rosenbloom, and their children, Henry and Molly, are now our beloved surrogate children and grandchildren. We are devoted to them, as they are to us.

Danny, who studied at the North Carolina School of the Arts, the University of North Carolina at Chapel Hill, and Brown University, is one of the most imaginative and innovative young men I've ever known. Currently the Managing Director of Brand New School, an internationally acclaimed production studio, Danny co-produced Project Discovery, one of One World Foundation's most exciting initiatives back in the 1990s. Distance learning was a new concept in those days and Danny was well ahead of his time. I remain astounded by his impressive creative talent, which is surpassed only by his marvelous enjoyment of playing with his family. As the patriarch of his little family of four, Danny communicates love to his wife and children in so many ways… and I find the enthusiastic playfulness of their family to be absolutely delightful. It is a joyful quality of family life that I missed growing up a "little rich boy" in a household of stiff formality with parents who consumed too much alcohol and vented their frustrations on one another at the dinner

Molly Rosenbloom! Wow!

table. Being included in the playtime atmosphere at the residence of Ruth A. and Danny and their great kids has been one of the true pleasures of my life.

Ruth A. is a strong advocate of women's issues and backs up her views on human rights with activism, having produced a documentary several years ago about Alternate Ways of Procreation. She is currently involved in exploring the complexities of child rearing in today's society and has garnered first-hand knowledge through being the devoted mother of a middle-school-aged daughter and high school-aged son. In her "spare" time, Ruth A. lends her considerable film and theatre expertise to a select group of IT clientele seeking to enhance their internet and arts knowledge. A devoted wife and mother, Ruth A. is also an independent woman of depth and high intellect. She is one of the most fascinating people I know.

At age 12, Molly has inherited her mother's beauty, spirit, and intelligence. It shines from her eager face and brings a smile on the coldest day in New York. Molly aims at becoming an actress like her late grandmother, Mary Doyle, but in the meantime, she enjoys playing soccer and is looking forward to being on a traveling team in 2013. Nancy is convinced that Molly is channeling Mary, and that very well may be true. When we spoke with her in the spring of 2013, Molly was planning to try out for the school play, *I Am*, and was completely confident that she would earn a leading role.

Molly's older brother, Henry, is already a leader in that he is a top student at one of the finest schools in New York City. Stuyvesant High School, founded in 1904, is one of the oldest, largest and most prestigious high schools in the nation. Henry, now 15,

Scott and Cousin Dee - Toddlers

writes for the school newspaper and is involved in the drama department as a director. He emulates both his father and mother in his vision, humor and intelligence.

The wonderful freedom of expression shared by the Rosenbloom family is a new kind of democracy to me – one that, as I said, I never had the privilege of experiencing as a boy. Together and separately, each of them is exciting, articulate and wonderful. Their camaraderie, at first, was so unexpected to me that I was in awe. Now, I simply bask in their enthusiasm and love it!

Even during those years I once considered wasted, life handed me some fabulous opportunities for growth and knowledge. Learning to appreciate the depth of the great Wagner operas was good, deep education for me. Admiring Roman Polanski as Mozart in *Amadeus* in a Parisian theater was an unforgettable experience, as was *Sarah et le cri de la Langouste*, riveted into my mind by Georges Wilson and Delphine Seyrig, France's greatest actors performing their perfect tour de force roles in Paris and at the Edinburgh Festival in 1984.

From childhood on, I have been most grateful for the life lessons provided by my mother, Hamilton (Hammie), whom I loved deeply.

When I look back, I'm also eternally grateful to my father who saved my life by killing a poisonous snake about to clamp his teeth on my left foot, and earned my admiration from that moment on.

I remember, fondly, and continue to keep in touch with my cousin Dee (Dorothea Meriwether) who still lives in a fine house in Kansas, just over the border from Missouri. Dee and I were playmates sharing games and ghost stories, from the time we were toddlers. We remain close to this day.

Life has been good to me even from the very first, when I was born at the beginning of the Great Depression and yet, remained one of the few of my generation who was unaffected by the poverty that swept the nation. I was raised in a privileged, private school atmosphere, as were my childhood chums, "Berky" Welch, George Ketcham, Joe Hall, and Dicky Durwood. My godfather was "Uncle Billy" Kemper. My cousins, Mary Gamble Meriwether and her sister, Dee, completed the circle.

I was too young to be involved in World War II, except as the son of an officer, but I remember how eager my Uncle Gilmer Meriwether was to serve his country in the Army Air Corps B25 Squadrons in Europe. As an intelligence officer, he was obliged to fly on some of the raids of Northern Italy, through the terrible flack fired up in defense of targeted factories. He discovered to his shame that crews sometimes dumped their bombs into the Mediterranean instead of on military targets. This haunted him, as did the early death of his and Aunt Dorothea's son, Buddy. Although he suffered post-war anxieties, he forgave family members and other associates for their cowardice during those five years of hellish war.

My father also flew missions as a planning officer in the Air Transport Command, sending aircraft to Great Britain from northern airfields in the U.S., Canada, and Newfoundland.

And while war was raging, I was experiencing three years of challenging prep school, during which I experienced impressive events such as a most impressive debate by two recently returned servicemen about learning responsibility and the true meaning of citizenship. Next came my gratitude to my parents for their choices of new marriage partners. I also enjoyed meeting and getting to know my new step-relations and then plunged into the world of professional theater, which deeply affected my creative life, even as I become 84 years old.

Ironically, after my carefree youth, I was destined to be the oldest draftee (at age 27) in my company at Fort Dix in 1955. I did, however, serve my country proudly and well, also learning a great deal about teaching with television. My years in the service prepared me in many areas for successful careers in advertising and broadcasting.

My parents had the good taste to name me after my prominent and prosperous grandfather, Walter Scott McLucas, who ended his days as President of the National Bank of Detroit and left me a legacy of honor and wealth. Throughout my youth, my grandfather was the powerful patriarch of our family, to whom everyone paid homage. One photograph of Grandfather McLucas that is dramatically descriptive of his status at the National Bank of Detroit was taken just 13 days following the Japanese bombing of Pearl Harbor on December 20, 1941. All eyes were on my grandfather as he presented a solemn Christmas message to a large assemblage of bank employees. The historic photo had been stored in the records department of the National Bank of Detroit for years before being shared with me, his only surviving grandson.

With my family history going back to the American Revolution and my maternal grandfather's fascination for historic military figures such as

W. Scott McLucas addressing the employees of the National Bank of Detroit

December 20, 1941

Napoleon Bonaparte, it is no wonder that I have spent a lifetime observing the world through the eyes of an historian.

During my eight plus decades, people of great significance have enriched my appreciation for history, often allowing me to be part of the process. At this time in the 21st century, as our country approached the year 2013 and I approached the final chapter of my memoir, a tumultuous upheaval occurred that changed the course of my personal history as well as impacting countless other lives. As Hurricane Sandy swept away the homes of people along the shores of the East Coast, it also swept away any doubts in my head regarding the next extensive project of One World Foundation, which focuses on preserving our environment.

For years, when Nancy and I traveled up the coast from Florida to the mountains of North Carolina, I expounded loudly as we passed seashore after seashore burdened by the blight of huge homes and buildings teetering precariously near the ocean, as if beckoning the next hurricane to blow them away. A pet peeve that, until now, was mainly for the ears of my long-suffering wife, was the encroachment of humanity onto the natural beauty of the beach as evidenced by the enormous expanse of buildings as far as the eye could see. Then, to top it off, there was the rebuilding and rebuilding again of these same buildings on that shrinking beach property after storms attacked from the sea. A horrendous error has occurred here, I reasoned. Inevitably, somewhere along the way, I'd turn to Nancy, shake my head, and comment wryly, "It'll be high tide in Hickory pretty soon!"

For those who don't recognize the humor in that statement, let me explain that Hickory, North Carolina, is so far inland and at a mountainous elevation that flooding is not yet a concern, though tornado damage cannot be ruled out.

With Sandy's destruction, my concern about the economic and human loss incurred by people who build on the beaches, year after year, found a voice! That voice appeared, loud and clear, in a November 8, 2012 New York Times article written by Dr. Orrin H. Pilkey, Emeritus Professor of Earth Sciences at Duke University, author of more than a dozen books, and co-author of The Rising Sea.

Dr. Pilkey's article, with headlines shouting WE NEED TO RETREAT FROM THE BEACH, follows, in its entirety:

AS ocean waters warm, the Northeast is likely to face more Sandy-like storms. And as sea levels continue to rise, the surges of these future storms will be higher and even more deadly. We can't stop these powerful storms. But we can reduce the deaths and damage they cause.

Hurricane Sandy's immense power, which destroyed or damaged thousands of homes, actually pushed the footprints of the barrier islands along the South Shore of Long Island and the Jersey Shore landward as the storm carried precious beach sand out to deep waters or swept it across the islands. This process of barrier-island migration toward the mainland has gone on for 10,000 years.

Yet there is already a push to rebuild homes close to the beach and bring back the shorelines to where they were. The federal government encourages this: there will be billions available to replace roads, pipelines and other infrastructure and to clean up storm debris, provide security and emergency housing. Claims to the National Flood Insurance Program could reach $7 billion. And the Army Corps of Engineers will be ready to mobilize its sand-pumping dredges, dump trucks and bulldozers to rebuild beaches washed away time and again.

But this "let's come back stronger and better" attitude, though empowering, is the wrong approach to the increasing hazard of living close to the rising sea. Disaster will strike again. We should not simply replace all lost property and infrastructure. Instead, we need to take account of rising sea levels, intensifying storms and continuing shoreline erosion.

I understand the temptation to rebuild. My parents' retirement home, built at 13 feet above sea level, five blocks from the shoreline in Waveland, Miss., was flooded to the ceiling during Hurricane Camille in 1969. They rebuilt it, but the house was completely destroyed by Hurricane Katrina in 2005. (They had died by then.) Even so, rebuilding continued in Waveland. A year after Katrina, one empty Waveland beachfront lot, on which successive houses had been wiped away by Hurricanes Camille and Katrina, was for sale for $800,000.

That is madness. We should strongly discourage the reconstruction of destroyed or badly damaged beachfront homes in New Jersey and New York. Some very valuable property will have to be abandoned to make the community less vulnerable to storm surges. This is tough medicine, to be sure, and taxpayers may be forced to compensate homeowners.

But it should save taxpayers money in the long run by ending this cycle of repairing or rebuilding properties in the path of future storms. Surviving buildings and new construction should be elevated on pilings at least two feet above the 100-year flood level to allow future storm overwash to flow underneath. Some buildings should be moved back from the beach.

Respecting the power of these storms is not new. American Indians who occupied barrier islands during the warm months moved to the mainland during the winter storm season. In the early days of European settlement in North America, some communities restricted building to the bay sides of barrier islands to minimize damage. In Colombia and Nigeria, where some people choose to live next to beaches to reduce exposure to malarial mosquitoes, houses are routinely built to be easily moved.

We should also understand that armoring the shoreline with sea walls will not be successful in holding back major storm surges. As experience in New Jersey and elsewhere has shown, sea walls eventually cause the loss of protective beaches. These beaches can be replaced, but only at enormous cost to taxpayers. The 21-mile stretch of beach between Sandy Hook and Barnegat Inlet in New Jersey was replenished between 1999 and 2001 at a cost of $273 million (in 2011 dollars). Future replenishment will depend on finding suitable sand on the continental shelf, where it is hard to find.

And as sea levels rise, replenishment will be required more often. In Wrightsville Beach, N.C., the beach already has been replenished more than 20 times since 1965, at a cost of nearly $53 million (in 2011 dollars). Taxpayers in at least three North Carolina communities — Carteret and Dare Counties and North Topsail Beach — have voted down tax increases to pay for these projects in the last dozen years. The attitude was: we shouldn't have to pay for the beach. We weren't the ones irresponsible enough to build next to an eroding shoreline.

This is not the time for a solution based purely on engineering. The Army Corps undoubtedly will be heavily involved. But as New Jersey and New York move forward, officials should seek advice from oceanographers, coastal geologists, coastal and construction engineers and others who understand the future of rising seas and their impact on barrier islands. We need more resilient development, to be sure. But we *also need to begin to retreat from the ocean's edge.*

Since reading his article, I have had several telephone conferences with Dr. Pilkey and we have agreed to meet in the near future regarding how One World Foundation, Inc. can advance the cause of changing the coastal attitude and, thus, saving lives and property from further devastation.

It is my contention that we must begin immediately to make exploratory visits to the interior of our country in order to establish new outposts of living which will replace our coastal homes. Time is of the essence. Climate change is here and it is imperative that attitude change must follow. Once again, it is about something lost and something found… this time, lives and property were lost, and, hopefully, common sense will be used generously.

Dr. Pilkey and I agree that Hurricane Sandy actually heralded good news in that people are beginning to take seriously the evidence that the retreat from the beach must begin now. By connecting One World Foundation with prestigious and knowledgeable people such as Dr. Orrin Pilkey and his associates, Nancy and I hope to help "stem the tide" of destruction and "shore up" the economy for future generations. I've joked for years about "High Tide in Hickory," thinking of it as a phrase somewhat akin to "When hell freezes over," but with climate change making such dramatic advances on this century, that high tide is not so inconceivable any longer. With my past focus on the arts, I have come to realize that without the basis of terra firma, support for the arts will become moot. One World Foundation will continue its support of the arts; at this time, however, environmental concerns will take precedence as we go forward.

It is my intention to encourage a maximum of research in collaboration with other organizations, charitable and commercial, to assist the population wishing to relocate inland from the coasts of our country. This should involve a minimum of cost and a maximum of economy and facility. Plans for family travel will be established to provide the greatest ease and least friction possible between the transitioning communities and their new neighbors. Prior to accomplishing anything of that magnitude, however, there are a couple of major concerns that must be dealt with: 1) There must be research conducted regarding the availability of strong leadership to carry out the vision of Dr. Pilkey, One World Foundation;

and governmental organizations concerned with population migration. 2) The fresh water and the sea water authorities must confer and seek agreement on common goals going forward.

These are ambitious and daunting projects on which to embark at any age, and I am now in my 80s. However, I believe I still have a few years left to continue work in the arts and in study of environmental changes and their consequences. In 2012, Hurricane Sandy also heralded the onset of mass destruction unless we come to our senses, and treat our climate and homeland with genuine respect. We should also consider a well-planned movement inland with our families, safe from the ravages of devastating storms and vast high seas in the future.

Addenda

ADDENDUM A

Volume 4, pages 1999-2002 of A Standard History of Kansas and Kansans – Excerpts of Narrative by Samuel Newell Simpson:

"In 1855 members of the Territorial Legislature of Kansas were elected by the votes of the citizens of the state of Missouri, who came into the Kansas territory by thousands to vote, carrying every voting district but one, and returning immediately after voting to Missouri. This Legislature passed a code of slave laws to govern the territory and the United States officials and the Army were aiding the territorial officers to execute these laws. The United States government protected every slave state movement. By the summer of 1856 one-third of the free-state settlers had left the Kansas territory because of the enormities of the slave power."

"At this time when there seemed to be total darkness, a man [Simpson] commenced shaping events without knowing it himself or attracting any attention from even his neighbors."

"...In September, 1854, he arrived in what is now called Lawrence, having walked through Missouri."

"... On the first Sabbath after he arrived he organized a Bible class. On the first Sabbath in 1855 he gathered the few children in town together in his office and commenced a Sunday school, which became the Sunday school of the Plymouth Congregational Church of Lawrence."

"In the winter of 1855 and 1856, the Plymouth Congregational church asked this man to go East to raise money for a church building. He accepted, and in raising this money came in contact with Dr. Post of St. Louis; Dr. Thompson, of Buffalo; Henry Ward Beecher and Dr. Bellows in New York and Brooklyn; Dr. Todd, in Pittsburg; Eli Thayer, J. M. S. Williams, Amos A.

Lawrence, Leonard Bacon, Dr. Cabbott, Dr. Webb, Edward Everett, Robert Winthrop, Dr. Wallace and many others in New England."

"… During the dark period in 1856 there were some 30 young men from different southern states scattered throughout Douglass county, boarding with families from Southern states. These young men received 30 dollars per month from the states from which they came. Their occupation was to create such a state of society by burning houses, barns, hay and grain stacks, killing stock and occasionally killing a man, as in the case of Barber, Hoyt and Dow, that free state settlers would cease to come to the territory and many of those already there would leave rather than live under such conditions."

"Dr. Charles Robinson and several other free state men were held as prisoners by United States troops in a camp about eight miles west of Lawrence. Dr. Robinson was the leader of the free-state cause and party in Kansas Territory during the struggle. This unnamed man visited the camp and talked over the conditions. They agreed that a vigilance committee should be formed with two by-laws, viz: To obey orders and to keep secrets and to make it their first business to force out of the country the men who were committing the depredations and murders."

"This man returned to Lawrence and invited to his office Turner Sampson, a democrat from the State of Maine, and Milton Guest, of Indiana, both men being over 45 years of age. The conditions in the county were discussed and it was agreed to organize a vigilance committee with the above by-laws. The three agreed to meet that evening after dark at a vacant house near the Blood Mill. They met and decided upon three persons who should be invited to meet at the same place the next night. At the next meeting there were six persons present and at the next 12. In a short time the committee had grown to have 200 members and they wished to elect this man dictator. He refused and a Mr. Green, who operated a saw mill, was elected dictator. Mr. Green was true and brave and very quiet. His orders were law. It is only when society is in desperate straits that it consents to a dictatorship. The organization did its work well and after a few of the marauders had been visited at night the rest left for Missouri."

"One day soon thereafter, when this man was superintending his Sunday school at Franklin, a Southern man, whose children attended the school, asked him to step to one side and said: 'I think that I ought to tell you that an army from Missouri will be up here in a short time to destroy Lawrence.

They are using a certain log cabin in town as a fort, and already have a cannon there to use against the town when they come up. Please do not give me away.'"

"This unnamed man went up to the camp the next day and informed Dr. Robinson. It was agreed that the fort at Franklin and any others which might be learned of should be taken before the army arrived from Missouri and the cannon secured. The free state party had been on the defensive long enough, and besides, it was known that a company of men under General Lane from the free states was on its way through Iowa and Nebraska to help the free state settlers of Kansas. It was thought well to strike a blow before assistance came. This man returned to Lawrence and the order came to 80 men of the vigilance committee to meet at two points near Franklin after dark the next night. Upon arriving at the points designated one party was to attack the fort at Franklin from the south side and the other party from the north side, and to take it. The men drew near upon their hands and knees so as not to be seen and to expose themselves as little as possible.

They all had Sharps rifles and they used them but to no good purpose. A space had been left open between the logs of the fort about five feet from the ground and those inside could fire through this opening. One free-state man was killed and others wounded. The free-state men were obliged to withdraw. And now what should be done? Some said the fort could not be taken without a cannon.

The men were wet with the dew upon the grass. It was nearly midnight. The pale moonlight and the dying companions afforded a sad picture. This man declared that the fort must be taken if they had to pry the logs apart. The cannon within must come into their hands. It was finally decided to load upon a wagon some hay and dry fencing and what tar and rosin could be found in town to set the log fort on fire. When the load was ready a call was made for volunteers to draw the fuel against the fort. Captain Bickerton, Caleb Pratt, S. C. Smith, Reuben Randall, Edward Russell, this man and two or three others took hold and drew the wagon close to the fort, then lighting the hay. The light illumined the town. It was agreed that a stream of bullets should be fired steadily into the door of the fort to prevent those inside from pushing the wagon away from the building. Soon a white flag was run up over the fort, and the cannon captured and taken out with gun carriage and wheels. In the moment of success and victory the cost of victory is forgotten. The men embraced the cannon even in that dark hour."

"After further deliberation it was planned to take by storm before daylight the fort on Washington Creek, six miles south of Lawrence; and that the cannon should be moved west upon the California road to Fort Titus 12 miles west of Lawrence. Kimball brothers and this man returned to Lawrence and fished out of the Kansas river the type which the border ruffians had taken from the office of the Herald of Freedom, the Kansas Tribune and the Kansas Free State, a few weeks before and thrown into the Kansas river at the time they destroyed the Free State Hotel and burned Dr. Charles Robinson's house. The lead was run into three bullets [cannon balls] for the cannon to be used at the taking of Fort Titus. All the forces with the cannon must be brought against the last fort and it must be taken before night."

"The company which had come through Nebraska arrived during the night that Franklin and Washington Creek forts were taken and assisted the free-state army in taking the last of the three forts. The news of the two victories in the night spread with the morning light and the free-state army numbered several hundred armed men before it reached Fort Titus. Colonel Shombry, of General Lane's party, in behalf of himself and his men, offered to take the fort by storm. They were not successful and the colonel lost his life in the attempt. The free-state army, out of range of the rifles in the fort now waited for the cannon with the three bullets."

"A man was found who had served in the English army—Captain Bickerton. The cannon was placed in his hands and after loading it he announced that he would give the enemy a copy of Kansas Herald of Freedom. The bullet went through the log fort. The cannon was loaded again and with a voice that all could hear the Captain announced that they should have a copy of the Kansas Tribune. After this bullet went through the fort up came a white flag. Titus and 18 prisoners were taken. The return to Lawrence in the latter part of the afternoon with the prisoners and the triumph of the three victories cannot be described."

"… The battle of Franklin was the Bunker Hill in the Kansas warfare, except that the victory was more telling and the results came sooner."

"… The people of Missouri went on preparing for the taking of Lawrence, for they realized it would be impossible to hold slaves in a state with such a town as Lawrence in it."

"… The successful capture of the fort at Franklin and the other two forts was the death knell of the introduction of slavery into Kansas. The loss of

Kansas to the South brought secession. Secession brought the war, and the war brought emancipation. Thus Providence often seemingly employs the most insignificant means to bring about very important results."

ADDENDUM B

NARCISSISM - As defined by the American Psychiatric Association's Diagnostic and Statistical Manual of Mental Disorders (DSM), Narcissistic Personality Disorder is a condition whereby the patient has an excessive need for admiration and affirmation, overestimating his or her abilities. (*DSM's definition of Narcissism is slated for change in 2013). A number of the prominent traits of Narcissistic Personality Disorder that characterized John M. Johnson, are summarized below:

1. Arrogance: By arrogantly debasing or degrading someone else, the narcissist pumps up his own precarious ego.

2. Shamelessness: The narcissist is unable to process shame, thus denying that it exists (although it is the underlying factor in all unhealthy narcissism).

3. Self-Delusion: In order to see oneself as perfect, the narcissist employs self-delusion continually, placing blame and shame on others rather than accepting it.

4. Envy: When faced with superior ability, the narcissist uses contempt to minimize another while maximizing his own abilities.

5. Entitlement: Because the narcissist is "special," it is a given that favorable treatment and automatic compliance will always be given. Non-compliance is considered an attack on the superiority of the narcissist, and rage toward the perpetrator often results.

6. Exploitation: With no regard for the feelings or interests of others, the narcissist demands subservience from those persons close to him. Resistance to those demands can often be nearly impossible.

7. Breaking/Ignoring Boundaries: The narcissist does not recognize his own boundaries and, therefore, considers others to be merely extensions of himself - existing only to meet his needs. When those needs are not met, he is unforgiving.

ADDENDUM C

Scott McLucas/One World Foundation Honors
a. City of Moscow Medal (in conjunction with the United Nations Medal)
b. Society of Writers Medal - United Nations
c. Ville de Vence Medal – Hommage de La Ville de Vence a Mr. Scott McLucas

Scott and his medals

Index of Images

Collaborator
Susan D. Brandenburg

Award winning biographer Susan D. Brandenburg lives in Ponte Vedra Beach, Florida, and has the great privilege of collaborating on full-length biographies about fascinating people like W. Scott McLucas.

A seasoned journalist, genealogist, speaker and researcher, she has written weekly columns and feature articles for local newspapers, as well as articles for local, state and national magazines. As president of Susan the Scribe, Inc., Susan is a pioneer in the field of writing and publishing. Having produced a dozen published works, she now takes your story from concept to completion.

Susan's words are a gift from God. She thanks Him daily for allowing her to help preserve the amazing legacies of His children.

www.susanthescribe.vpweb.com

Acknowledgements

To **Nancy**, my loving spouse, who has been with me every step of the way.

To **Susan D. Brandenburg**, who knows how to describe on a page the good and the bad, the ugly and the beautiful, or any of the myriad special types one wants to read about. I would not have been able to write this book without her sensitive assistance.

To **Dee (Dorothea) Morris**, my dear friend and first cousin, and to her brave and kind husband, Bud.

To **Joe Schwarz**, my good friend with whom I have a partnership for joint theater projects and the Horton Foote Legacy Foundation.

To **Hallie Foote and family**, who are near the top of the major theater families in every important way. Your father's biography inspired this one, and you inspire me even more. In observing your personal acting style, I've found that you gently dramatize your connection with your audience whether you are a single performer musing to yourself or are performing with others. Please never stop making magnificent stage drama.

To **NALL**, whose insightful portrait of me is the cover of my book and a touching reminder of days gone by.

To **Errol Girdlestone**, one of the finest conductors I've ever known, and a man who has brought the joy of fine music into our lives and our hearts.

To Sue Girdlestone, an industrious and inspirational woman.

To Charlotte Moore, whose keen instincts continue to make "must-see" destinations of the Irish Rep and its W. Scott McLucas Studio Theatre, and whose beautiful foreword graces this book.

To Ruth A., Danny, Henry and Molly Rosenbloom, our surrogate children and grand-children of whom we are inordinately proud.

To Chef Jean-Stephane Poinard and his family, who bring the finest of French customs and cuisine to St. Augustine, Florida.

To Leigh Cort, whose publicity talents and enthusiasm are boundless.

To Maggie Fitzroy, who put Nancy and me in the North Florida spotlight through a thoughtful and well-written article about us and One World Foundation.

To Dana Ivey, a dear friend and a fine actress with whom we have spent many enjoyable times – both at home and abroad.

To Aprille & Bill Glover, who taught us that cave life in France can be elegant.

To Fred and Michel Natale, who helped us maintain and enhance our wonderful house in Cagnes sur-Mer.

To Carlos Rodriguez, who has been a sympathetic and helpful friend.

To Preston Haskell, for his sense of loyalty and his generosity to his community here in North Florida.

To Arthur Milam, for his superb executive sense in resolving cultural, legal and organizational issues.

To Benjamin Casey Herring, for his imagination and loyalty.

To Barbara and Bill Miller, for their wisdom and talent.

To Jacques Renoir, for his book Le tableau amoureaux, and his beautiful inscription inside.

To Robert Cogo-Fawcett, for his expertise as an artistic director and theater producer, and for his management of One World Foundation in the U.K.

To Susan Barrow, L.C.S.W., for her humanity, compassion and sense of humor.

To Dr. Thomas Tomlin, for his willingness to study a long-term medical problem of mine and for discovering a definitive and curative solution to it.

To Dr. Michael Till, for his diplomacy, sense of humor and judgment.

To Dr. Morris Dees, for following a family problem-solving tradition.

To Trish Diggins, for her professional completion of the physical book model of Lucky Life, with its many important details and parts.

To Rona Brinley, owner of The Bookmark in Neptune Beach, for her ongoing friendship to Nancy and me, and our One World Foundation.

To Montana Buss, for her valuable research into Narcissism.

To George Rondo, for his loyalty in the early days of our foundation, and his imagination.

To the Officers on the Board of Directors,
One World Foundation, Inc.

W. Scott McLucas, President/Director
Nancy McLucas, Vice President/Director
David Miron, Vice President, Director
Mary Marx, Vice President/Director
Samuel B. Tannahill, Vice President/Director
Claude Brun, Vice President/Director & European Representative
Adam Buss, Secretary/Legal Counsel
Paula Buss, Treasurer

CPSIA information can be obtained at www.ICGtesting.com
Printed in the USA
LVOW10s2014071013

355747LV00002B/6/P